# Architektur *Architecture*

**EXPO 2000 Hannover**

# Architektur *Architecture*

## EXPO *2000* Hannover

Hatje Cantz Verlag

# Inhalt
# Contents

# Grußwort
## A Word of Welcome

Die EXPO 2000 bietet mit ihrem Motto »Mensch – Natur – Technik: Eine neue Welt entsteht« eine Leitidee, an der sich ein Großteil aller Länderbeiträge orientiert. Die erste Weltausstellung im neuen Jahrtausend ist eine ausgezeichnete Gelegenheit, deutlich zu machen, über welche Potenziale die Menschheit verfügt, ihre Zukunft im Sinne einer nachhaltigen Entwicklung zu gestalten und einen Bewusstseinswandel hin zu einer Harmonie von Mensch, Natur und Technik zu initiieren.

Der Gedanke der Nachhaltigkeit durchzog so auch die gesamten Planungen der EXPO 2000. Uns war von Anfang an klar, dass es nicht ausreichen würde, nur vorangegangene Weltausstellungen zu kopieren. Zu viele negative Aspekte, vor allem in der Nachnutzung anderer Expo-Areale, standen uns vor Augen. Die Entscheidung, das weltgrößte Messegelände mit seiner Infrastruktur für die Weltausstellung mitzunutzen und an die EXPO 2000-Entwicklung anzupassen, hat sich als richtig erwiesen. Von dem 160 Hektar großen Expo-Areal mussten nur etwa 70 Hektar neu erschlossen werden, und für alle Bereiche ist eine sinnvolle Nachnutzung sichergestellt.

Diesen Mut, neue Wege zu gehen, haben wir auch in der Architektur bewiesen. Alle Bauvorhaben, die im Zuge der EXPO 2000 realisiert wurden, sind zukunftsorientiert. Hier wurden neue Konzepte der Energieeinsparung entwickelt, natürliche Ressourcen optimal genutzt und etwa Holz als nachwachsender Rohstoff verwendet. Wir haben beispielgebende Lösungen in Bereichen verwirklicht, in denen private Bauherren im Zweifelsfall kaum bereit sind, Risiken einzugehen, weil viele Techniken noch im Versuchsstadium stehen. Wir konnten dadurch Anstöße für die gesamte Architektur geben und haben auch als Vorbild für die teilnehmenden Nationen und Investoren gewirkt. Viele der Pavillons, von denen ein großer Teil nach der Weltausstellung in Hannover weitergenutzt wird, sind ebenfalls mit besonderer Weitsicht geplant worden und vermitteln spannende Einblicke in ungewöhnliche Konstruktionen. Landestypische Elemente und Bauweisen sowie Designideen auf internationalem Niveau sorgen zudem dafür, dass die EXPO 2000 auch zu einem sinnlichen Erlebnis wird. Wir zeigen in Hannover, dass die Architektur des 21. Jahrhunderts ökonomisch und ökologisch sinnvoll geplant werden und gleichzeitig höchsten gestalterischen Ansprüchen genügen kann.

In diesem Sinne bietet das vorliegende Buch eine umfangreiche Dokumentation zahlreicher architektonischer Highlights. Möge es Anregungen geben, den eingeschlagenen Weg weiterzugehen und das Motto »Mensch – Natur – Technik: Eine neue Welt entsteht« auch zukünftig in der Architektur sinnvoll umzusetzen.

Sepp D. Heckmann

With the theme of "Humankind – Nature – Technology: A New World Arising," EXPO 2000 proposed a guiding concept which the majority of national presentations have adopted and applied in their contributions. The first World Exposition in the new millennium offers a perfect opportunity to emphasize humanity's vast potential for shaping its own future in keeping with the principle of sustainable development and for achieving a change of consciousness that will bring about a harmony between humanity, nature and technology. The ideas of sustainable development and resource conservation had an appreciable impact upon virtually every aspect of planning for EXPO 2000 as well. We knew from the outset that we could not be content with merely imitating previous World Expositions. There were too many negative aspects of past experience to ignore, especially in the use of other Expo sites once they had outlived their original purpose. The decision to make use of the world's largest trade fair grounds and the existing infrastructure and to adapt them to the development of EXPO 2000 has proven to be a wise one. Of the 160 hectares now occupied by the Expo site, only 70 had to be newly acquired and developed, and we are now assured that all of the areas will be put to good use after the World Exposition closes.

We find this firm resolve to pursue new directions reflected in the architecture as well. All of the construction projects realized for EXPO 2000 are oriented toward the future. New energy-saving concepts have been developed, and natural resources have been used with optimum efficiency. Builders have relied on such renewable materials as wood. We have implemented exemplary solutions in areas in which builder-clients are rarely willing to take risks, as too many of the technologies in question are still in the experimental phase. This has enabled us to offer valuable stimulus to architects everywhere and to serve as an example for participating nations and investors. Many of the pavilions, of which the majority will be dedicated to new purposes after the World Exposition, were planned with almost visionary far-sightedness, and they offer exciting insights into unusual structures. Building components and methods typical of the participating countries and design concepts of international caliber have also ensured that EXPO 2000 will also be a fascinating sensory experience as well. We demonstrate clearly in Hanover that the architecture of the 21st century can be planned in keeping with both economic and ecological principles while still achieving the highest standards of quality in design. In this sense, the present volume presents a comprehensive documentation of numerous architectural highlights. It is our hope that it provides inspiration to others to pursue the paths marked out here and to achieve the objectives implicit in the thematic slogan "Humankind – Nature – Technology: A New World Arising" in the architecture of the future.

Sepp D. Heckmann

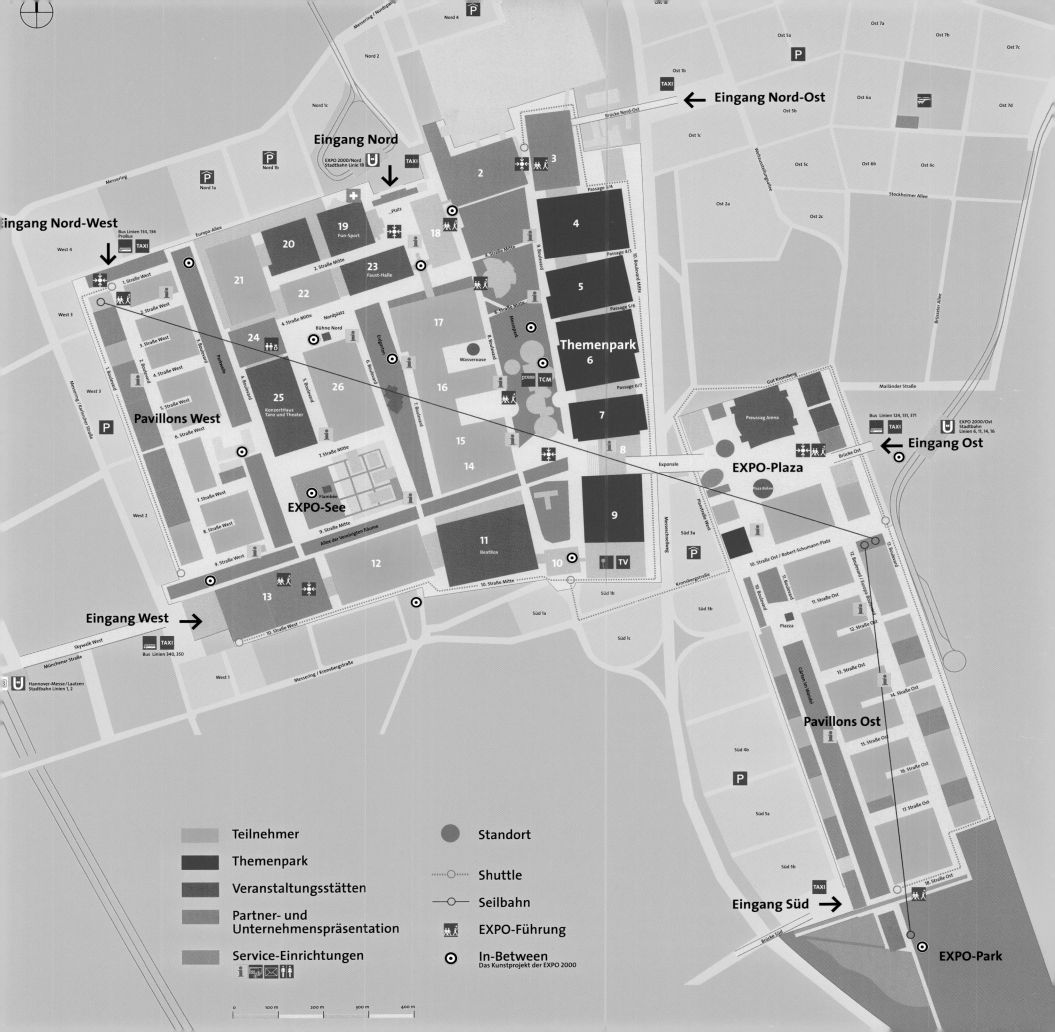

# Vorwort
## Foreword

Seit sich am 1. Juni 2000 die Tore geöffnet haben, erleben wir eine der größten Kulturveranstaltungen in der Geschichte. Das Fest hat begonnen – EXPO 2000 – die erste Weltausstellung in Deutschland.

Wir erleben gemeinsam fünf Monate lang ein Ereignis internationaler Kultur. Das Spannungsfeld von Tradition und Exotik, von Technik und Innovation bis hin zu Visionär-Utopischem wird ein einmaliges und unvergleichliches Erlebnis werden. Wir erwarten vor allem auch ein farbenfrohes, heiteres und friedliches Miteinander der Kulturen, denen das Weltausstellungsgelände bis Oktober eine Plattform bietet – eine Bühne für Musik, Tanz und Theater, für Begegnungen, Austausch und Beziehungen.

Der Bereich Planen und Bauen hatte die Aufgabe, diese Plattform, diese Bühne zu gestalten und vorzubereiten. Es galt, adäquaten Raum für Präsentationen und Veranstaltungen zu schaffen und natürlich eine angenehme Umgebung für die Besucher. Das Ergebnis ist unsere Botschaft aus Hannover: anspruchsvolle Architektur, kreative und sensible Landschaftsgestaltung und hohe Ingenieurkunst.

Eine über fünfjährige Vorbereitung ist abgeschlossen. In der Planungsphase hatte für uns die Gestaltungsqualität der gebauten Umwelt eine zentrale Bedeutung. Frühzeitig wurde die Philosophie einer Gesamtgestaltung des Geländes mit Hilfe von Grundsätzen zum übergreifenden visuellen Erscheinungsbild entwickelt und durch Leitlinien präzisiert. Diese Steuerungsinstrumente waren mit genügend großer Offenheit versehen, sodass der Spielraum zur gewünschten kreativen Entfaltung auf Planerseite jederzeit gegeben war.

Die Ausführungsphase war stark geprägt durch die Einbeziehung der Pavillons der Nationen. Die Begleitung der Teilnehmer während der Vorbereitung ihrer Präsentationen war eines der Highlights in dieser Zeit. Das eingangs erwähnte Spannungsfeld zwischen Traditionellem und Utopischem war hier schon in seiner ganzen Bandbreite spürbar. Herangehensweisen der einzelnen Nationen, wie sie unterschiedlicher nicht sein konnten, haben gerade diesen Teil unserer Aufgabe zu einer der spannendsten und schönsten Herausforderung gemacht, der sich Planer überhaupt stellen können.

Mittlerweile sind alle Projekte abgeschlossen, die gesamte Bühne für das Fest der Völker dieser Welt ist fertig gestellt. Jetzt sind im Zusammenspiel von »Mensch« und »Natur« für den Besucher thematisch inspirierte Landschaftsarchitekturen erlebbar; jetzt kann der Begriff »Technik« anhand innovativer Projekte wie dem Expo-Dach oder modernster Ausstellungshallen neu definiert werden. Beweise für eine nachhaltige Entwicklung sind – in den Gebäuden auf der One World Plaza, dem zentralen Ort mit internationaler Präsenz und dem Sitz des Hauses des Gastgebers – ebenso zu finden wie flexible, multifunktionale Bauformen, etwa bei den Service- und Gastronomiegebäuden. Eingebettet sind alle Projekte in eine Landschaft visueller Kommunikation, die Elemente des Public Design.

Since opening our gates on June 1, 2000, we have experienced one of the greatest cultural events in history. The festivities have now begun – EXPO 2000 – the first World Exposition in Germany.

For five months, we will together experience an international cultural event. The interaction of the traditional and the exotic, technology and innovation and visionary-utopian dreams is destined to culminate in a unique and unforgettable experience. We anticipate above all a colorful, happy and peaceful intermingling of the cultures for which the grounds of the World Exposition will provide a platform until October – an immense stage for music, dance and theater, for encounter, exchange and the forging of new relationships.

The Department of Planning and Construction was tasked with the job of designing and preparing this great platform, this world stage. Its goal was to provide sufficient space for presentation and events and, of course, to create a pleasant environment for visitors. The outcome is our statement from Hanover: high-quality architecture, creative, sensitive landscape design and superior engineering accomplishments.

Five years of preparation have now come to completion. During the planning phase, a high premium was placed upon achieving quality of design in our constructed environment. Thus we embraced the philosophy of a total design achieved on the basis of principles devoted to the creation of an integrated visual image and specified our objectives in guidelines. These controlling tools were made flexible enough to ensure that sufficient room for creativity remained for planners at all times.

The implementation phase bore the marked imprint of the process of integrating the national pavilions. Assisting the participants during preparations for their presentations was truly one of the highlights of this phase. The full bandwidth of the creative tension that emerged from the encounter between the traditional and the utopian was evident even at this stage. The approaches pursued by the individual nations could hardly have differed more, and this made our task one of the most exciting and gratifying challenges a planner could possibly imagine.

At this writing, all of the projects have been completed. The whole stage for the great festival of the peoples of our world is finished. Now thematically inspired landscape architectures are ready to be experienced by visitors in the context of interplay between "humankind" and "nature," and now the concept of "technology" can be redefined on the basis of innovative projects such as the Expo Roof or state-of-the-art exhibition buildings at EXPO 2000. Irrefutable evidence of sustainable development will be just as easy to find – in the buildings at One World Plaza, the central site with its international representation and the headquarters of the host – as flexible, multipurpose building solutions as they appear in the many service and restaurant buildings, for example. All of

Mittelpunkt des Geschehens sind die Präsentationen der Nationen und internationalen Organisationen – in Form nachnutzbarer oder temporärer Pavillons oder in Form von Ausstellungsbeiträgen in vorhandenen Hallen. Deshalb ist ein großer Teil dieses Buches auch diesen Projekten gewidmet. Von zentraler Bedeutung ist natürlich auch der eigene Ausstellungsbeitrag der EXPO 2000, der Themenpark, dessen Inhalte teilweise von Architekten wie Szenografen mitgestaltet wurden.

Wenn am 31. Oktober 2000 die Tore des Geländes endgültig schließen, ist die Weltausstellung EXPO 2000 in Hannover Geschichte. Was bleiben wird, sind Erinnerungen an ein einmaliges Ereignis und die Bilder des Geländes, die fortan Geschichte gegenwärtig erscheinen lassen.

Dieses Buch soll einen kleinen Beitrag dazu leisten.

Hubertus von Bothmer und Klaus Wenzel

these projects are embedded in a landscape of visual communication comprising the elements of public design.

The focal points of activity are the presentations of the various nations and international organizations – in the form of reusable or temporary pavilions or as exposition contributions in existing buildings. And that is why a significant portion of this book is dedicated to these projects. Equally important, of course, is the presentation of the EXPO 2000 Committee itself: the Thematic Area, whose attractions have been designed in a cooperative effort involving both architects and scenographers.

When the gates to the grounds finally close on October 31, 2000, the World Exposition EXPO Hanover 2000 will become history. What remains will be memories of an unparalleled experience and images of an exposition site that will continue to make history a part of the present for many years to come.

It is hoped that this book will make its own small contribution to that end.

Hubertus von Bothmer and Klaus Wenzel

# Masterplan Planen und Bauen EXPO 2000
# Planning and Construction Site Plan EXPO 2000

Der erste Masterplan für die EXPO 2000 in Hannover entstand 1994 als Gemeinschaftsarbeit der Wettbewerbsgewinner Arnaboldi/Cavadini (Locarno) mit den Büros AS & P Albert Speer & Partner (Frankfurt am Main) und Kienast Vogt Partner (Zürich). In diesem ursprünglichen Masterplan wurden sowohl die grundlegenden städtebaulichen Ziele der Weltausstellung formuliert als auch erste Festlegungen für die wesentlichen funktionalen Aspekte getroffen, wie Verkehrsplanung, Lage der Besuchereingänge, Belange der Sicherheit, Baukosten und Termine.

Ziel und Anspruch war eine »EXPO des neuen Typs«, eine EXPO, die nicht nur ein temporäres Ereignis ist, sondern ein bestehendes Gelände und dessen Infrastruktur als Ressource und Chance nutzt und gleichzeitig als Motor für die Stadtentwicklung von Hannover dient. Außerdem sollten alle Planungen in ein sinnvolles Nachnutzungskonzept eingebunden werden.

Die Vielschichtigkeit dieser Aufgabenstellung erforderte ein einfaches, robustes städtebauliches Konzept, das trotz immer neuer Fragestellungen und Änderungen eine konsistente Planungsgrundlage blieb. Dazu wurde das Messegelände nach einem orthogonalen System neu geordnet und um zwei Pavillonflächen ergänzt. Um der Vielfalt der Nationenpavillons einen übersichtlichen Rahmen zu geben, wurden diese Pavillonflächen ebenfalls orthogonal gegliedert. Eine Allee verbindet die verschiedenen Geländeteile. Sie endet auf der Expo-Plaza, dem zentralen Veranstaltungsort und damit einem der Höhepunkte auf dem Gelände.

Die Bauvolumen der Hallen und Pavillons wurden auf bestimmte Bereiche konzentriert, um eine EXPO mit urbanem, geschlossenem Charakter zu schaffen. Im Kontrast dazu stehen großzügige Grünräume, die als Parks und Gärten aufwändig gestaltet wurden. Dadurch entsteht ein klar gegliedertes, übersichtliches »Stück Stadt«, in dem sich die Besucher leicht orientieren können. Aber auch der Betrieb der EXPO profitiert von der Funktionalität des Geländes, vor allem in Hinblick auf den internen Transport, die Logistik und die Steuerung der Besucherströme.

Der Masterplan wurde seit 1995 vom Büro AS & P Albert Speer & Partner kontinuierlich weiterentwickelt und aktualisiert. Alle sechs Monate wurde der jeweilige Planungsstand dokumentiert und als neuer Masterplan veröffentlicht, eine Vorgehensweise, durch die der gesamte Planungsprozess organisiert und strukturiert wurde. Der Masterplan dient damit als zentrales Planungs- und Koordinationsinstrument der Weltausstellung, in dem Ziele und Visionen, aber auch Ansprüche und Bedürfnisse aller an der EXPO Beteiligten zusammengefasst wurden.

Albert Speer und Frank Höf

The first Master Plan (officially, the "Planning and Construction Site Plan") for EXPO 2000 in Hanover was prepared in 1994 as a cooperative effort involving the competition winner Arnaboldi/Cavadini (Locarno) and the offices of AS & P Albert Speer & Partner (Frankfurt am Main) and Kienast Vogt Partner (Zurich). This original plan included both an articulation of the fundamental urban architectural goals of the World Exposition and specifications regarding essential functional aspects, such as traffic and transportation planning, the location of visitors entrances, security matters, construction costs and scheduling.

The goal and the intent were to present a new type of EXPO, an EXPO that would not be merely a passing event but a permanent site that would take advantage of its infrastructure as a resource and an opportunity and serve as a motor for urban development in Hanover. In addition, all planning measures were to be integrated into a feasible and purposeful concept for continued use after the end of EXPO 2000.

The complexity of these objectives required a simple, robust urban architectural concept that would ensure a consistent planning foundation despite numerous, inevitable reassessments and changes. Accordingly, the trade fair grounds were restructured as an orthogonal system, and lots for two more pavilions were added. In order to provide a clear, comprehensible framework structure for the diverse national pavilions, the pavilion lots were also laid out in an orthogonal configuration. A broad avenue connects the different sections of the grounds. It ends at the Expo-Plaza, the central venue for events and thus one of the major attractions at EXPO 2000.

The architectural volumes of the halls and pavilions were concentrated in specific areas in order to give EXPO the character of a compact, urban setting. A contrast is provided by the expansive green areas, which were designed with a great deal of effort as parks and gardens. The result is a clearly ordered urban microcosm offering easy orientation for visitors. Day-to-day operations at EXPO 2000 will also profit from the functional layout of the grounds, particularly in terms of transportation inside the grounds, logistics and the management of visitor flows.

The Master Plan was continuously developed and regularly updated by the office of AS & P Albert Speer & Partner beginning in 1995. Planning status was reviewed and documented every six months and published as a new Master Plan, an approach that helped organize and structure the overall planning process. Thus the Master Plan serves as a central planning and coordination tool for the World Exposition, an instrument in which the goals and visions as well as the needs and requirements of all participants at EXPO 2000 are reflected in a unified whole.

Albert Speer and Frank Höf

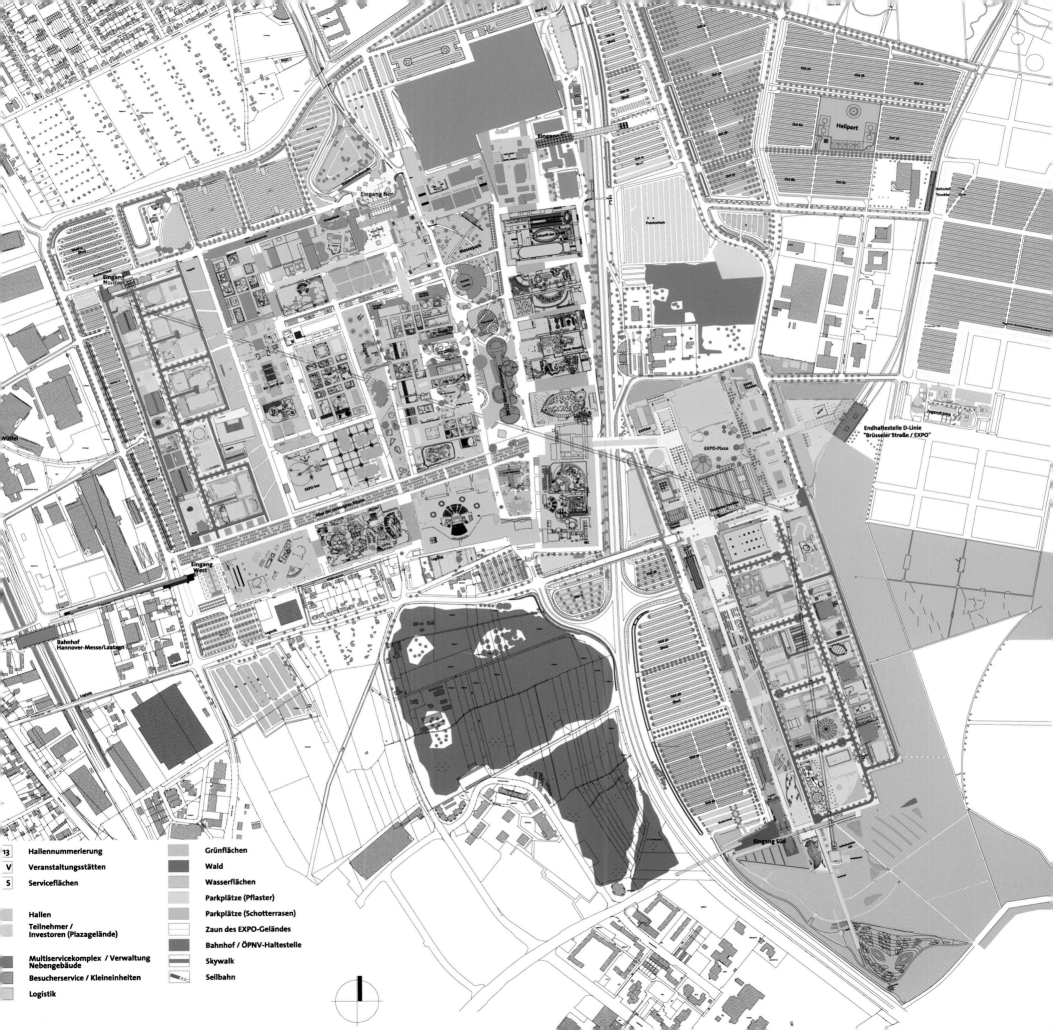

Heliport

Eingang Nord

Eingang Nordwest

Eingang West

Eingang Süd

Endhaltestelle D-Linie
"Brüsseler Straße / EXPO"

Bahnhof
Hannover-Messe/Laatzen

EXPO-Plaza

**13** Hallennummerierung
**V** Veranstaltungsstätten
**S** Serviceflächen

Hallen
Teilnehmer /
Investoren (Plazagelände)

Multiservicekomplex / Verwaltung
Nebengebäude
Besucherservice / Kleineinheiten
Logistik

Grünflächen
Wald
Wasserflächen
Parkplätze (Pflaster)
Parkplätze (Schotterrasen)
Zaun des EXPO-Geländes
Bahnhof / ÖPNV-Haltestelle
Skywalk
Seilbahn

# Das übergreifende Erscheinungsbild
## The Total Image

Aspekte eines übergreifenden visuellen Erscheinungsbildes für das Weltausstellungsgelände wurden von der Deutschen Messe AG und der EXPO 2000 Hannover GmbH schon frühzeitig thematisiert. Seit 1994 wurden alle grundsätzlichen Gestaltungsthemen im Büro für Gestaltung von Prof. Eberhard Stauß und Ursula Wangler bearbeitet. Dabei stand die räumliche Verbindung von Architektur und Landschaft im Vordergrund, unterstützt und ergänzt durch ein differenziertes Gestaltungskonzept im Bereich Public Design. Das Gelände wurde als »Gesamtraum« gesehen und großer Wert auf kommunikationsfördernde Außenräume gelegt. Um diese komplexe Gestaltungsphase zu begleiten, wurde der Gestaltungskreis der EXPO 2000 ins Leben gerufen. Hier wurden von verschiedenen Fachleuten alle relevanten Fragen des Städtebaus, der Architektur, der Landschaftsplanung, des Designs, der Kunst und der visuellen Kommunikation behandelt. Aus dieser Arbeit wurden konkrete Leitlinien und Grundsätze für die Gestaltung der Freiräume, der Verkehrsbauwerke, der Ausstellungsgebäude, der Beleuchtung, der Serviceeinrichtungen, der Möblierung und der Beschilderung entwickelt.

Mitglieder des Gestaltungskreises:

Uta Boockhoff-Gries, Stadt Hannover
Dr. Wilfried Dickhoff, Berater EXPO 2000 Hannover GmbH
Prof. Meinhard von Gerkan, Architekt BDA
Sepp D. Heckmann, Deutsche Messe AG und EXPO 2000 Hannover GmbH
Prof. Thomas Herzog, Architekt BDA
Prof. Dieter Kienast, Landschaftsarchitekt (verstorben am 23. Dezember 1998)
Prof. Albert Speer, Architekt BDA
Prof. Eberhard Stauß, Büro für Gestaltung (verstorben am 28. Juni 1998)
Ursula Wangler, Büro für Gestaltung

Zu den prägenden Elementen gehört das städtebauliche Konzept mit seinem rechtwinkligen Ordnungssystem. Die Allee der Vereinigten Bäume bildet dabei als axiale West-Ost-Verbindung das Rückgrat der Anlage, und die orthogonal dazu stehenden Grünfinger strukturieren das Gelände und bilden Freiräume. Diese Freiräume sind Orte der Begegnung, der Kommunikation, des Dialogs, der Entspannung und der Ruhe, sie sind weit gefasst und übersichtlich. Auch die Verkehrsräume wurden nach den Gestaltungsleitlinien entwickelt. So sind sie nicht nur Funktionsräume für den fließenden Verkehr, sondern gleichzeitig auch Orientierungs- und Erlebnisräume. Alle wichtigen Erschließungsstraßen sind nach einem Gestaltungsprinzip ausgebildet, um ein räumlich durchgängig wirksames Zeichen zu erhalten, das dem Stadtbild, der EXPO 2000 und der Messe gleichermaßen dient. Bei den neuen Ausstellungshallen wurden hohe

Aspects of a total visual image for the grounds of the World Exposition were addressed early on by the Deutsche Messe AG and EXPO 2000 Hannover GmbH. Prof. Eberhard Stauss and Ursula Wangler of the Design Office began work on all of the major design themes in 1994. Emphasis was placed upon the spatial integration of architecture and landscape, an approach that was supported and augmented by a highly differentiated concept for Public Design. The grounds were viewed as an organic whole, and considerable effort was invested in the development of open spaces that would foster communication. The EXPO 2000 Design Circle was formed to provide accompanying guidance for this complex phase of the design process. Within the group, all of the relevant aspects of urban development, architecture, landscape planning, design, art and visual communication were examined and discussed by a team of experts from various fields. Their work produced concrete guidelines and basic principles to be applied to the design of outdoor spaces, traffic and transportation areas, exhibition buildings, lighting, service facilities, furnishings and informative signs.

The Design Circle was composed of the following members:

Uta Boockhoff-Gries, city of Hanover
Dr. Wilfried Dickhoff, consultant, EXPO 2000 Hannover GmbH
Prof. Meinhard von Gerkan, architect, BDA
Sepp D. Heckmann, Deutsche Messe AG and EXPO 2000 Hannover GmbH
Prof. Thomas Herzog, architect, BDA
Prof. Dieter Kienast, landscape architect (died on December 23, 1998)
Prof. Albert Speer, architect, BDA
Prof. Eberhard Stauss, Design Office (died on June 28, 1998)
Ursula Wangler, Design Office

One of the most striking features is the urban development concept based on an orthogonal ordering system. United Trees Avenue, the axial east-west link, forms the backbone of the whole, while the fingers of green which branch off at right angles from it give structure to the grounds and create open spaces. These open spaces are settings for encounter, for communication, for dialogue, rest and relaxation. They are expansive and clearly structured. The traffic and transport routes were also developed in keeping with the design guidelines and are thus not only functional spaces that accommodate the flow of traffic but areas of orientation and encounter as well. All of the major access roads are based upon a principle of design dedicated to the creation of a symbol of spatial consistency that effectively enhances the image of the city, EXPO 2000 and the trade fair grounds. Demanding technical and environmental standards

In den großzügig angelegten Freiräumen ist, wie hier bei der Allee der Vereinigten Bäume, das rechtwinklige Ordnungsprinzip spürbar.
The underlying orthogonal order is evident in the expansive open areas, as in this view of United Trees Avenue.

technische und ökologische Maßstäbe angelegt. Sie sind geprägt von klaren Formen, wieder verwendbaren Materialien, natürlicher Belichtung und Belüftung, von freundlicher Ausstrahlung, interessanter Raumwirkung und auf den Menschen bezogener Maßstäblichkeit.

Von großer Bedeutung für das durchgängig wirksame Erscheinungsbild des Weltausstellungsgeländes sind auch die häufig wiederkehrenden Elemente der Beleuchtung, des Leit- und Orientierungssystems, der Serviceeinrichtungen und der Möblierung. Sie werden im Kapitel »Servicegebäude und Public Design« näher vorgestellt. Grundlage für die Orientierung auf dem Gelände ist der Lageplan auf Seite 9, der mit seiner einfachen und klaren Darstellung einem Stadtplan ähnelt: Verzeichnet sind übergeordnete Bereiche, Straßen und die Nummern der Messehallen. In der dazugehörigen Legende sind die offiziellen und nichtoffiziellen Teilnehmer, der Themenpark, Partner- und Unternehmenspräsentationen sowie Veranstaltungsstätten und Serviceeinrichtungen aufgeführt. Auf den Schildern des Leit- und Orientierungssystems ist der Expo-Lageplan in Deutsch und Englisch erläutert.

were applied to the design and construction of the new exhibition halls. Their most noteworthy characteristics are clarity of form, the use of recyclable materials, natural lighting and ventilation, their inviting appearance, interesting spatial effects and a people-oriented scale.

Significant aspects of the consistent total image of the World Exposition grounds are the regularly recurring elements of lighting, the orientation and guidance system, service facilities and furnishings. These are discussed in greater detail in the Chapter entitled "Service Buildings and Public Design." The basis for orientation within the grounds is the layout plan on page 9, which resembles a city map in its simplicity and clarity. It shows major areas of interest, streets and the numbers of the trade fair halls. The key lists the official and non-official participants, the Thematic Area, partner and corporate presentations as well as event sites and service facilities. The details of the Expo layout are explained in German and English on the signs which form the orientation and guidance system.

# Freiraumplanung und Landschaftsgestaltung
## Open-Spaces Planning and Landscape Design

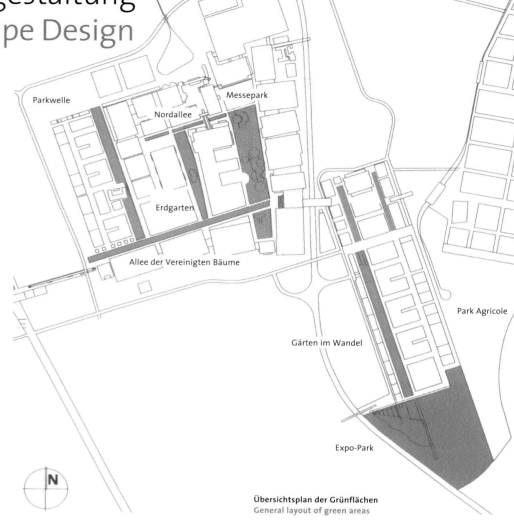

Die Grün- und Freiflächen sind elementare Bestandteile des Weltausstellungsgeländes und von großer Bedeutung für seine Aufenthaltsqualität. Ihre Gestaltung ist geprägt von den Ideen zweier Planer. Der 1998 verstorbene Schweizer Freiraumplaner Dieter Kienast entwarf die Grünanlagen auf dem bereits bestehenden Ausstellungsgelände, und der in Berlin lebende algerische Landschaftsarchitekt Kamel Louafi entwickelte das Konzept für den neuen Bereich am Kronsberg. Sie haben sich an dem übergeordneten Freiflächenkonzept des Masterplans orientiert, der ein Netz aus rechtwinklig angeordneten grünen Bändern vorgab, die sich fingerartig zwischen die Ausstellungsbereiche schieben. Sie strukturieren das Gelände durch den rhythmischen Wechsel von bebauten und unbebauten Flächen. Die Umsetzung der Entwürfe von Dieter Kienast erfolgte in einer Arbeitsgemeinschaft mit dem Hildesheimer Umweltplanungsbüro Heimer + Herbstreit.

Als konzeptionelles Rückgrat und grüne Haupterschließungsachse verbindet die Allee der Vereinigten Bäume das westliche und östliche Ausstellungsgelände. Nördlich dieser Allee schließen sich völlig unterschiedlich gestaltete Grünzonen an. Neben dem bereits vorhandenen Messepark und der Nordallee laden die neu gestaltete Parkwelle, der Erdgarten und der Expo-See Besucher zum Verweilen ein. Am Kronsberg bildet die Expo-Plaza den Ausgangspunkt für eine kulturgeschichtliche Entdeckungsreise durch die Gärten im Wandel, und der Expo-Park markiert den südlichen Abschluss des Weltausstellungsgeländes. Auch die ansprechenden Platzgestaltungen sind Bestandteil des Gesamtkonzepts.

**Planung der Allee der Vereinigten Bäume,**
**der Parkwelle, des Erdgartens und des Expo-Sees:**
**Arbeitsgemeinschaft der Landschaftsarchitekten**
**Kienast Vogt Partner, Zürich**
**Heimer + Herbstreit, Hildesheim (ARGE KVHH)**
Planning for United Trees Avenue, Park Wave,
Earth Garden and Expo Lake:
joint project involving the landscape architects
Kienast Vogt Partner, Zurich
Heimer + Herbstreit, Hildesheim (ARGE KVHH)

**Übersichtsplan der Grünflächen**
General layout of green areas

Green and open areas are fundamental parts of the World Exposition grounds and contribute significantly to their quality as an ambiance for visitors. The design of these areas bears the imprint of the ideas of two planners. The Swiss landscape planner Dieter Kienast, who died in 1998, developed the plans for the parks and gardens on the existing trade fair grounds, while the Berlin-based Algerian landscape architect Kamel Louafi created the concept for the new site on the Kronsberg. Their point of departure was the general open-spaces concept formulated in the Planning and Site Construction Plan, which called for a network of green bands arranged at right angles that would extend like fingers through the exhibition areas. They imposed structure on the grounds by means of the rhythmic pattern of alternation between developed and undeveloped lots. Dieter Kienast's proposals were put into final form in cooperation with the Hildesheim environmental planning office of Heimer + Herbstreit.

As the conceptual backbone and a green, main access route, United Trees Avenue connects the eastern and western exposition sites. North of this avenue are several green areas with very different designs. Adjacent to the existing trade fair park and Nordallee (Northern Avenue) are the newly created Park Wave, Earth Garden and Expo Lake. Expo-Plaza, on the Kronsberg, is the point of departure for a journey of discovery through cultural history and evolving gardens, and Expo Park marks the southern boundary of the World Exposition grounds. The appealing design of plazas is also part of the overall concept.

# Allee der Vereinigten Bäume
## United Trees Avenue

Die Allee der Vereinigten Bäume ist die grüne Verbindung zwischen dem westlichen und östlichen Geländeteil. Über eine Distanz von 900 Metern leitet sie Besucher vom Eingang West bis zum Übergang zur Expo-Plaza. Die Pflanzungen erfolgten bereits 1998, um den Bäumen Zeit zum Eingewöhnen zu geben. Entstanden ist eine Art Baumgarten mit insgesamt 460 Bäumen aus 273 Gattungen, die in unseren Breitengraden gedeihen. Auf einer Gesamtbreite von 26 Metern sind sie in vier Reihen angeordnet, die Abstände richten sich nach dem individuellen Platzbedarf. Eine unterirdisch installierte Bewässerungsanlage sorgt zusammen mit einer speziellen Nährstoffzufuhr für die optimale Versorgung jedes einzelnen Baumes. Als Schutz bei Stürmen halten Anker und Spanngurte die Wurzelballen der hochstämmigen Bäume, die beim Pflanzen bereits einen Stammumfang von 50 bis 60 Zentimetern und eine Höhe zwischen 5 und 9 Metern besaßen.

**Um die lebendige Vielfalt dieses einmaligen Baumgartens in Ruhe genießen zu können, laden zahlreiche Bänke Besucher zum Verweilen ein.**
Numerous benches offer visitors an opportunity to enjoy the living diversity of this unique garden of trees in an atmosphere of serenity.

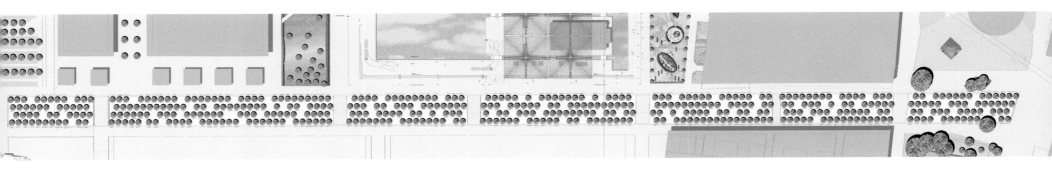

**Planausschnitt**
**Planning detail**

United Trees Avenue is the green link between the East and West Pavilion Sites. Nine hundred meters long, it leads visitors from the West Entrance to the walkway to Expo-Plaza. The trees were planted in 1998 in order to give them sufficient time to adjust to their new conditions. The result is a kind of arboreal garden comprising a total of 460 trees of 273 different species, all native to our latitudes. They are arranged in four rows covering a total width of 26 meters. Intervals between the trees vary depending upon their individual space requirements. An underground irrigation system and a special fertilizing setup ensure an optimum supply of water and nutrients to each tree. The roots of the tall trees, which were 50 to 60 centimeters thick and between five and nine meters long at planting, are secured with anchors and tension belts as protection against high winds.

**Abends wird die Allee durch im Boden
eingelassene Scheinwerfer stimmungsvoll
illuminiert.**
Floodlights set in the ground provide
atmospheric lighting for the Avenue after
dark.

**Blick von Westen auf die Allee der
Vereinigten Bäume**
View of United Trees Avenue from the
west

# Parkwelle
## Park Wave

**Hängebuchen auf der Insel im See**
Hanging beeches on the island in the lake

Mit ihrer stark modellierten Topografie erstreckt sich die Parkwelle entlang des Pavillongeländes West und wird auf der anderen Seite begrenzt von den Ausstellungshallen 21, 24 und 25. Dieser rund 3 Hektar große Grünfinger stellt eine Komposition aus sanften Hügeln und Tälern dar, die dem Besucher beim Gehen immer neue Perspektiven erschließen. Im Süden lehnt sich die Bepflanzung aus dicht stehenden Eichen, Buchen und Lebensbäumen an die angrenzende Allee der Vereinigten Bäume an. Während eines leichten Anstiegs lichten sich die Bäume, und der Besucher erreicht einen von Tulpen umgebenen, kiesbedeckten Platz. Im Folgenden markiert ein Birkenwald die höchste Erhebung der Parkwelle. Säuleneichen führen schließlich zur tiefsten Stelle. Hier versteckt sich ein von amerikanischen Eichen eingefasster See mit einer kleiner Insel, auf der sich drei rotblättrige Hängebuchen befinden. Über ein altes Industriegleis führt der Weg durch weitere Wellentäler zu Lindenkegelstümpfen und einheimischen Waldpflanzungen. Auf ihrer gesamten Länge ist die Parkwelle von 30 bis 60 Grad geneigten Böschungen eingefasst. Sie sind bepflanzt mit einheimischen Heckenpflanzen, Hainbuchen, Feldahorn, Liguster und Schlehdorn.

Park Wave, with its markedly undulating topography, runs along the West Pavilion Site and is bordered on the other side by Exhibition Halls 21, 24 and 25. Covering some three hectares, this green finger is a composition of gently rising hills and valleys that offers visitors a series of changing perspectives. Toward the south, dense groves of oaks, beeches and trees of life approach the nearby United Trees Avenue. As the terrain gradually rises, the trees become more sparse, and visitors arrive at a gravel-covered clearing surrounded by tulips. Further on, a birch grove marks the highest elevation in Park Wave. Rows of stately oaks lead down to the lowest point in the park. Hidden there is an oak-lined pond with a small island planted with three red-leafed hanging beeches. The path leads from this point over the tracks of an old industrial railhead through a series of valleys toward patches of linden cone stumps and groves of indigenous trees. Park Wave is bordered along its entire length by embankments with slopes ranging from 30 to 60 degrees. These are planted with native hedge shrubs, common beeches, common maples, privet and blackthorn.

**Blick von der Brücke auf den nördlichen Teil der sanft geschwungenen Parkwelle**
View of the northern section of the gently undulating Park Wave, seen from the bridge

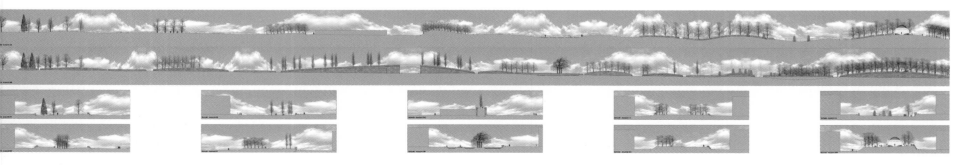

**Plan der Parkwelle**
Map of Park Wave

# Erdgarten
## Earth Garden

**Kleine Heckengärten laden zum Ausruhen ein.**
Small hedged gardens invite visitors to stop and rest.

Der circa 2 Hektar große, von Hainbuchen gesäumte Erdgarten längs der Hallen 14 bis 17 verbindet die Nordallee und die Allee der Vereinigten Bäume. Im gesamten Erdgarten, der sich in drei unterschiedliche Bereiche gliedert, können Besucher über hoch strapazierfähigen Rasen laufen. Den markantesten Blickfang bilden im nördlichen Bereich sieben rasenbewachsene Erdkegel. Sie haben eine Neigung von 60 bis 70 Grad, sind zwischen 5,5 und 13 Meter hoch und besitzen Spitzen aus glänzendem Chromstahl. Im mittleren Bereich stehen kastenförmig geschnittene Linden in einem regelmäßigen Raster. Sie bilden einen angenehmen, halbschattigen Aufenthaltsbereich. Im Süden schließlich findet der ruhesuchende Besucher ideale Rückzugsmöglichkeiten. Hecken aus 3,5 Meter hohem Zierobst bilden kleine, geschlossene Räume mit runden, eckigen und elliptischen Grundformen. Sie sind jeweils unterschiedlich gestaltet und bepflanzt. In einem dieser Heckengärten wachsen rot und gelb blühende Dickblattgewächse, in einem anderen leuchten blaue Hortensien und in einem weiteren spiegeln sich riesenblättrige Stauden in einem kleinen Wasserbecken.

Covering about two hectares, the beech-lined Earth Garden extends along Halls 14 through 17 and connects Nordallee (Northern Avenue) with United Trees Avenue. Visitors can stroll over the robust lawn throughout this garden, which comprises three different sections. The most striking feature of the park is a group of grassy earthen cones located in the northern section. They have slopes of between 60 and 70 degrees, heights ranging from 5.5 to 13 meters and are topped with caps of polished chromium steel. Box-shaped linden trees form a regular grid pattern in the central section and offer visitors a pleasant, semi-shaded setting for rest and relaxation. Visitors also find an ideal place of retreat in the southern section, where 3.5-meter-high hedges of decorative fruit bushes form small, enclosed, circular, rectangular or elliptical spaces. Each of these small havens has a different design and different vegetation. Red- and yellow-flowering crassulae grow in one of these hedge gardens, blue hortensias in another, and giant-leafed herbaceous perennials are mirrored in a small pool in yet another.

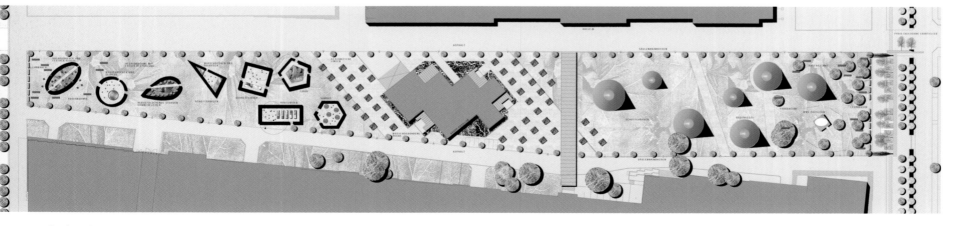

**Plan des Erdgartens**
Map of Earth Garden

**Die Erdkegel haben dem Garten seinen Namen gegeben.**
These earthen mounds give the garden its name.

# Expo-See
## Expo Lake

Eingefasst von der Parkwelle, dem Erdgarten und der Allee der Vereinigten Bäume bildet der 42.000 Quadratmeter große Platz am Hermesturm mit dem Expo-See einen herausragenden Veranstaltungsbereich. Für die allabendlichen Flambée-Vorstellungen steht nördlich des Sees eine Tribüne für rund 10.000 Zuschauer zur Verfügung. Drei breite Betonstufen und die Uferpromenade bieten zahlreichen weiteren Besuchern Platz. Sie führen von der Allee der Vereinigten Bäume hinab auf das Niveau des Wasserplatzes. Aus der Seefläche tauchen quadratische Inseln von 36 Metern Seitenlänge auf, die als Ausstellungs- und Aufenthaltsbereiche dienen und über Brücken aus dicken Betonplatten miteinander verbunden sind. Sie bilden ein System aus Grachten, die den großen See am Hermesturm mit einem kleinen im Südosten verbinden. Große, schirmartige Dachelemente bieten Witterungsschutz: Sie bilden das so genannte Expo-Dach.

Bordered by Park Wave, Earth Garden and United Trees Avenue, the park near the Hermes Tower, covering 42,000 square meters and encompassing Expo Lake, is one of the most prominent venues for events on the grounds. A grandstand seating approximately 10,000 spectators has been erected for the "flambée shows" presented each evening. The broad concrete steps and the lakeside promenade provide additional space for many more visitors. They lead down from United Trees Avenue to shore level. Square islands measuring 36 meters on each side emerge from the water's surface and serve as exhibition sites and visitor rest areas. They are joined by thick concete-slab bridges. Together they form a system of canals that link the large lake at Hermes Tower with a smaller one located to the southeast. Broad, umbrella-style roof elements forming the Expo Roof provide shelter against sun and rain.

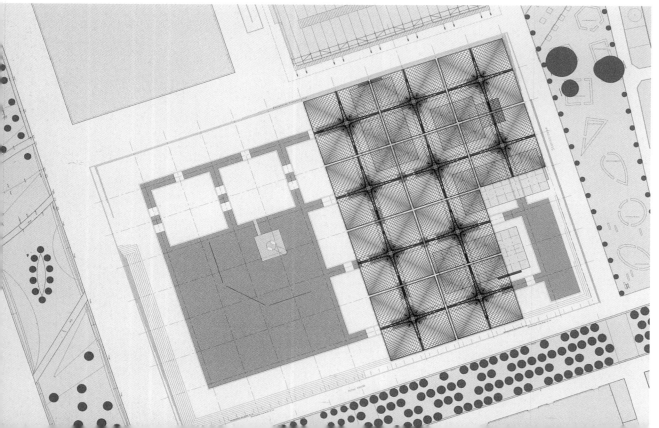

**Plan des Platzes am Hermesturm**
Map of the square at the Hermes Tower

**Bei den allabendlichen Flambée-Veranstaltungen verwandelt sich die Wasseroberfläche des Expo-Sees in eine Projektionsfläche für Lichtspiele.**
The surface of the lake becomes a projection screen for light shows at the "flambée shows" presented every evening.

# Expo-Dach
## Expo Roof

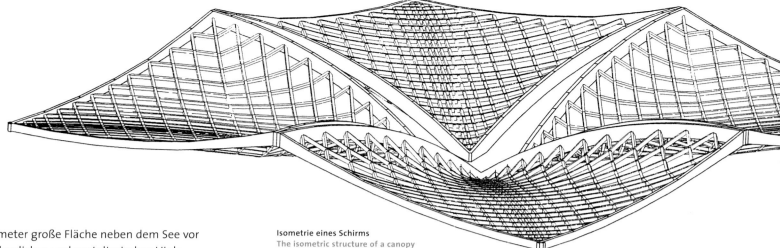

**Isometrie eines Schirms**
The isometric structure of a canopy

Das Expo-Dach, das die 16.000 Quadratmeter große Fläche neben dem See vor den Launen des Wetters schützt, ist ein bauliches und gestalterisches Highlight. Es wird aus zehn Holzschirmen gebildet, die mit einer Höhe von über 20 Metern und einer Größe von 40 x 40 Metern beeindruckende Ausmaße haben. Für den Architekten Thomas Herzog aus München bedeutete dieser Entwurf eine konstruktive Herausforderung. Zweifach gekrümmte Gitterschalen aus Holz bilden das Grundgerüst. Pro Dach reicht eine zentral stehende Stütze aus, um die anfallenden Lasten nach unten abzuleiten. Ein solches Tragwerk ist für den Holzbau in dieser Größenordnung absolut neuartig. Mit dieser Demonstration baulichen Könnens und der Schönheit der gefundenen Form sind die Schirme selbst ein markantes Exponat der Weltausstellung. Die Dachhaut besteht aus einer voll recycelbaren Kunststoffmembran, die das Tageslicht durchlässt, aber gleichzeitig vor zu großer Sonneneinstrahlung schützt. Regenwasser wird als eine Art Wasserspiel an den Stützen abgeleitet. Unter diesem weiten, leicht und transparent wirkenden Dach können Darbietungen und Aktionen vor großem Publikum im Freien und dennoch geschützt stattfinden. Für die Gastronomie stehen unter dem Dach Pavillons, ebenfalls entworfen vom Büro Herzog + Partner, zur Verfügung.

Architekten: Herzog + Partner Diplomingenieure
Architekten BDA, GbR, München
Prof. Thomas Herzog, Hanns Jörg Schrade mit
Roland Schneider
Tragwerksplanung: IEZ Natterer GmbH, Wiesbaden
Prof. Dipl.-Ing. VBI Julius Natterer
Architects: Herzog + Partner Diplomingenieure
Architekten BDA, GbR, Munich
Prof. Thomas Herzog, Hanns Jörg Schrade in cooperation with Roland Schneider
Structural framework design: IEZ Natterer GmbH, Wiesbaden
Prof. Dipl.-Ing. VBI Julius Natterer

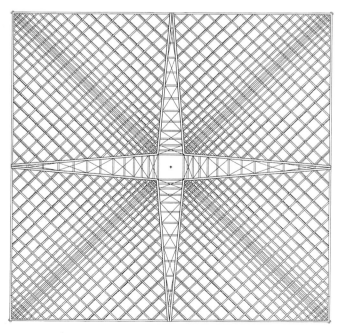

**Grundriss eines Schirms**
Basic shape of a canopy

The Expo Roof, which protects an area of some 16,000 square meters near the lake from the capricious whims of the weather, is a genuine architectural and aesthetic highlight. It comprises ten huge wooden umbrellas, each over 20 meters tall and spanning an area of 40 x 40 meters. The task of designing the roof represented a major engineering challenge for architect Thomas Herzog of Munich. The basic framework consists of wooden lattice shells with two angular bends. Each roof element requires only a single central vertical support, which transfers the entire weight of the structure to the ground. This particular type of load-bearing construction is an absolute novelty in wooden structures of this magnitude. This demonstration of architectural skill and the formal beauty of these umbrellas make them a prominent feature of the World Exposition. The roof covering consists of a fully recyclable membrane that allows sunlight to pass through but blocks excessive solar radiation. Rainwater is diverted down along the supports, creating a fountain effect. This broad, light, transparent roof offers space and shelter for performances and activities of all kinds for the pleasure of outdoor audiences that are nevertheless protected against inclement weather. Restaurant pavilions also designed by the office of Herzog + Partner are located beneath the Expo Roof.

**Modellaufnahme eines Schirmelements**
Model photo of a canopy element

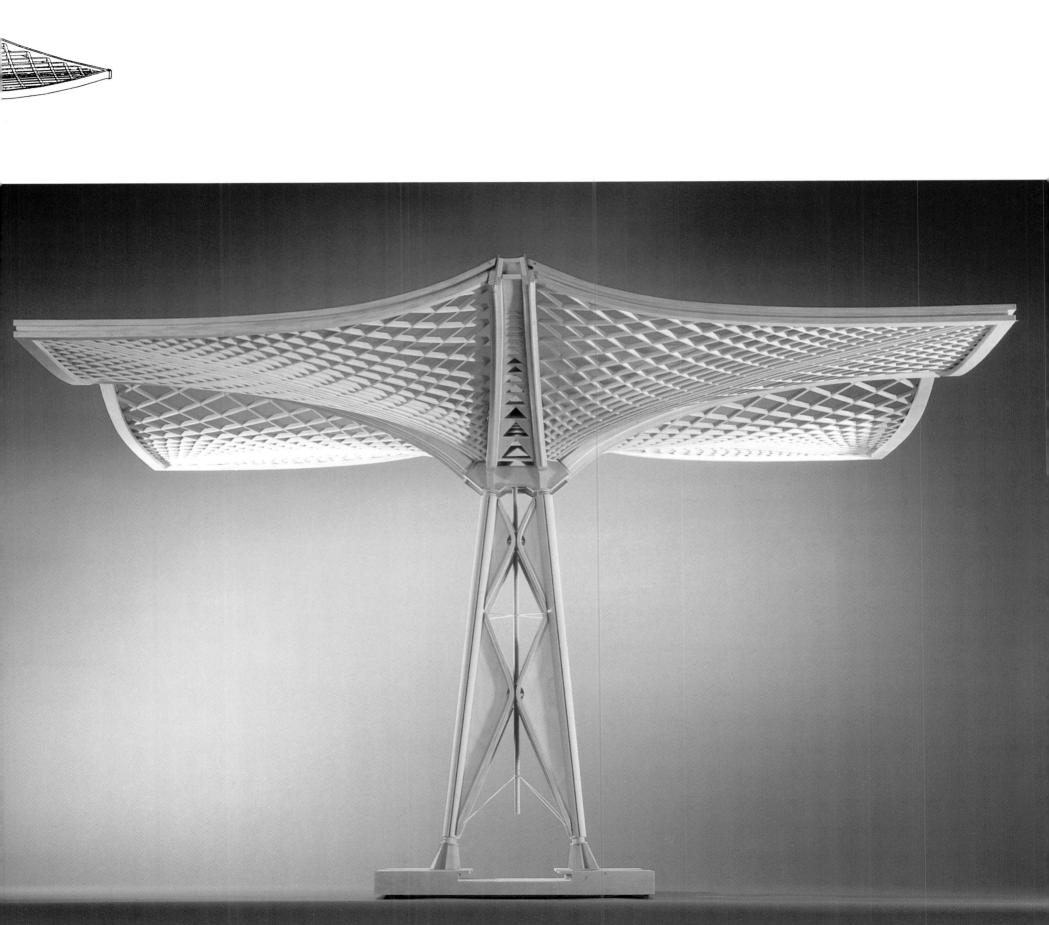

Blick von der Allee der Vereinigten Bäume
auf das Expo-Dach
View of the Expo Roof from United Trees
Avenue

Vom Hermesturm bietet sich Besuchern
eine interessante Perspektive.
The Hermes Tower offers visitors an interesting view of the grounds.

Blick unter die Schirmkonstruktion
View of the canopy construction from below

# Grünanlagen am Kronsberg
## Parks and Gardens on the Kronsberg

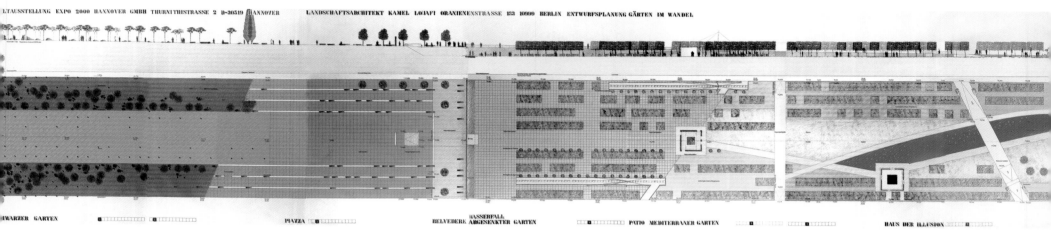

**Plan der Gärten im Wandel**
Map of the Evolving Gardens

Für die Gestaltung der weitläufigen Grünanlagen im Bereich des südlichen Kronsbergs wurde 1995 ein landschaftsplanerischer Realisierungswettbewerb ausgelobt. Unter 55 Teilnehmern aus ganz Europa ging im April 1996 der Berliner Landschaftsarchitekt Kamel Louafi als Sieger hervor. Er entwickelte ein schlüssiges Gesamtkonzept für den Bereich des Pavillongeländes Ost, den Expo-Park und den außerhalb des Weltausstellungsgeländes liegenden Parc Agricole: eine spannende Abfolge von unterschiedlichen Landschaftsräumen, ein fließender Übergang von intensiv zu extensiv genutzten Flächen.

A competition for landscape planning and realization of the expansive green areas around the southern part of the Kronsberg was announced in 1995. The Berlin-based landscape architect Kamel Louafi emerged as the winner from a group of 55 competitors from all over Europe. He developed a convincing total concept for the area encompassing the East Pavilion Site, Expo Park and Parc Agricole just outside the World Exposition Site: a fascinating sequence of different landscapes arranged in a seamless flow from intensive to extensively developed areas.

**Planung der Gärten im Wandel, des Expo-Parks und des Parc Agricole: Landschaftsarchitekt Kamel Louafi, Berlin**
Planning for the Evolving Gardens, Expo Park and Parc Agricole: Landscape architect Kamel Louafi, Berlin

# Gärten im Wandel
## The Evolving Gardens

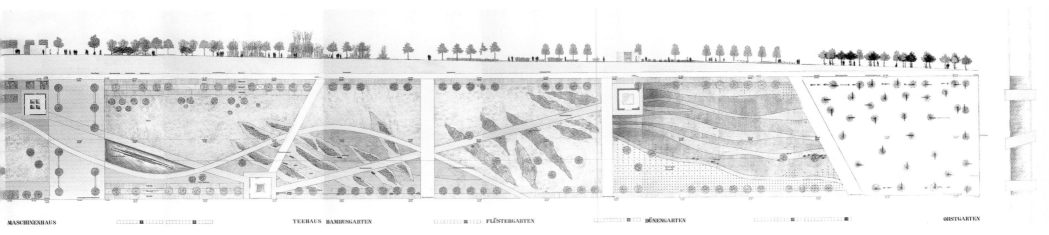

MASCHINENHAUS                     TEEHAUS   BAMBUSGARTEN          FLÜSTERGARTEN         DÜNENGARTEN                OBSTGARTEN

Die Gärten im Wandel ziehen sich als schmales grünes Band von der Expo-Plaza das gesamte Pavillongelände Ost entlang bis zum Expo-Park. Von Norden nach Süden verändern sich dabei schrittweise die Dichte, Intensität und Formenstrenge der Bepflanzung; Besucher werden mit immer neuen, völlig unterschiedlichen Gartentypen überrascht. Der von zahlreichen Schwarzkiefern umgebene Schwarze Garten, geprägt durch dunkelgraue Felsblöcke, geht in eine Piazza über, auf der Steinquader zum Sitzen einladen. In unmittelbarer Nähe stürzt ein Wasserfall 3,5 Meter senkrecht in die Tiefe. Von einer Brüstung bietet sich ein reizvoller Blick auf die tiefer liegenden Gartenteile. Über zwei Rampenanlagen oder einen Einstieg von der Piazza führt der Weg in den Abgesenkten Garten, in dem in einer unterirdischen Grotte der Wasserfall von innen erlebbar ist. Duftende Zypressen und Orangenbäume leiten über in den Mediterranen Garten, der in seiner Form- und Farbgestaltung der maurischen Kultur entlehnt ist. Im anschließenden Bambusgarten symbolisieren die elastischen Stämme der Bambuspflanze, die sich im Wind bewegen und immer wieder aufrichten, die Kunst des Überlebens im Einklang mit der Natur. Auch der Dünengarten thematisiert eindringlich das Motiv der Bewegung. Sanddünen zeigen die Erosion und stehen für langsame und kontinuierliche Veränderung. Der daran angrenzende Obstgarten markiert den Übergang zum Expo-Park und schließt den Kreis zur heimischen Kulturlandschaft. An ausgewählten Orten und Übergängen ergänzen Klanginstallationen oder Wasserspiele die Gartengestaltung. In Form von offenen Räumen sind Schleusen als inszenierte Stationen eingerichtet. Auf quadratischer Grundfläche überlagern sie den »Fluss« des Gartens als Orte der Stille. In kleinen Nischen, die nur einem oder zwei Besuchern Platz bieten, kann man sich in kontemplativer Atmosphäre entspannen und für kurze Zeit zurückziehen.

The Evolving Gardens form a narrow, green band that runs from Expo-Plaza across the entire East Pavilion Site to Expo Park. Visitors walking through them from north to south observe gradual changes in the density, intensity and formality of the vegetation and its presentation as they proceed through a series of very different gardens. Surrounded by numerous black pines, the Black Garden with its striking dark-gray stone blocks opens onto a plaza, where stone cubes invite visitors to stop and sit. Nearby, a waterfall sends a 3.5-meter cascade of water plunging into the depths. A balustrade offers a charming view of the garden areas below. Two ramps and a stairway from the plaza lead visitors down to the Sunken Garden, where the water from the fall flows into an underground grotto. Fragrant cypresses and orange trees mark the transition to the Mediterranean Garden, whose formal design and coloration are adapted from Moorish culture. Swaying in the wind, yet always returning to their upright position, the elastic stocks of the bamboo plants in the adjacent Bamboo Garden symbolize the art of survival in harmony with nature. The Dune Garden also offers a compelling illustration of motion in the form of eroding sand dunes as symbols of slow, constant change. The Orchard next to the Dune Garden stands at the entrance to Expo Park and closes the circle with a return to a local cultivated landscape. Waterworks and sound installations at selected spots and points of transition complement the garden designs. Gateways in the form of open spaces are set in scene as stations along the way. They lie upon the flowing garden as spots of tranquillity on squares of green. In these small niches, large enough to accommodate no more than one or two people, visitors can retreat for a moment of relaxation in an atmosphere conducive to contemplation.

**Am Wasserfall**
At the Waterfall

**Im Dünengarten**
In the Dune Garden

**Im Schwarzen Garten**
In the Black Garden

Das Teehaus im Bambusgarten lädt zum
Ausruhen ein und vermittelt Einblicke in
asiatische Lebensphilosophie und Kultur.
The Teahouse in the Bamboo Garden
invites visitors to stop and rest, while
offering impressions of Asian philosophy
and culture.

# Expo-Park
## Expo Park

Zwischen den Gärten im Wandel und dem Expo-Park verläuft ein Kanal und weist damit auf das zentrale Thema des Parks hin, die Gestaltung und der Umgang mit Wasser. Neben dem Kanal sind ein Wassergarten mit hölzernen Stegen, ein Regenrückhaltebecken und eine bewaldete Anhöhe die gestalterischen Hauptelemente. Auf dem höchsten Punkt der im Westen modellierten Anhöhe lädt ein 15 Meter hoher, erdfarbener Himmelsturm den Besucher dazu ein, seine Blicke schweifen zu lassen. Von hier gewinnt er einen Überblick über die Dimensionen des Parks und, in der Rückschau, über die Gärten im Wandel. Entlang eines Weges, der von der Anhöhe sanft hinabführt, liegen drei weitere, kleinere Aussichtstürme. Im Osten grenzt der ebenfalls von Kamel Louafi entwickelte Parc Agricole an den Expo-Park. Mit seinen gestalteten und gewachsenen Landschaftsteilen bildet er im Anschluss an die Gärten im Wandel und den Expo-Park die dritte und letzte Etappe auf dem Weg in die freie Landschaft.

A canal running between the Evolving Gardens and Expo Park calls attention to the main theme of the park – water as a resource and an element of design. Located along the canal are the park's most important features: an aquatic garden with wooden piers, a rain-catchment basin and a wooded rise. At the highest point on the hill, which is shaped on its western side, the 15-meter, earth-colored Sky Tower invites visitors to gaze out over the scenery below. From here, visitors gain an impression of the dimension of the park and can look back over the Evolving Gardens. Three more outlook towers are positioned along the path leading down a gentle slope from the hill. In the eastern section, Parc Agricole, also designed by Kamel Louafi, borders on Expo Park. With its combination of shaped and natural landscape segments, it represents the last stage on the route through the Evolving Gardens and Expo Park toward the open landscape.

**Blick aus dem Expo-Park in den Parc Agricole**
**View of Parc Agricole from Expo Park**

**Das Regenrückhaltebecken zählt zu den prägenden Elementen des Parks.**
**The rain-catchment basin is one of the most striking features of the park.**

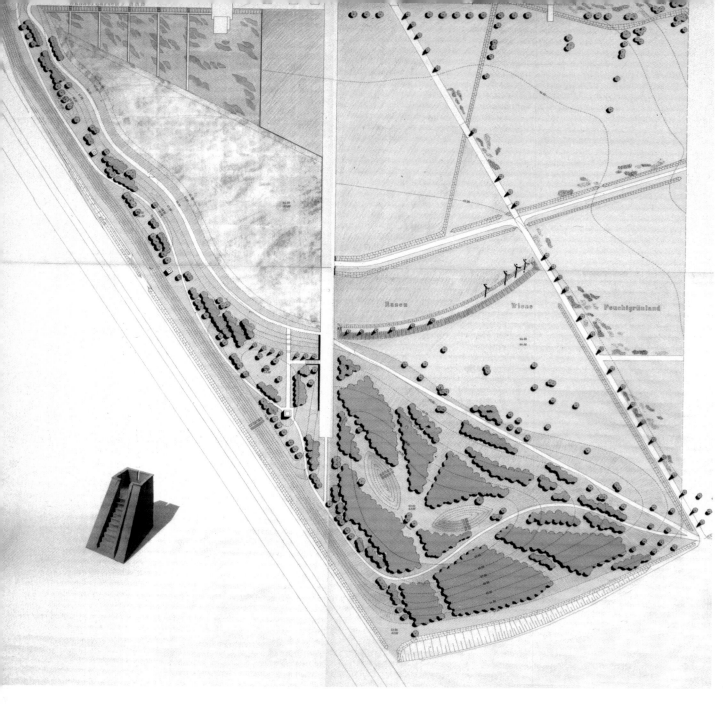

Rasen          Wiese          Feuchtgrünland

**Plan des Expo-Parks**
Map of Expo Park

Der Himmelsturm ist ein interessanter Aussichtspunkt.
The Sky Tower is an interesting outlook point.

# Expo-Plaza
## Expo-Plaza

**Modellaufnahme des Wettbewerbsmodells von 1996**
**Photo of the model submitted for the competition in 1996**

Im städtebaulichen Konzept des Weltausstellungsgeländes nimmt die Expo-Plaza eine zentrale Rolle ein. Mit ihrer großzügigen Gestaltung stellt sie einen besonderen Veranstaltungsort und Empfangsraum dar. Die Plaza ist zudem ein Bindeglied zwischen den beiden Geländeteilen des bereits vorhandenen Messeareals und der neu erschlossenen Fläche am Kronsberg. Besucher, die den Eingang Ost benutzen, werden mit Hilfe zweier attraktiver Fußgänger-brücken mitten über die Plaza zum westlichen Teil des Ausstellungsgeländes geführt. Seine urbane Grundstruktur macht den Platz zu einem ansprechenden Stadtraum, der zum Verweilen einlädt.

Das Konzept für die Plaza-Gestaltung wurde von dem Hamburger Architektur-büro gmp von Gerkan, Marg & Partner entwickelt, das 1996 den städtebau-lichen Wettbewerb Expo-Plaza gewonnen hat. Der quadratische Platz, der mit 110.000 Quadratmetern größer ist als der Petersplatz in Rom, erinnert in seiner Form an einen südländischen Stadtplatz. Er ist an allen Seiten bebaut und erhält dadurch klare Raumkanten. Die unteren Geschosse der Gebäude wurden durch die Ausgestaltung von Sockelbereichen betont, sodass der Blick der Besucher geführt wird. Auch nach der Weltausstellung wird die Plaza als attrak-tiver Stadtraum weiter Bestand haben, denn die Gebäude an der Plaza sind fast alle auf Dauer angelegt und werden im Rahmen eines modernen Edutain-ment- und Dienstleistungszentrums sinnvoll nachgenutzt.

An der Süd- und Nordseite der Plaza liegen sich der Deutsche Pavillon und die Arena gegenüber. Die Bebauung im Westen besteht aus dem Global House, dem Christus Pavillon, dem Bertelsmann-Pavillon Planet m, dem Radisson SAS Hotel und dem Plaza-Café. Die östliche Begrenzung bilden das EuropaHaus und das NILEG Plaza Forum. Während der Weltausstellung ergänzt ein tempo-rärer Bau dieses Ensemble: ein Theater, in dem zwei große Festivals stattfinden. Die Höhen aller Gebäude sind nach Empfehlungen des Gestaltungskreises der EXPO 2000 genau aufeinander abgestimmt. Der Deutsche Pavillon ist 18 Meter, die Arena 25 Meter und alle anderen Gebäude maximal 22,5 Meter hoch.

The Expo-Plaza plays a key role in the urban architectural concept for the grounds of the World Exposition. Its dimensions and design make it a particu-larly important site for events and receptions. Moreover, the Plaza forms a link between the two parts of the existing trade fair grounds and the newly developed area around the Kronsberg. Visitors arriving through the East Entrance are guided along two attractive pedestrian bridges over the heart of the Plaza to the western section of the exposition grounds. The Plaza's fundamental urban character makes it an appealing spot for visitors to stop and spend some time.

The concept for the design of the Plaza was developed by the Hamburg archi-tecture office gmp von Gerkan, Marg & Partner, winner of the 1996 urban architecture competition for the Expo-Plaza. The form of the square Plaza, which occupies 110,000 square meters of ground and is thus even larger than St. Peter's Square in Rome, calls to mind a typical southern European city plaza. It is framed on all sides by buildings, giving it clearly defined spatial bound-aries. The lower stories of the buildings are emphasized by the design of their base segments, which tend to focus the gazes of visitors. The Plaza will remain as an attractive urban space after the close of the World Exposition, since nearly all of the buildings are permanent structures and are to be used to good purpose as elements of a modern edutainment and service center.

The German Pavilion and the Arena stand opposite one another on the north and south sides of the Plaza. Buildings on the western side include the Global House, the Pavilion of Christ, the Bertelsmann Pavilion Planet m, the Radisson SAS Hotel and the Plaza Café. The eastern boundary is formed by the Europe-House and the NILEG Plaza Forum. A temporary structure joins this ensem-ble during the World Exposition: a theater which will host two major festivals. In keeping with the recommendations of the EXPO 2000 Design Circle, the heights of the buildings relate to one another in a harmonious pattern. The German Pavilion is 18 meters tall, the Arena rises to 25 meters and the other buildings have maximum heights of 22.5 meters.

**Luftaufnahme der Expo-Plaza**
**Aerial view of Expo-Plaza**

# Innere Platzfläche
## Plaza Interior

Die Gestaltung der inneren Platzfläche ist ein entscheidender Faktor für die besondere Aufenthaltsqualität der Expo-Plaza. Im Osten wird die leicht geneigte
Fläche von einer dreireihigen und im Westen von einer fünfreihigen Platanen-
allee eingefasst. Die stark raumbildenden Alleen bilden grüne Platzkanten,
deren Strenge an einigen Stellen durch alte vereinzelte Bestandsbäume wie
Apfel, Ahorn oder Linde unterbrochen wird. Auf dem Platz wurden zahlreiche
alte Linden und Pappeln erhalten. Sie tragen zur Maßstäblichkeit der Plaza
bei und werden gleichzeitig zu Orten der Begegnung, denn die Hälfte ist von
Sitzstufen umgeben, teils abgesenkt und teils erhöht zu Sitzpyramiden. In
der Dunkelheit werden einige Stufenringe von unten beleuchtet und lassen
die Baumkronen optisch über dem Platz schweben. Auf der gesamten Platzfläche sind helle, quadratische Betonvorsatzsteine verlegt, in der Mitte größere
(75 × 75 Zentimeter) und am Rand kleinere (25 × 25 Zentimeter). Ihrer Oberfläche
sind glitzernde Glimmerplättchen und Edelstahlsplitter beigemischt.
Vor dem Deutschen Pavillon liegt eine große Stufenanlage mit einer überdachten Bühne, die unter anderem für die Nationentage genutzt wird. Zum gestalterischen Repertoire gehört auch das Element Wasser. So erzeugen 98 tan-
zende Fontänen ein beruhigendes Plätschern und sorgen für ein angenehmes
Klima. An heißen Tagen steigt Nebel an den Bäumen auf und bewirkt am
Abend zusammen mit den Lichteffekten eine geheimnisvolle Atmosphäre. Eine
runde Wasserfläche, das Wasserauge, liegt unterhalb einer Baumgruppe und
vermittelt Ruhe und Besinnung. So bietet die Plaza, deren platzgestaltende
Elemente auf Bewegung ausgelegt sind, auch Bereiche, die zum Verweilen einladen, wodurch ihre stadtprägende Funktion unterstrichen wird.

The design of the interior of the Plaza has a significant impact upon the quality of Expo-Plaza as a setting for visitors. In the eastern section, the slightly
sloping surface is bordered by an avenue formed by three rows of plane
trees. Another avenue with five rows of plane trees borders the area to the
west. These avenues have a marked space-shaping character and form a green
edging for the Plaza. Their strict uniformity is broken up at certain points
by isolated, old, long-standing maples, apple and linden trees. A substantial
number of old linden and poplar trees were left in place on the Plaza. They
contribute to its formal regularity and also serve as points of encounter, as half
of them are surrounded by stepped seats, some descending below ground
level, others rising to form seating pyramids. Several of these rings of steps are
illuminated from below after dark, creating the impression that the treetops
above hang suspended above the Plaza. The entire surface of the Plaza is paved
with light-colored, square concrete facing stones, larger ones in the middle
(75 × 75 centimeters) and smaller ones along the edges (25 × 25 centimeters).
Glittering sequins and stainless steel splinters were mixed into their surfaces
layers.
Located in front of the German Pavilion is a large grandstand with a canopied
stage, which is to be used for National Day festivities and other events. The
repertoire of design elements includes water. Ninety-eight dancing fountains
produce pleasant sounds reminiscent of a softly babbling brook. On hot days,
fog rises into the trees, combining with the lighting effects to create an atmosphere of mystery during the hours of darkness. A round pool of water, known
as the Water Eye, lies beneath a group of trees, evoking a sense of reflective
tranquillity. Thus although the Plaza's defining elements are designed with
movement in mind, it also offers places to stop and spend time, a feature that
underscores its urban function.

Platzgestaltung: Landschaftsarchitekten WES Wehberg,
Eppinger, Schmidtke & Partner, Hamburg
Plaza design: Landschaftsarchitekten WES Wehberg,
Eppinger, Schmidtke & Partner, Hamburg

Baumorte werden zu Treffpunkten und
laden zum Ausruhen ein.
Tree areas form meeting points and inviting places to stop and rest.

Die Platzfläche ist seitlich von Platanen-
alleen eingefasst.
The plaza is bounded on two sides by tree-
lined avenues

# Bühnenüberdachung
# Stage Canopy

Die 1.800 Quadratmeter große Membranüberdachung der Bühne bietet Zuschauern und Akteuren Schutz vor Witterungseinflüssen. Gleichzeitig dient das Dach auch wartenden Besuchern des Deutschen Pavillons als Unterstand bei Regenwetter. Nebenräume für die Künstler liegen, durch zwei Treppen erreichbar, unter der Bühne. Den höchsten Punkt der Dachkonstruktion bildet ein von Süd nach Nord geneigter Zugring aus Stahlrohr mit einem Durchmesser von 16 Metern, der direkt über der Bühnengrube liegt. Das zweite Element ist ein von Nord nach Süd geneigter Druckring mit einem Durchmesser von 29 Metern, der von sieben V-förmigen Stützen getragen wird. Durch die Verschränkung und gegenseitige Verschiebung der Ringe sowie durch deren Wirkung als kraftschlüssige Systeme ist es möglich, eine Membran mit hoher Zugkraft zwischen den äußeren und inneren Ring zu spannen. Die Membran besteht aus weißem, teflonbeschichtetem Glasfasergewebe (PTFE).

Measuring 1,800 square meters, the large membrane canopy above the stage offers spectators and performers protection against inclement weather. The roof also provides shelter for visitors waiting to enter the German Pavilion on rainy days. Dressing rooms for the artists are located beneath the stage, accessible from two stairways. The highest point in the roof structure is formed by a steel pull ring inclined on a north-south plane. It measures 16 meters in diameter and is positioned directly over the stage pit. The second element is a pressure ring, also inclined on a north-south plane, with a diameter of 29 meters, which is supported by seven V-shaped columns. The dual configuration and the push-and-pull of the rings, combined with their function as force-binding systems, makes it possible to span a membrane between the inner and outer rings with considerable tension. The membrane itself consists of white fiberglass fabric (PTFE) with a Teflon coating.

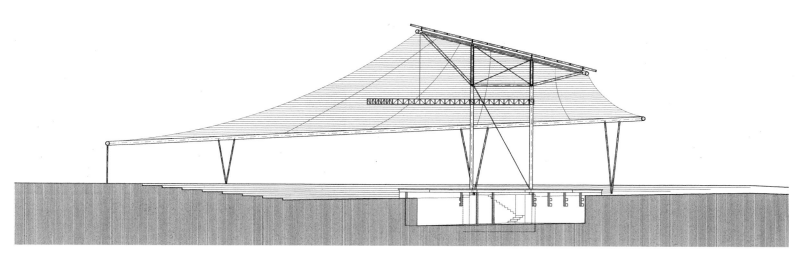

**Schnitt durch die Bühnenüberdachung**
Cross-sectional view of the stage roof

**Architekten: Schulitz + Partner, Braunschweig**
**Prof. Helmut C. Schulitz, Johannes König, Jürgen Schade**
**Tragwerksplanung: Werner Sobek Ingenieure, Stuttgart**
Architects: Schulitz + Partner, Braunschweig
Prof. Helmut C. Schulitz, Johannes König, Jürgen Schade
Supporting structure design: Werner Sobek Ingenieure,
Stuttgart

**Die leichte Membrankonstruktion setzt
einen Akzent auf der Plaza.**
The light membrane construction lends
a special accent to the Plaza.

# Expo-Brücken
## Expo Bridges

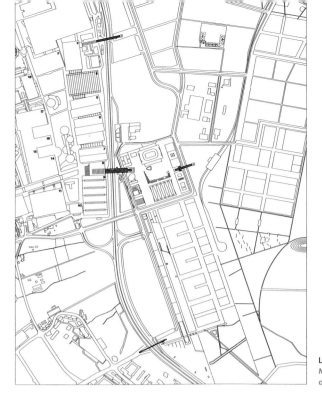

**Lageplan aller vier Brücken**
Map showing the locations
of all four bridges

Für die Erschließung der Plaza und zur Verbindung der beiden Geländeteile wurden insgesamt vier neue, einheitlich gestaltete Brücken gebaut. Bei der Ankunft am Eingang Ost leitet eine 90 Meter lange und 15 Meter breite Fußgängerbrücke die Besucher über Höhenunterschiede im Gelände auf die Expo-Plaza. Von der Westseite der Plaza führt eine großzügig gestaltete, 127 Meter lange und 30 Meter breite Fußgängerbrücke über den Schnellweg zur Allee der Vereinigten Bäume. Die stegähnlichen Brücken überraschen durch ihre außergewöhnlichen Dimensionen und hohe Gestaltqualität. Die Konstruktion besteht aus schlanken 8 bis 14 Meter langen Stahlstelen, die masthoch über die Brücken hinausragen und wie ein Begrüßungsspalier wirken. Architektonisch zeichnet sich der Entwurf durch seine klare Eleganz und durch ansprechende Details aus. Bei Dunkelheit verwandeln sich die Stelen in ein weithin sichtbares Meer aus Leuchtstäben, die aus bedruckten Acrylglaszylindern bestehen. Der Aufbau der Brücken unterliegt einem einfachen, streng modularen System. Die Stelen sind in einem Raster von 7,5 x 7,5 Metern zu einem »Mastenwald« zusammengestellt und bei größeren Spannweiten, etwa bei der Überbrückung des Schnellwegs, in ein abgespanntes Tragwerk eingehängt. Das Raster ermöglicht eine vielseitige Gestaltung der Gehflächen. Holzbohlen werden mit Betonflächen kombiniert, und auch Rampen, Treppen oder Podeste lassen sich leicht einbinden. Um eine hohe Flexibilität in Bezug auf die Weltausstellungs- und Nachnutzung zu erreichen, sind die Brücken so konstruiert, dass sie den verschiedenen Anforderungen an Länge und Breite, Umbau oder Abbau ohne Veränderung der Gestaltung gerecht werden und temporär, wie am Eingang Ost, mit schützenden Membrandächern überspannt werden können.

| | | |
|---|---|---|
| Brücke Mitte (»Exponale«): | Länge: 127,5 Meter | Breite: 30,0 Meter |
| Brücke Ost: | Länge: 90,0 Meter | Breite: 15,0 Meter |
| Brücke Nordost: | Länge: 142,5 Meter | Breite: 15,0 Meter |
| Brücke Süd: | Länge: 90,0 Meter | Breite: 7,5 Meter |

A total of four new, uniformly designed bridges were constructed to provide access to and from the Plaza and to link the two separate parts of the grounds. Visitors arriving at the East Entrance walk over a pedestrian bridge (90 meters long and 15 meters wide) above rising and falling terrain elevations to the Expo-Plaza. Those approaching from the west cross an expansive pedestrian bridge (127 meters long and 30 meters wide) over Schnellweg to United Trees Avenue. These walkway-style bridges exhibit astonishingly unusual dimensions and a surprisingly appealing design. The superstructure consists of slim steel steles in lengths ranging from 8 to 14 meters, which tower like masts above the bridges and evoke the effect of a welcoming guard of honor. The outstanding features of the architectural design are its elegant clarity and appealing details. Darkness transforms the steles into a sea of luminous rods consisting of printed acrylic-glass cylinders that can be seen from a great distance.

The bridges are constructed on the basis of a simple, strictly modular system. The steles are arranged in a grid pattern measuring 7.5 x 7.5 meters, forming a "forest of masts." For longer span distances – where the bridge crosses Schnellweg, for example – they are hung in a guyed support structure. The grid pattern allows for great diversity in the design of the walking surfaces. Wooden planks are combined with concrete segments, and ramps, stairs and pedestals are easily integrated. In order to ensure sufficient flexibility with respect to use both during and after the World Exposition, the bridges are constructed in such a way that they meet the various different requirements with regard to length, width, conversion or dismantling without affecting the quality of design. They can also be covered temporarily, as is the case at the East Entrance, with protective membrane roofs.

| | | |
|---|---|---|
| Central Bridge ("Exponale"): | length: 127.5 meters | width: 30.0 meters |
| East Bridge: | length: 90.0 meters | width: 15.0 meters |
| Northeast Bridge: | length: 142.5 meters | width: 15.0 meters |
| South Bridge: | length: 90.0 meters | width: 7.5 meters |

Die »Exponale« verbindet das westliche
Ausstellungsgelände mit der Plaza.
The "Exponale" connects the West Pavilion
Site with the Plaza.

Stele mit Leuchte
Stele with lamp

Architekten: gmp von Gerkan, Marg & Partner,
Hamburg
in ARGE mit Schlaich, Bergermann und Partner + SIAT
Entwurf: Prof. Volkwin Marg mit Prof. Jörg Schlaich
Sponsor: Preussag AG, Hannover
Architects: gmp von Gerkan, Marg & Partner, Hamburg
in cooperation with Schlaich, Bergermann und
Partner + SIAT
Design: Prof. Volkwin Marg and Prof. Jörg Schlaich
Sponsor: Preussag AG, Hanover

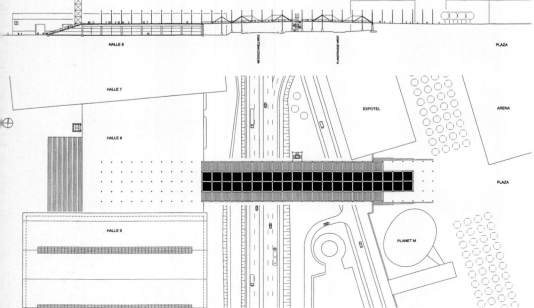

Grundriss und Schnitt der Brücke Mitte
(»Exponale«)
Floor plan and cross section of the Central
Bridge (the "Exponale")

Blick durch den Stützenwald
View through the forest of pillars

# Deutscher Pavillon
## German Pavilion

Als offizieller Beitrag der Bundesrepublik Deutschland ist der Deutsche Pavillon von besonderer Bedeutung und dementsprechend von hoher architektonischer Qualität. Die Ästhetik des gläsernen Baukörpers spiegelt Großzügigkeit und repräsentative Offenheit. Für den Friedrichshafener Architekten und Investor des Deutschen Pavillons, Josef Wund, symbolisiert diese Transparenz Demokratie und Fortschritt. Er entwarf ein Gebäude, in dem sich Deutschland weltoffen und aufgeschlossen präsentieren kann.

Der Pavillon ist 130 Meter lang, 90 Meter breit und 18 Meter hoch und besteht aus Stahl, Glas und Holz. Eine technische Innovation stellen die konkav nach innen gebogene Glasfassade und ihre Aufhängung dar. Glasstützen mit Stahlkern stoßen durch die Fassade durch, liegen das eine Mal vor, das andere Mal hinter dem Glas. Insgesamt 14 Stützen tragen sechs hölzerne, geschwungene Dachelemente. Der Schwung der Fassade und des Daches setzt sich im Innern des Gebäudes fort, in dem es, abgesehen von einigen Brandwänden, in allen Bereichen nur geschwungene Wände und Decken gibt. Diese reichen nicht bis an die Fassade heran, sodass immer ein Blick in den Nachbarraum oder nach unten möglich ist. Der gesamte Pavillon ist von einem Wassergraben umgeben, dessen Boden aus Edelstahl interessante Spiegelungen erzeugt. Während der Weltausstellung ist der Pavillon aufgeteilt in drei Ausstellungs- und Showbereiche sowie in Theater, Empfangs- und VIP-Bereiche, Büros, Presseräume und ein Restaurant, das sich nach außen auf die Plaza ausdehnt. Nach der EXPO 2000 wird das Gebäude voraussichtlich als »Forum für Wissenschaft und Technik« weiter für Ausstellungszwecke genutzt werden.

Architekt: WUND EXPO Pavillon Hannover GmbH,
Friedrichshafen
**Josef Wund**
Architect: WUND EXPO Pavillon Hannover GmbH,
Friedrichshafen
Josef Wund

Das Dach mit seinem Überhang von 6 Metern bietet Besuchern Wetterschutz. With its six-meter overhang, the roof offers visitors shelter against inclement weather.

As the official presentation of the Federal Republic of Germany at EXPO 2000, the German Pavilion assumes a status of particular importance, and its architectural quality is entirely commensurate with its significance. The aesthetics of the glass edifice reflect expansiveness and representational openness. In the opinion of Josef Wund, the Friedrichhafen investor and pavilion architect, its transparency symbolizes both democracy and progress. Wund has designed a building in which Germany can present itself to the world with open arms. The pavilion is 130 meters long, 90 meters wide and 18 meters high. It is built of steel, glass and wood. The concave glass face and its mounting structure represent a genuine technical innovation. Steel-core glass support beams jut through the facade, appearing outside the glass in some places, behind it in others. A total of 14 supports bear the weight of six curved, wooden roof elements. The sweepings curves of the facade and the roof are mirrored inside the building as well, where – with the exception of a few fire barriers – all of the walls and ceilings are curved. Since they do not abut against the outside walls, it is possible everywhere to look into the next room or down to the floor below. The entire pavilion is surrounded by a water-filled moat with a stainless-steel bottom that creates interesting mirror effects. During the World Exposition, the pavilion will be divided into three exhibition and show areas in addition to a theater, reception and VIP areas, offices, press rooms and a restaurant that opens onto the Plaza outside. According to current plans, the building will continue to be used for exhibition purposes as "Forum for Science and Technology" after the end of EXPO 2000.

Die Glasfassaden ermöglichen von allen
Seiten Einblicke in das Geschehen im
Gebäude.
The glass facades offer a view of activity
inside the building from all sides.

Im Wassergraben spiegelt sich die Glasfassade.
The glass facade is reflected in the moat.

**Die Nordfassade des Deutschen Pavillons
an der Plaza**
The north facade of the German Pavilion
on the Plaza

# Global House
## Global House

Das Erscheinungsbild des Gebäudes ist geprägt durch seine klare Form und die Fassaden aus Glas und Aluminium. Einen besonderen Blickfang bietet die Verkleidung aus gehobelten Lärchenbrettern auf der Westseite. Der eigentliche Reiz des Gebäudes liegt in seinem vollverglasten Atrium, das als sechsgeschossige Halle die beiden angrenzenden Riegelbauwerke miteinander verbindet. Es dient gleichzeitig als Eingang, Veranstaltungs- und Ausstellungsfläche. Das Klima des Atriums ist durch entsprechende Lüftungselemente im Dach und in der Fassade dem Außenklima angenähert. Durch die Nutzung von Sonnenenergie ist das Atrium im Winter frostfrei und kann in den Ausstellungsbereichen bei Bedarf temperiert werden.

Der Entwurf konnte nachhaltig über die Zeit der Weltausstellung hinaus entwickelt werden, da die Nachnutzung durch die Fachhochschule für Design und Medien in Hannover frühzeitig feststand. Aus Sicht der Planer hat die Ambivalenz zwischen der Expo-Nutzung für die Ausstellung der Weltweiten Projekte und der Nachnutzung einen Gebäudetypus ermöglicht, der in dieser Form sonst weder als reiner Expo-Pavillon noch als Fachhochschule hätte entstehen können. Seine Transparenz lässt das Leben im Gebäude auch nach außen sichtbar werden.

The outward appearance of the building is characterized by its formal clarity and its glass-and-aluminum facades. A particularly striking feature is the layer of planed larchwood boards on the western face. The most appealing aspect of the building is its all-glass atrium, a six-story edifice that connects the two adjacent building wings. The atrium serves as an entrance, an exhibition area and a venue for events. The air in the atrium is continuously adjusted to approximate outdoor temperatures by ventilation units in the roof and the facade. The use of solar energy keeps the atrium frost-free during the winter, and the exhibition areas can be heated when the need arises.

The design was developed with an eye for viability beyond the end of the World Exposition, as the decision to turn the building over to the Fachhochschule für Design und Medien in Hanover was made quite early on. From the standpoint of the planners, the dual objectives of utilization at EXPO 2000 for the exhibition of global projects and providing for later use as well enabled them to design a building that would otherwise have been inconceivable as either a conventional EXPO pavilion or an institution of higher learning. Its transparency allows those outside the building to catch a glimpse of life inside it.

**Architekten: SIAT Architektur + Technik, München**
**Architects: SIAT Architektur + Technik, Munich**

**Südfassade des Global House**
The south facade of Global House

Blick in das Atrium
View of the atrium

# Christus Pavillon
## Pavilion of Christ

Für die gemeinsame Expo-Präsentation der evangelischen und katholischen Kirche mit dem Thema »Jesus Christus – gestern, heute und in Ewigkeit« haben die Hamburger Architekten gmp von Gerkan, Marg & Partner ein Gebäude entworfen, das an ein Kloster erinnert. Klare geometrische Formen und die Reduzierung auf wenige Materialien geben dem Pavillon ein ansprechendes, unverwechselbares Erscheinungsbild. Über die gesamte Länge von 75 Metern begrenzen 16 Meter hohe, stählerne Kolonnaden als Säulenwand den Pavillon zur Plaza und bilden gleichzeitig den Rahmen für die Brücke, über die die Besucher das Gebäude betreten.

Ein 3,6 Meter breiter und 7,2 Meter hoher Kreuzgang umgibt den Gesamtkomplex und dient als Wandel- und Ausstellungsbereich. Der zentrale Bereich, ein großer kubischer Sakralraum, ist von kleinen Ausstellungsräumen umgeben. Der Pavillon ist als Ort der Stille und Besinnung angelegt; Lichtinszenierungen in der Krypta im Untergeschoss und im Sakralraum betonen den meditativen Charakter. Im Sakralraum tragen die Wände aus lichtdurchlässigen Alabasterplatten zur indirekten Beleuchtung und zu der kontemplativen Stimmung des Raumes bei.

Der Christus Pavillon wurde aus einheitlichen Modulen aus verzinktem Stahl, Sichtbeton und Glas erbaut und zeigt offen seine Konstruktion und Details. Er ist das einzige Gebäude auf der Plaza, das nach der EXPO 2000 wieder abgebaut und an einem anderen Standort weitergenutzt wird. Es wurde so konzipiert, dass es für die Erweiterung des Zisterzienserklosters Volkenroda in Thüringen verwendet werden kann.

**Architekten: gmp von Gerkan, Marg & Partner, Braunschweig**
**Prof. Meinhard von Gerkan**
Architects: gmp von Gerkan, Marg & Partner, Braunschweig
Prof. Meinhard von Gerkan

**Blick von der Plaza auf den Christus Pavillon**
View of the Christ Pavilion from the Plaza

For the joint EXPO presentation on the theme of "Jesus Christ – Yesterday, Today and for all Eternity" organized by the Evangelical and Catholic Churches, the Hamburg architects gmp von Gerkan, Marg & Partner designed a building resembling a monastery. Clearly defined geometric forms and the use of a limited number of materials contribute to the unique and appealing appearance of the pavilion. Along the entire length of 75 meters, steel colonnades measuring 16 meters in height border the pavilion as a columned wall. They also form the frame of the bridge over which visitors enter the building.

The entire complex is surrounded by a cloistered hall 3.6 meters wide and 7.2 meters high, which serves as a walking and exhibition area. The central area, a large, cubic ecclesiastical room, is surrounded by small exhibition rooms. The pavilion is conceived as a setting of tranquillity and contemplation. Light shows in the basement crypt and in the church room underscore the meditative character of the atmosphere. Walls made of translucent alabaster panels in the church room provide indirect lighting and contribute to the prevailing contemplative mood.

The Pavilion of Christ was built of uniform modules constructed of galvanized steel, exposed concrete and glass. It openly exhibits its underlying structure and details. It is the only building on the Plaza that is scheduled for dismantling and further use at a different location after the end of EXPO 2000. The pavilion was designed specifically as an extension to the Cistercian monastery in Volkenroda in the state of Thüringen.

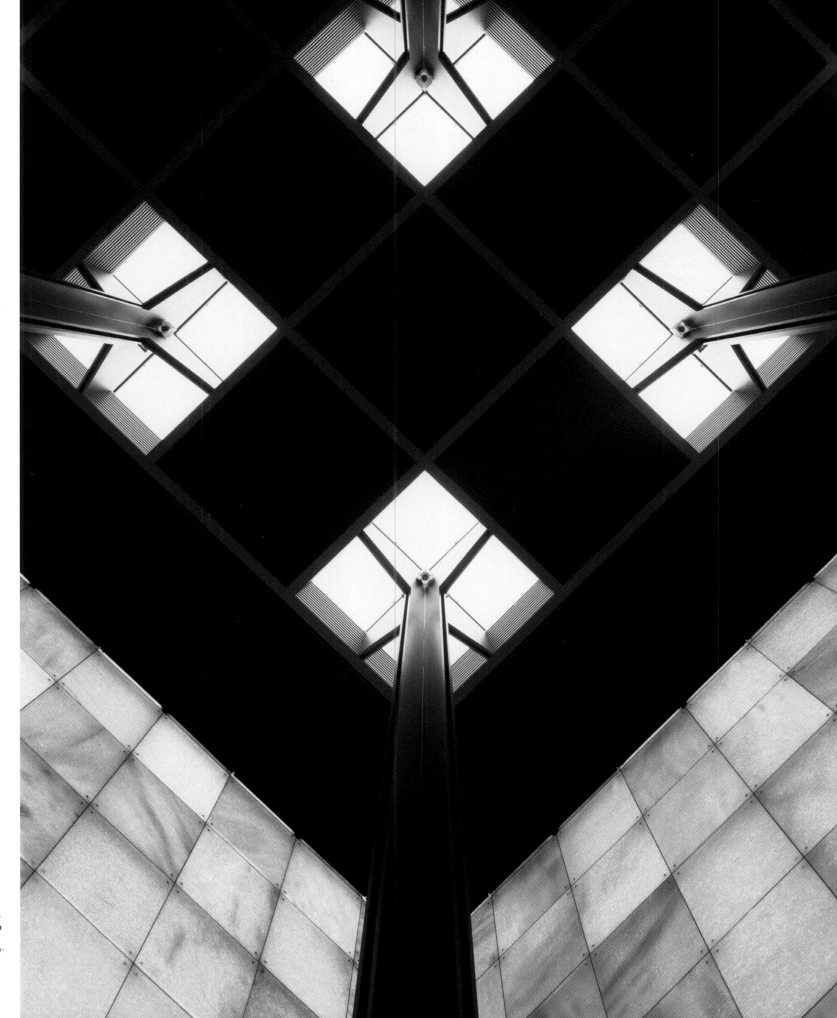

Die 18 Meter hohen, kreuzförmigen Stahlstützen münden in Oberlichter, aus denen Streiflicht in den Sakralraum fällt.
The 18-meter-high, cross-shaped steel supports culminate in skylights that admit beams of light into the church interior.

**In der Krypta, dem Raum der Stille, dringt
Licht durch schmale Schlitze und umläuft
als leuchtendes Band den Boden.**
In the crypt, the Room of Silence, light
enters through small slits and creates a
luminous band around the edges of the
floor.

**Die zweischalige Glasfassade des Kreuzgangs ist als
Vitrine mit unterschiedlichen Materialien gefüllt,
die je nach Dichte die Lichtstimmung beeinflussen.**
The double-shelled glass facade of the cloister forms a
showcase filled with a variety of different materials,
which generate diverse moods of light by virtue of their
varying density.

# Planet m – medien für menschen
# Planet m – media for people

Der Pavillon des Medienkonzerns Bertelsmann stellt durch seine ungewöhnliche Gestaltung einen Blickfang auf der Plaza dar. Er besteht aus einem klaren und kompakten Haupthaus und einem aufgeständerten »Planeten«. Beide Bauteile sind durch eine geschlossene Brücke miteinander verbunden. An der Westseite wird der Komplex von einer 8 Meter hohen Glaswand begrenzt.

Das Haupthaus ist ein schlichter kubischer Baukörper mit einer Länge von 50 Metern, einer Breite von 12 Metern und einer Höhe von 21,5 Metern. Mit seiner einfachen Holzverschalung erinnert das Gebäude an einen Hafenschuppen und bildet damit bewusst einen starken Gegensatz zu dem Planeten, dessen Konstruktion dem Schiffsbau entlehnt ist. Der Planet ist ein amorpher Körper mit einem Tragwerk aus umlaufenden Stahlspanten. Ähnlich wie die Längen- und Breitengrade auf einem Globus bilden diese Spanten 84 Einzelfelder mit einer Größe von ungefähr 5,4 x 5,4 Metern. Der Planet misst in seiner größten Ausdehnung 46 x 36 Meter und hat eine Stichhöhe von 26 Metern. Eine Hubbühne, der so genannte Space-Lift, kann gleichzeitig 200 Besucher 8 Meter hoch in die Ausstellungsbereiche des Planeten befördern.

Die Außenhaut des Planeten besteht aus einem dreidimensionalen, spiralförmigen Edelstahlgewebe. Zusammen mit über 800 innen liegenden Halogenstrahlern bewirkt dieses neue Material den Effekt, dass der Planet im Dunkeln zu glühen und zu schweben scheint. Ein Steuerungsprogramm kann zahlreiche unterschiedliche Farbstimmungen erzeugen, von einem kalten Weiß über Gelb und Orange zu einem glühenden Rot und schließlich zu einem kühlen Dunkelblau.

The pavilion of the media corporation Bertelsmann presents a particularly unusual and eye-catching design on the Expo-Plaza. It comprises a clear-lined, compact main building and an elevated "planet." The two elements are joined by a covered bridge. To the west, the complex is bordered by an eight-meter-high glass wall.

The main building is an unpretentious oblong structure, measuring 50 by 12 meters, with a height of 21.5 meters. With its simple wooden facade, the building bears a certain resemblance to a waterside shed and thus presents a deliberate, stark contrast to the planet, a model constructed on the basis of principles of the shipbuilder's craft. The planet is an amorphous shape with an encircling framework of steel rings. Like the lines of longitude and latitude on a globe, these rings form 84 fields measuring approximately 5.4 by 5.4 meters. At its greatest circumference, the planet is 46 by 36 meters thick. An elevator platform, the so-called Space Lift, carries up to 200 visitors at a time up to the exhibition areas inside the planet.

The outer skin of the planet is made of three-dimensional, spiral, woven stainless steel. In combination with the more than 800 halogen spotlights inside, this novel material creates the effect of a planet that glows in the dark and appears to hover in suspension. A programmed control system generates a wide selection of different atmospheric color combinations ranging from cold white to yellow and orange to glowing red or cool dark blue.

**Architekten: Triad mit Becker Gewers Kühn & Kühn, Berlin,**
**Karl Karas, Wolf-Rüdiger Kehrer**
Architects: Triad in cooperation with Becker Gewers Kühn & Kühn, Berlin
Karl Karas, Wolf-Rüdiger Kehrer

**Das Erscheinungsbild des Pavillons ist geprägt durch zwei sehr unterschiedliche Baukörper.**
The pavilion comprises two very different building structures.

Bei Dunkelheit lassen Lichtinszenierungen den Planeten scheinbar über der Plaza schweben.
Staged lighting effects give the Planet the appearance of hovering above the square during the hours of darkness.

# Radisson SAS Hotel
## Radisson SAS Hotel

**Blick von der Plaza auf das Hotel**
View of the hotel from the Plaza

Das Vier-Sterne-Haus der Hotelkette Radisson SAS Hotels Worldwide verfügt über 252 Zimmer, eine Präsidentensuite, Juniorsuiten, Tagungs-, Kongress- und Seminarräume, ein Restaurant, eine Bar, Ladengeschäfte, ein Fitnesscenter und ein Parkhaus. Der fünfgeschossige, großzügig gestaltete Komplex besteht aus zwei parallel angeordneten Gebäuderiegeln, die durch einen dritten, auf der Mittelachse liegenden Bauteil verbunden sind. Der Entwurf ist geprägt durch die Lage des Eckgrundstücks und nutzt einen Geländesprung von knapp 6 Metern für zwei Eingänge. Von der Plaza ist das Hotel nur für Fußgänger zugänglich, die Zufahrt für PKW, Busse oder Lieferfahrzeuge erfolgt über das tiefer gelegene Niveau der Zufahrtsstraße. Die gesamte vertikale Erschließung des Hotels ist in dem auf der Mittelachse liegenden Gebäudeteil untergebracht. Dieser Mittelbau ist über alle Geschosse offen ausgebildet und ermöglicht den Hotelgästen durch seine Transparenz eine einfache Orientierung. Mit den zur Außenfassade gerichteten Höfen zählt die Ausbildung der Mittelachse zu den besonderen architektonischen Merkmalen des Hotels.

Nach amerikanischem Vorbild können die Gäste des Hotels bei der Buchung unter vier verschiedenen Themenzimmern wählen. Der »Italian«-Stil vermittelt mit seinen Intarsienarbeiten und aus Italien importierten Dekorationsgegenständen eine Mischung aus Tradition und Eleganz. Der »Scandinavian«-Stil wirkt freundlich und unkompliziert, und im »Maritim«-Zimmer erinnert die Ausstattung aus Mahagoniholz, Leder und Messing an frühere luxuriöse Ozeanreisen. Das »High-Tech«-Zimmer mit seinem hochmodernen Ambiente ist auf das 21. Jahrhundert ausgerichtet.

The four-star facility representing the Radisson SAS Hotels Worldwide chain has 252 rooms, a presidential suite, junior suites, meeting, conference and seminar rooms, a restaurant, a bar, shops, a fitness center and a parking garage. The five-story, lavishly designed complex consists of two parallel building wings joined by a third structure linking them at their midpoints. The design reflects the topography of the corner lot and exploits a drop in elevation of some six meters to incorporate two entrances. The hotel is accessible from the Plaza only to pedestrians. Cars, busses and delivery trucks arrive at the lower level via a roadway. All of the vertical access routes inside the hotel are accommodated in the central building linking the two wings. This middle segment is open on all floors; its transparency contributes to complete ease of orientation for hotel guests. With its courtyards facing the outer facade, the design of the central axis is one of the most striking architectural features of the hotel.

As in many American hotels, guests booking accommodations may choose from among four different room themes. The "Italian" style, with its wood inlay work and decorative items imported from Italy, offers a mixture of tradition and elegance. The "Scandinavian" style presents a friendly, uncomplicated ambiance, and guests in the "Maritime" rooms find themselves reminded by the mahogany, leather and brass furnishings of the luxury ocean voyages of bygone days. The "High-Tech" rooms offer an ultra-modern atmosphere in a decidedly 21st-century style.

**Architekten: Freitag, Kaltenbach & Partner, Karlsruhe**
Architects: Freitag, Kaltenbach & Partner, Karlsruhe

# Plaza-Café
## Plaza Café

Mit seinen gläsernen Fassaden wirkt das Café einladend und freundlich.
The Café's glass walls give it an open, inviting appearance.

Das Café ist ein einladend wirkendes Gebäude aus Stahl, Glas und Holz, das über alle drei Geschosse vollverglast ist. Diese Transparenz schafft eine Verbindung zwischen Innen und Außen. Der freundliche und offene Eindruck des Gebäudes wird durch das Glasdach, das von einer Stahlkonstruktion getragen wird, verstärkt. Das Gebäude ist 28 Meter lang, 20,5 Meter breit und 12 Meter hoch. Im ersten und zweiten Obergeschoss liegen zur Plaza hin Terrassen mit einem Bodenbelag aus Lärchenholzdielen. Die Erschließung der beiden oberen Etagen erfolgt über außen liegende Treppen an den Seiten des Gebäudes. Im obersten Geschoss befinden sich neben dem Gastraum auch mehrere geschlossene VIP-Lounges. Insgesamt bietet das Café rund 200 Gästen Platz.

The café is an inviting structure of steel, glass and wood. Glass facades surrounding all three floors create a transparency that links inside and outside together. The appealing impression of openness evoked by this building is enhanced by the glass roof, which is supported by a steel construction. The building is 28 meters long, 20.5 meters wide and 12 meters high. Rooms on the second and third floors have balconies overlooking the Plaza, with larchwood deal floors. Visitors reach the upper levels via exterior stairways on the sides of the building. Aside from the main dining room, the top floor contains several enclosed VIP lounges. The café accommodates about 200 guests.

Architekten: Schulitz + Partner, Braunschweig
Prof. Helmut C. Schulitz, Wolf Bartuszat, Matthias Rätzel, Markus Riebschläger
Tragwerksplanung: Ingenieurbüro Sprysch + Partner, Braunschweig
Olaf Duddek

Architects: Schulitz + Partner, Braunschweig
Prof. Helmut C. Schulitz, Wolf Bartuszat, Matthias Rätzel, Markus Riebschläger
Supporting structure design: Ingenieurbüro Sprysch + Partner, Braunschweig
Olaf Duddek

# Preussag Arena
## Preussag Arena

Die multifunktionale Veranstaltungshalle ist eine Arena der so genannten vierten Generation, die den Zuschauern modernste Technik und größten Komfort bietet. Das klassisch-moderne Gebäude ist 128 Meter lang und 115 Meter breit. Von den 34 Metern Gesamthöhe sind 25 Meter sichtbar, und 9 Meter liegen unter dem Plaza-Niveau. Die Fassade besteht aus Aluminium, Glas und terrakottafarbenen Keramikplatten. Ein gläserner Vorbau lässt die Arena zur Plaza hin besonders einladend erscheinen. Im Innern bieten drei übereinander liegende Zuschauerränge je nach Nutzung der Arena bis zu 13.500 Besuchern Platz. Besondere Annehmlichkeiten bieten 34 Clublogen und sechs Partylogen, insgesamt 26 Cateringbereiche sorgen für das leibliche Wohl.
Die Arena ist für unterschiedlichste Veranstaltungen – Fernsehshows, Konzerte, Kongresse oder Sport-Events – geeignet. Alle Hallensportarten wie Basketball, Handball, Reiten, Boxen oder Hallenfußball können hier ausgetragen werden, für die Nutzung als Eishockeystadion ist die Einrichtung einer permanenten Eisfläche möglich. Ein ausgefeiltes Licht- und Akustikkonzept sorgt für optimale Beleuchtung und Beschallung. Auf einem von der Decke abgehängten Videowürfel liefern vier je 12 Quadratmeter große Leinwände Nahaufnahmen, Zeitlupen- oder Stimmungsbilder und ermöglichen damit einen engen Blickkontakt zu den Stars auf der Bühne.

This multipurpose hall is an arena of the "fourth generation" offering audiences the utmost in comfort and state-of-the-art technology. The classical-modern building is 128 meters long and 115 meters wide. Of its total vertical length of 34 meters, 25 are visible, while the remaining nine meters lie below the level of the Plaza. The facade is made of aluminum, glass and terracotta-colored ceramic tiles. A glass front extension toward the Plaza gives the arena a particularly inviting look from this perspective. Inside, three levels of seats arranged one above the other provide seating for up to 13,500 persons, depending upon nature of each specific event. Thirty-four club boxes and six party lounges offer extra comforts, and 26 catering areas provide for food and drink.
The arena is designed to accommodate a wide range of different events – television shows, concerts, conferences or sports events. All indoor sports such as basketball, team handball, horseback riding, boxing or indoor soccer can be presented here. The option of installing a permanent ice surface has been planned in to allow for use as a hockey arena as well. A sophisticated lighting concept and finely tuned acoustics ensure optimum lighting and sound. A video cube suspended from the ceiling has four screens, each measuring 12 square meters, for close-ups, slow-motion replays and video impressions, and thus ensures audiences a close look at the stars on stage.

**Architekt: Büro Dr. Helmut Sprenger, Hannover**
**Architect: Büro Dr. Helmut Sprenger, Hanover**

**Blick in den Zuschauerraum**
View of the grandstand
area inside the Arena

**Der dreiseitig verglaste Vorbau verleiht dem Haupteingangsbereich der Arena eine eigene Identität.**
The main entrance to the arena derives its unique identity from the glassed-in porch.

# NILEG Plaza Forum und EuropaHaus
## NILEG Plaza Forum and EuropeHouse

Das NILEG Plaza Forum und das EuropaHaus bilden die Ostschiene der Plaza-Bebauung und geben der Platzkante durch ihre horizontale Gliederung und einheitliche Fassadengestaltung ein homogenes Erscheinungsbild.
Beide Gebäude sind 50 Meter breit und knapp 22 Meter hoch, das Plaza Forum ist 100 Meter lang und das EuropaHaus genau 30 Meter länger. Die Gliederung in unterschiedliche Bauteile ermöglicht eine große Multifunktionalität, die auch im Hinblick auf die Nachnutzung als World Trade Center Hannover (WTCH) oder Gewerbe-, Büro- und Hochschulgebäude von Bedeutung ist. Während der Weltausstellung werden beide Komplexe teilweise als Eingangsgebäude genutzt. Außerdem sind hier unter anderem eine Großdiskothek, die Ausstellung der Europäischen Union und der Club der Generalkommissare zu finden.

NILEG Plaza Forum and EuropeHouse form the eastern line of Plaza buildings and lend the boundary of the Plaza a homogeneous appearance by virtue of their horizontal configuration and their uniform facade design. Each of these buildings is 50 meters wide and roughly 22 meters high. Plaza Forum is 100 meters long, precisely 30 meters shorter than EuropeHouse. Subdivision into different building sections provides for a high degree of multifunctionality – an important aspect in view of the projected use of the buildings as the World Trade Center Hanover (WTCH) or a commercial, office and university facility after EXPO 2000. During the World Exposition, the two complexes will be used in part as entrance buildings. They also house a large discotheque, the exhibition of the European Union and the Commissioner Generals' Club.

**Architekten: Determann & Martienssen, Hannover**
**Architects: Determann & Martienssen, Hanover**

Zwischen dem Plaza Forum und dem EuropaHaus führt die Brücke Ost auf die Plaza.
The East Bridge between Plaza Forum and EuropeHouse leads to the Plaza.

Blick von der Plaza auf die nebeneinander liegenden Gebäudekomplexe
View of the adjacent building complexes from the Plaza

# Pavillons der Nationen und Organisationen
## Pavilions of Nations and Organizations

Zum Bau eigener Pavillons zur EXPO 2000 konnten die teilnehmenden Nationen und Organisationen zwischen zwei unterschiedlichen Geländebereichen wählen. Auf dem 18 Hektar großen Pavillongelände West wurden temporäre Bauten errichtet, von denen einige an anderer Stelle weitergenutzt werden oder deren Materialien wieder verwendet beziehungsweise recycelt werden können. Auf dem 27 Hektar großen Pavillongelände Ost sind teilweise dauerhafte Pavillons entstanden, die größtenteils nach der Weltausstellung im Rahmen eines modernen Gewerbeparks sinnvoll nachgenutzt werden.

Participating countries and organizations were given a choice of two different areas in which to erect their pavilions for EXPO 2000. The West Pavilion Site, comprising 18 hectares, was used for the construction of temporary structures, several of which will be made available for further use at other locations. Materials from some of the other pavilions on this site will be recycled. Many of the pavilions erected on the East Pavilion Site (27 hectares) are permanent buildings, the majority of which are to assume functions within a modern industrial park after the World Exposition.

# A. Pavillongelände West · Offizielle Teilnehmer
## A. West Pavilion Site · Official Participants

# Australien
# Australia

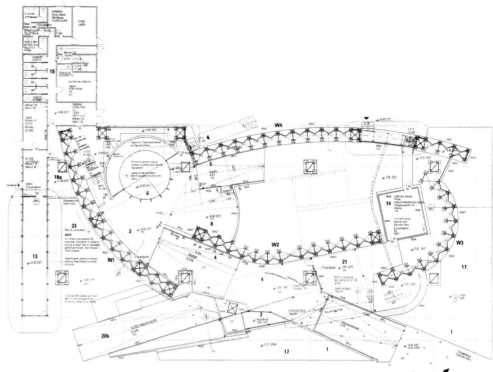

**Grundriss des australischen Pavillons**
Floor plan of the Australian Pavilion

Das Erscheinungsbild des australischen Pavillons ist geprägt durch Transparenz und Leichtigkeit, ein Gestaltungskonzept, durch das die Offenheit des Landes und seiner Bewohner symbolisiert werden soll. Das Gebäude besteht aus einer einfachen Gerüstkonstruktion aus Stahl, die mit einem hochmodernen transparenten Stoff umhüllt ist. Es spiegelt Farben und Formen des Kontinents wider und ist so gestaltet, dass sowohl sein Äußeres als auch sein Inneres die Besucher ansprechen. Nachts werden die textilen »Wände« angestrahlt, sodass sie sanft leuchten. Tagsüber erlauben sie von außen Einblicke in das Innere des Pavillons und machen damit neugierig auf die Ausstellung, unterstützt durch eine Kombination aus audiovisuellen Elementen und Live-Performances. Der Überstand des großen, fließenden Daches gewährt bei jedem Wetter Schutz.

Innen setzt sich das Gestaltungsprinzip in gleicher Weise fort. Gebogene Wände, die teilweise genauso aufgebaut sind wie die Pavillonhülle selbst, bilden unterschiedliche, offene Ausstellungsbereiche und machen die Konstruktion erlebbar. Licht, Farben, Geräusche sowie die gesamte Atmosphäre und Gestaltung des Pavillons wurden so gewählt, dass sie ein möglichst vielschichtiges Bild Australiens präsentieren. Unter dem Motto »Vom Boomerang zum bionischen Ohr« informiert das Land über seine Geschichte ebenso wie über moderne soziale und technische Errungenschaften. Die effiziente Nutzung der Solarenergie, die Vereinbarkeit von Tourismus und Umweltschutz oder der Einsatz moderner Kommunikationstechniken, die zur Überbrückung der großen Entfernungen im Land genutzt werden, gehören neben den Olympischen Spielen in Sydney zu den vorgestellten Projekten. Der Anspruch der Nachhaltigkeit in Bezug auf den Pavillon wird dadurch dokumentiert, dass das Stahlskelett und die Außenhaut rückbaufähig sind und komplett wieder verwertet werden können.

Architekten: Tonkin Zulaikha Architects, East Sydney
Kontaktarchitekt: Obermeyer Planen + Beraten, Hannover
Grundstücksgröße: 2.500 Quadratmeter
Bebaute Fläche: 1.800 Quadratmeter
Architects: Tonkin Zulaikha Architects, East Sydney
Contact Architect: Obermeyer Planen + Beraten, Hanover
Lot size: 2,500 square meters
Constructed area: 1,800 square meters

The outward appearance of the Australian Pavilion communicates an impression of transparency and lightness, a design concept meant to symbolize the openness of the country and its people. The building consists of a simple steel framework covered with an ultramodern transparent material. It reflects the colors and shapes of the continent and is designed in such a way that both its interior and its exterior present an appealing face to visitors. The textile "walls" are illuminated at night, giving them a soft glow. During the day, they offer a view from outside into the interior of the pavilion, arousing curiosity about the exhibition, which is complemented by a combination of audiovisual elements and live performances. The canopy formed by the extension of the large, streamlined roof offers protection against sun and rain.

The underlying design principle is evident inside the building as well. Curving walls, some of which are structured exactly like the shell of the pavilion itself, provide for a variety of different open exhibition spaces and enable visitors to experience the design concept. Light, colors, sounds and the entire atmosphere and configuration of the pavilion were selected with an eye to presenting as diverse an image of Australia as possible. Under the thematic slogan "From the Boomerang to the Bionic Ear," the country informs visitors about its history and about its modern social and technological accomplishments. Aside from the Olympic Games in Sydney, exhibition projects include such topics as the efficient use of solar energy, the compatibility of tourism and environmental awareness and the application of modern communication technologies to bridge the great distances between different parts of this vast country. The commitment to long-term conservation as it relates to the pavilion is documented by the fact that the steel skeleton and the outer skin can be dismantled and reassembled for further use in their entirety.

Textile Wände prägen das Erscheinungsbild.
Textile walls are among the pavilion's most
striking features.

# Bhutan
## Bhutan

Bhutan nimmt zum ersten Mal an einer Weltausstellung teil und präsentiert sich in dem Nachbau eines »Lhakhang«, eines buddhistischen Tempels. Das Ausstellungskonzept steht unter dem Motto »Umwelt und Bildung« und vermittelt den Besuchern die kulturellen und religiösen Traditionen des Landes. Der Buddhismus weist den Menschen die Rolle als Bewahrer der Natur zu – der Schutz der Artenvielfalt steht in seiner religiösen Tradition. So zeigt Bhutan in einer Ausstellung Modellprojekte zum Umweltschutz, der hier Vorrang vor kurzfristigem wirtschaftlichem Gewinn genießt.

Der Entwurf für den Pavillon Bhutans stammt von einem Architekten aus der Schweiz, der seit vielen Jahren in Bhutan lebt und mit der Kultur vertraut ist. Die einzelnen Bauelemente des Tempels mit zum Teil sehr komplexen Holzverbindungen wurden von einheimischen Handwerkern vorproduziert und nach Hannover gebracht. Unter Aufsicht eines buddhistischen Priesters setzten bhutanische und deutsche Fachleute die zahlreichen Einzelteile dann auf dem Weltausstellungsgelände zusammen. Wie bei der traditionellen Tempelarchitektur wurde eine Holzkonstruktion mit Lehmbauelementen kombiniert. Zu dem symmetrisch angelegten Komplex mit dem zentralen Gotteshaus, dem »Lhakhang«, und zwei Ausstellungsgebäuden gehört ein offener Hof als Ort zum Ausruhen und Meditieren. Besuchern stehen drei Eingänge, einer davon als zentrales Eingangstor gestaltet, zur Verfügung. Außerhalb der Anlage befinden sich links und rechts zwei kleine Bauwerke. Der »Dunghkor« enthält ein sechssilbiges Mantra, ein Gebet zur Befreiung aller Lebewesen von geistiger und körperlicher Knechtschaft. Die Form des »Chorten« stellt den gekrönten Buddha meditierend auf seinem Thron dar.

A first-time participant at a World Exposition, Bhutan is presenting itself in a replica of a *Lhakhang*, a Buddhist temple. The exhibition concept is focused on the theme of "Environment and Education" and offers visitors insights into the cultural and religious traditions of the country. Buddhism assigns human beings the role of guardians of nature – the preservation of species diversity is a part of its religious tradition. Thus Bhutan is presenting an exhibition of model projects in the field of environmental protection, a concern that is given priority in that country over short-term economic gain.

The design for the Bhutanese Pavilion was conceived by a Swiss architect who has lived in Bhutan for many years and is well acquainted with its culture. The individual structural elements of the temple, including a number of highly complex wooden connections, were prefabricated by native craftsmen and shipped to Hanover. Under the supervision of a Buddhist priest, Bhutanese and German specialists then assembled the numerous parts at the World Exposition site. As in traditional temple architecture, the building features a wooden structure combined with clay-construction elements. The symmetrically arranged complex with its central house of worship, the *Lhakhang*, and two exhibition buildings also includes an open courtyard for rest and meditation. Visitors may enter the building through any of three entrances, one of which is designed as a central entrance portal. Two small structures are located outside the complex. The *Dunghkor* contains a six-syllable mantra, a prayer for the liberation of all living beings from physical and spiritual bondage. The shape of the *Chorten* is that of a crowned Buddha meditating on his throne.

**Modell**
Model

**Grundriss**
Floor plan

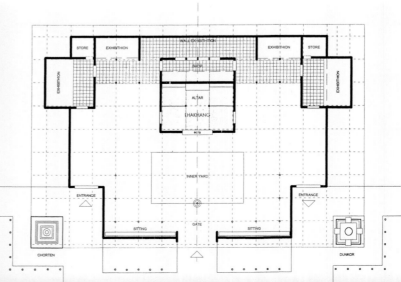

Ostfassade des »Lhakhang«
Eastern facade of the *Lhakhang*

**Architekt:** Peter Schmid, Bhutan Architectural Design, Thimphu
**Kontaktarchitekten:** Jabusch + Schneider Architektur, Hannover
**Grundstücksgröße:** 1.750 Quadratmeter
**Bebaute Fläche:** 250 Quadratmeter
Architect: Peter Schmid, Bhutan Architectural Design, Thimphu
Contact architects: Jabusch + Schneider Architektur, Hanover
Lot size: 1,750 square meters
Constructed area: 250 square meters

**Das Tor bildet den Haupteingang in den Pavillon Bhutans.**
The gateway is the main entrance to the Bhutanese
Pavilion.

**Ansicht**
View of the Bhutanese Pavilion

**Die Deckenkonstruktion zeugt von großer Handwerkskunst.**
The ceiling construction is an example of outstanding craftsmanship.

# Der Heilige Stuhl
# The Holy See

Das zentrale bauliche Thema dieses Pavillons lautet: »Einen Ort stiften«. Mit dem kreisrunden Gebäude, das nur einen kleinen Teil des Grundstücks im nördlichen Bereich einnimmt und sich nach allen Seiten öffnet, wurde es in sinnfälliger Weise umgesetzt. Der Pavillon des Heiligen Stuhles liegt in einem Hain aus hoch aufgeasteten Robinien, die ein transparentes Blätterdach bilden. Kleine Wasserspiele, ein überdachtes Forum mit vertieften Sitzstufen oder eine große runde Bank bilden ideale Treffpunkte und bieten sich als Orte zum Verweilen und Kommunizieren an. In den Bäumen sind unzählige Lichtpunkte aufgehängt und verleihen dem Hain auch in der Dunkelheit eine einladende Atmosphäre.

Der Pavillon aus Holz und Glas ist geprägt durch seine große Transparenz, die schon von außen Einblicke in den zentralen eingestellten Ausstellungsraum ermöglicht. Hier wird der Öffentlichkeit erstmals das Mandylion, eine Christus-Ikone aus der vatikanischen Kapelle Redemptoris Mater, präsentiert. Um diesen Bereich legt sich ein ringförmiger Ausstellungsraum, der von einem Glasdach überspannt wird und in dem Skulpturen die einzelnen Kontinente repräsentieren. Hier werden die Besucher empfangen und auf die Ausstellung mit dem Motto »Jesus Christus – gestern, heute und in Ewigkeit« vorbereitet. In einem weiteren, dem äußeren Ring sind die Themenbereiche der Ausstellung angeordnet. In Kabinetten werden die fünf Hauptthemen dargestellt: »Friede und Gerechtigkeit«, »Die Frau«, »Das Kind«, »Die Familie« und »Die Würde des Menschen«. Die Konstruktionsweise des Pavillons ermöglicht seine Demontage und den geplanten Wiederaufbau des Gebäudes als Gemeindezentrum in Lettland.

Architektur und Gesamtplanung: SIAT Architektur + Technik, München
Landschaftsarchitekten: WES Wehberg, Eppinger, Schmidtke & Partner, Hamburg
Bauherr: Der Heilige Stuhl, vertreten durch den Apostolischen Nuntius
Grundstücksgröße: 4.500 Quadratmeter
Bebaute Fläche: 1.400 Quadratmeter
Architecture and project planning: SIAT Architektur + Technik, Munich
Landscape architects: WES Wehberg, Eppinger, Schmidtke & Partner, Hamburg
Client: The Holy See, represented by the Apostolic Nuncio
Lot size: 4,500 square meters
Constructed area: 1,400 square meters

Grundriss mit Grünkonzept
Floor plan with layout of green areas

The central architectural theme of this pavilion is "Creating a Setting." The concept is realized in a readily visible manner in the open-sided circular building which occupies only a small part of the lot in the northern section. The Pavilion of the Holy See is located in a grove of robinias with high overhanging branches that form a transparent roof of foliage. Small fountains, a canopied forum with amphitheater-style stepped seats and a large round bench serve as ideal meeting places and settings for relaxation and communication. Countless small lights hung in the branches of the trees make the grove an inviting setting even after dark.

A striking feature of the wood-and-glass pavilion is its transparency, which permits visitors to look into the central interior exhibition rooms from the outside. Here, the *Mandylion*, an icon of Christ from the Vatican Redemptoris Mater Chapel is being presented to the public for the very first time. This area is surrounded by a ring-shaped exhibition space spanned by a glass roof, in which sculptures representing each of the continents are exhibited. It is here that visitors are welcomed and briefed on the exhibition entitled "Jesus Christ – Yesterday, Today and for all Eternity." The other themes covered in the exhibition are presented in an outside ring. The five major themes are displayed in showcases: "Peace and Justice," "Women," "Children," "The Family" and "Human Dignity." The pavilion is constructed in such a way that it can be easily disassembled. Plans call for the building to be re-erected for use as a community center in Latvia.

**Der zentrale Ausstellungsbereich**
The central exhibition area

**Blick durch den Hain auf den Pavillon**
View of the pavilion from the birch grove

**Ansicht von Süden**
View from the south

**Schnitt durch den Pavillon des Heiligen Stuhles**
Cross section of the Vatican Pavilion

**Über das Glasdach fällt Tageslicht in den ringförmigen Ausstellungsraum.**
Daylight enters through the glass roof into the ring-shaped exhibition room.

Der Mensch ist der Weg der Kirche
Christus ist der Weg des Menschen

# Indien
## India

Der Pavillon Indiens ist überspannt mit einem 10 Meter hohen Tonnengewölbe in Holzbinderkonstruktion. Den Eingang bildet eine 12 Meter große grafische Nachbildung eines »Namaskar«, einer Skulptur, die in traditioneller indischer Weise symbolisiert: »Ich grüße das Göttliche in dir.«

Im Innern machen Besucher einen Rundgang durch die Straßen und den Alltag Indiens. Der Weg führt an einem traditionellen Haus vorbei durch die »Parliament Street« zu einer alten Sternwarte und weiter durch die unterschiedlichen Landschaften Indiens.

In mehreren Ausstellungsbereichen werden Eindrücke von dem Land und seiner Philosophie vermittelt; Stadtplaner zeigen, wie sie sich die zukünftige Entwicklung Indiens vorstellen. Der Rundgang endet in einem Basar, auf dem Verkaufsstände, Handwerker und Künstler Einblicke in das indische Leben gewähren.

The Indian Pavilion is spanned by a ten-meter-high semicircular vault in wooden-truss construction. The entrance is formed by a 12-meter-high graphic replica of a Namaskar, a sculpture that illustrates in traditional Indian fashion the words: "I greet the divine in you."

Inside the pavilion, visitors take a tour through the streets and everyday life of India. The route leads past a traditional house along "Parliament Street" to an ancient observatory and on through the many different landscapes of India.

Visitors gain impressions of the country and its philosophy in several different exhibition areas. City planners show how they envision India's future development. The tour ends at a bazaar, where merchants' booths, artists and artisans offer insights into life in India.

**Architekt: D. R. Naidu**
**Design C Hindustan Thompson Ass., Neu-Delhi**
**Kontaktarchitekt: Generalunternehmer Kurth Bau,**
**Hannover**
**Grundstücksgröße: 3.700 Quadratmeter**
**Bebaute Fläche: 2.800 Quadratmeter**
Architect: D. R. Naidu
Design C Hindustan Thompson Ass., New Delhi
Contact architect: Generalunternehmer Kurth Bau,
Hanover
Lot size: 3,700 square meters
Constructed area: 2,800 square meters

In der Ausstellung
Inside the exhibition

Eingangsbereich des indischen Pavillons
Entrance area of the Indian Pavilion

# Island
# Iceland

Der isländische Pavillon besteht aus einer würfelförmigen, membranumspannten Stahlkonstruktion. Die Außenflächen aus einer doppelten Folienhaut – die innere Schicht blau und lichtdurchlässig, die äußere transparent – sind ständig von einem fließenden Wasserfilm überzogen und lassen den Pavillon wie einen würfelförmigen Wasserfall erscheinen. Das herunterfließende Wasser sammelt sich in einem umlaufenden Wassergraben und wird von dort wieder auf das Dach gepumpt. Um den Pavillon zu betreten, gehen Besucher über eine Brücke durch den Wasserfall hindurch. In der Mitte des Pavillons befindet sich ein Wasserbecken, auf dessen Oberfläche ein Film mit Aufnahmen der isländischen Natur projiziert wird. Höhepunkt der Ausstellung ist ein künstlicher Geysir, der als Wassersäule von der Oberfläche des Beckens 35 Meter in die Höhe schießt, weit über das Dach hinaus. Ein Bereich des Daches mit einem Durchmesser von 2 Metern öffnet sich bei jeder Eruption, um den Strahl ins Freie zu entlassen. Eine von der Decke abgehängte, spiralförmige Rampe windet sich um das Ausstellungszentrum des Pavillons nach oben; sie dient gleichzeitig der Erschließung des Gebäudes und als Zuschauerbereich.

The Icelandic Pavilion consists of a cube-shaped steel structure enveloped by a plastic membrane. The outside surfaces comprising a double-layer of plastic sheeting – the inner layer blue and translucent, the outer one transparent – are continuously covered by a flowing film of water, giving the pavilion the appearance of a cube-shaped waterfall. The cascading water is collected in a circular basin surrounding the building, from where it is pumped to the roof again. To enter the pavilion, visitors walk over a bridge through the waterfall. A pool of water is located in the middle of the pavilion, and a film showing Icelandic nature scenes is projected on it. The most spectacular attraction at the exhibition is an artificial geyser that propels a column of water from the surface of the pool to a height of 35 meters, far above the level of the rooftop. A section of the roof measuring two meters in diameter opens at each eruption, allowing the jet of water to pass through. A spiral ramp suspended from the ceiling winds upward around the pavilion exhibition center. It provides access to the building and serves at the same time as a space for spectators.

**Architekt:** Ámi Páll Jóhannsson, Reykjavík
**Kontaktarchitekt:** Akzente Architektur & Landschaftsplanung GbR, Hannover
**Grundstücksgröße:** 2.600 Quadratmeter
**Bebaute Fläche:** 1.300 Quadratmeter
Architect: Ámi Páll Jóhannsson, Reykjavík
Contact architect: Akzente Architektur & Landschaftsplanung GbR, Hanover
Lot size: 2,600 square meters
Constructed area: 1,300 square meters

**Die Rampe bietet Besuchern einen optimalen Blick auf die Ausstellung.**
The ramp offers visitors a perfect view of the exhibition.

Der blaue »Wasserwürfel« Islands
Iceland's "Blue Cube"

# Japan
## Japan

Längsschnitt
Longitudinal section

Japan präsentiert sich spektakulär mit einem mehrgeschossigen Pavillon ganz aus Papier. Der Entwurf für das von allen Seiten begehbare, voll recycelbare Gebäude stammt von dem Architekten Shigeru Ban, der für atemberaubende Bogenkonstruktionen und seine Experimente mit ungewöhnlichen Materialien bekannt ist. Der rund 90 x 45 Meter große Pavillon wird aus einem gekrümmten Flächentragwerk gebildet, das aus kreuzweise gegeneinander verschränkten gebogenen Papprhöhren mit einem Durchmesser von jeweils 20 Zentimetern besteht. Das Dach des Pavillons wurde von Stahlstützen hochgestemmt, bis die endgültige gewölbte Dachform erreicht war. Als Dachhaut dient eine lichtdurchlässige Membran aus Textilien und Papierkunststoff, die allen Witterungsbedingungen standhält. In Deutschland wurde mit diesem ungewöhnlichen Baustoff Neuland betreten, denn das Material »Papier« war hier bislang für Hochbauten nicht zugelassen. Erst eine so genannte »Zustimmung im Einzelfall« und zahlreiche Sondergenehmigungen haben diese einmalige Konstruktion ermöglicht.

Japan is making a spectacular presentation with a multistory pavilion built entirely of paper. The design for the fully recyclable building, which can be entered from all sides, comes from the drawing board of the architect Shigeru Ban, who has made a name for himself with breathtaking arch constructions and experiments with unusual materials. Measuring approximately 90 x 45 meters, the pavilion is formed around a curved planar load-bearing structure consisting of curving cardboard tubes, each 20 centimeters in diameter, interconnected in a crosswise pattern. The roof of the pavilion was raised on steel piles until the final vaulted form was achieved. The roofing surface is a translucent membrane made of textile and paper-plastic materials designed to withstand all types of weather. The use of this unusual building material is a daring innovation in Germany, as paper has never before been approved for use in high-rise construction in this country. The realization of this unique structure was made possible by the issuance of a "one-time approval" and a number of special permits.

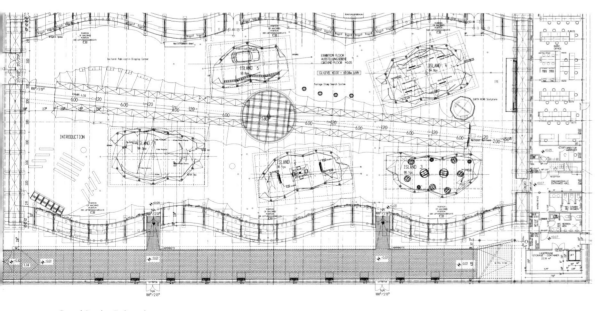

Grundriss des Erdgeschosses
Plan of the ground floor

**Architekt:** Shigeru Ban, Tokio
**Berater:** Prof. Frei Otto, Leonberg
**Kontaktarchitekt:** Schürmann Spannel Planungsgesellschaft mbH, Bochum
**Bauherr:** JETRO Japan External Trade Organization, Berlin
**Grundstücksgröße:** 5.450 Quadratmeter
**Bebaute Fläche:** 3.600 Quadratmeter
Architect: Shigeru Ban, Tokyo
Consultant: Prof. Frei Otto, Leonberg
Contact architect: Schürmann Spannel Planungsgesellschaft mbH, Bochum
Client: JETRO Japan External Trade Organization, Berlin
Lot size: 5,450 square meters
Constructed area: 3,600 square meters

Der Pavillon ist von einer lichtdurchlässigen Membran überspannt.
The pavilion is covered by a translucent
membrane.

**Im Ausstellungsraum**
Inside the exhibition area

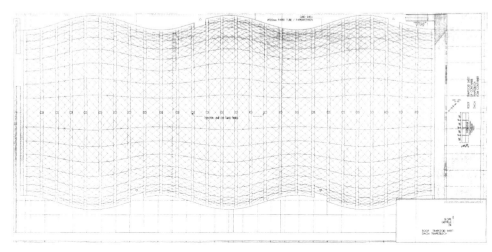

**Dachaufsicht**
View of the roof from above

**Detail der Röhrenkonstruktion**
Detail of the tubular construction

# Kolumbien
## Colombia

Der kolumbianische Pavillon gliedert sich in zwei getrennte Baukörper von völlig unterschiedlicher Gestaltung. Im Vordergrund steht der eigentliche Ausstellungsbereich, ein »Wald« aus 20 baumartigen Stützen. Dahinter liegt der zweite Bauteil mit Serviceeinrichtungen, eine schlichte und zurückhaltende Leichtbaukonstruktion.

Die Konstruktion des zentralen Pavillonbereichs besteht aus einem dreidimensionalen Rahmentragwerk, das aus den baumartigen Stützen und dem von ihnen getragenen Leichtbaudachsystem gebildet wird. Jede Stütze umfasst einen Stahlschaft, der auf einem Betoneinzelfundament ruht und aus dem zwölf Teakholzstangen als »Äste« hervorgehen. Diese sind mit Stahlrohr und Spannseilen ausgesteift und schließen mit einem Gelenk an die Deckenkonstruktion an. Für den Pavillon wurde bewusst Teakholz aus den Wiederaufforstungsgebieten im Norden Kolumbiens verwendet, um zu demonstrieren, dass Kolumbien diese gefährdete Tropenholzart intensiv anzubauen und damit vor dem Aussterben zu schützen versteht. Die Wände des Ausstellungsbereichs sind beidseitig mit Faserzementplatten verkleidet und besitzen an der Außenseite zusätzlich Holz- und Bambuslamellen.

Durch die Gestaltung von überdachten, aber offenen Bereichen kann der Pavillon weitgehend natürlich belichtet und belüftet werden. Durch seine modulare Konstruktion ist er zudem vollständig wieder verwendbar.

The Colombian Pavilion consists of two separate buildings, each featuring an entirely different design. The actual exhibition area stands in the foreground – a "forest" of 20 tree-shaped supporting columns. Located behind it is the building housing the service facilities, a plain, unpretentious, lightweight structure.

The central pavilion area consists of a three-dimensional framework comprising the tree-shaped supporting columns and the lightweight roof system mounted on them. Each column encloses a steel shaft that rests on a single concrete foundation pad. Twelve teakwood poles protrude from the shaft as "branches." These are reinforced with steel rods and tension cables and connected by a joint to the ceiling construction. The architects deliberately selected teak harvested from the reforested regions in northern Colombia in order to demonstrate Colombia's commitment to promoting the intensive cultivation of this endangered species of tropical tree and protecting it against extinction. The walls of the exhibition area are lined on both sides with fibercement plates. The exterior wall also has wood and bamboo slats.

Designed with both roofed and open areas, the pavilion can be illuminated and ventilated naturally for the most part. Its modular construction ensures that it can be made available for reuse in its entirety.

**Architekt: Daniel Bonilla, Arquitectura y Urbanismo, Bogotá**
**Grundstücksgröße: 2.000 Quadratmeter**
**Bebaute Fläche: 1.300 Quadratmeter**
Architect: Daniel Bonilla, Arquitectura y Urbanismo, Bogotá
Lot size: 2,000 square meters
Constructed area: 1,300 square meters

**Blick von Nordwesten in den kolumbianischen Pavillon**
View into the Colombian Pavilion from the northwest

Zwölf Teakholzstangen bilden die »Äste« der baumartigen Stützen.
Twelve teakwood poles form the "branches" of the tree-shaped supports.

# Korea
## Korea

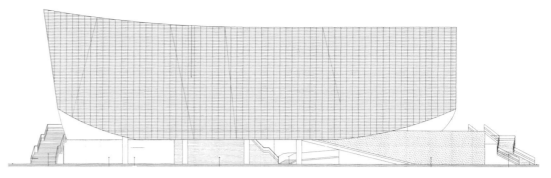

Ansicht des koreanischen Pavillons von Norden
View of the Korean pavilion from the north

**Architekt: Chul Kong, Kc Architectural Lab, Seoul**
**Kontaktarchitekt: Schürmann Spannel**
**Planungsgesellschaft mbH, Bochum**
**Grundstücksgröße: 3.700 Quadratmeter**
**Bebaute Fläche: 1.860 Quadratmeter**
Architect: Chul Kong, Kc Architectural Lab, Seoul
Contact architect: Schürmann Spannel
Planungsgesellschaft mbH, Bochum
Lot size: 3,700 square meters
Constructed area: 1,860 square meters

Beleuchtet kommt die Fassade aus farbigen
Fliesen besonders zur Geltung.
The facade of colored tiles is a particularly
striking sight at night.

Das äußere Erscheinungsbild des koreanischen Pavillons wird geprägt durch seine Fassade aus farbigen, in unterschiedlichen Winkeln angebrachten Fliesenelementen, die von innen angestrahlt werden.

Das Erdgeschoss des Pavillons ist größtenteils aufgeständert. Darüber entwickelt sich in unregelmäßiger Form das kompakte Gebäude, dessen Tragstruktur aus einer Stahlrahmenstruktur besteht. Über eine Rampe betreten Besucher den 19 Meter hohen zweigeschossigen Bau, in dem sich unterschiedliche Ausstellungsbereiche, ein Restaurant und ein Theater befinden. Unter dem Motto »Fließendes Land« präsentiert sich Korea zukunftsorientiert mit modernster Multimedia-Technik.

The most prominent feature of the outside of the Korean Pavilion is its facade composed of colored tile elements applied in a variety of different angles and illuminated from within.

Most of the ground floor of the pavilion is elevated. Above it, the compact building rises in an irregular pattern. The load-bearing structure consists of a steel framework. Visitors enter the 19-meter-high structure, which houses various exhibition areas, a restaurant and a theater, via a ramp. With its thematic slogan, "A Flowing Land," Korea presents itself as a nation with an eye to the future and a commitment to state-of-the-art multimedia technology.

Eingangsbereich des koreanischen
Pavillons
Entrance area of the Korean Pavilion

# Mexiko
## Mexico

Der mexikanische Pavillon gliedert sich in fünf separate, mehrgeschossige Bau-körper, in denen die Vielfalt des Landes, aber auch unterschiedliche Themen aus den Bereichen Verkehr und Kommunikation im nächsten Jahrtausend vor-gestellt werden. Unter dem Motto »Mexiko: ein Millenniumsbau« symbolisiert der Pavillon zudem die Verschmelzung unterschiedlicher Kulturen, ethnischer Gruppen und Glaubensrichtungen.

Die einzelnen Gebäude sind so angeordnet, dass Innenhöfe, so genannte Patios, entstehen, in denen die verschiedenen Ökosysteme Mexikos vorgestellt wer-den: die Wüste, das Meer und der Regenwald. Die Einzelbauten sind unter-schiedlich große Kuben aus Stahl und Glas, die eine große Transparenz gewähr-leisten. Die Abwechslung von hellen und dunklen Farben, durchsichtigen und undurchsichtigen Flächen bringt Bewegung in die Fassade. Durch das Spiel mit Licht, Farben und dem Material Glas erhält der mexikanische Pavillon ein bewusst fröhliches Erscheinungsbild. Über Rampen werden Besucher zu den unterschiedlichen Bereichen geführt und erleben den Komplex aus immer neuen, interessanten Perspektiven. Nach der Weltausstellung wird der mexi-kanische Pavillon voraussichtlich in Braunschweig von der Hochschule der Bildenden Künste als Erweiterung ihrer Bibliothek weitergenutzt.

The Mexican Pavilion comprises five separate multistory buildings in which the country is presented in all of its great diversity. Exhibits deal with various themes from the fields of transportation, travel and communication in the new millennium. In keeping with the thematic slogan "Mexico: a Millennium Project," the pavilion also symbolizes the intermingling of different cultures, ethnic groups and religions.

The individual buildings are arranged in such a way as to form inner court-yards, or patios, each presenting a view of one of Mexico's different ecosystems: desert, oceans and rain forest. Designed as different-sized steel-and-glass cubes, the buildings exhibit a substantial degree of transparency. The alterna-tion between light and dark colors and transparent and opaque surfaces brings an element of motion to the facade. The interplay of light, color and the material qualities of glass gives the Mexican Pavilion a decidedly cheerful look. Visitors are led along ramps to the different areas and can experience the complex from a series of constantly changing perspectives. According to cur-rent plans, the Mexican Pavilion is to be transferred to Braunschweig for use as an extension of the library of the Hochschule der Bildenden Künste after the close of the World Exposition.

**Ansicht von Norden**
View from the north

**Architekt: Ricardo Legorreta, Legorreta Arquitectos, Mexico City**
**Kontaktarchitekten: Bahlo-Köhnke-Stosberg & Partner GmbH, Hannover**
**Grundstücksgröße: 4.200 Quadratmeter**
**Bebaute Fläche: 3.000 Quadratmeter**
Architect: Ricardo Legorreta, Legorreta Arquitectos, Mexico City
Contact architects: Bahlo-Köhnke-Stosberg & Partner GmbH, Hanover
Lot size: 4,200 square meters
Constructed area: 3,000 square meters

**Wüsten-Patio**
Desert Patio

**Blick von Südosten**
View from the southeast

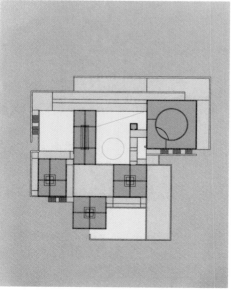

**Grundriss des Obergeschosses**
Floor plan of the upper level

**Regenwald-Patio**
Rain Forest Patio

# Nepal
## Nepal

Der Himalaja-Pavillon des Königreiches Nepal vereint zwei traditionelle Architekturrichtungen Asiens miteinander. Er kombiniert Elemente der buddhistischen Stupa mit Elementen des hinduistischen Pagoden-Tempels. Die runde Form des Stupa-Grundrisses symbolisiert gleichzeitig die Natur, die Erde, den Kosmos sowie die Schöpfung, die quadratische Grundform des Tempels steht für den Menschen und seine Kreativität. Das Thema der Ausstellung ist das seit über 2.500 Jahren praktizierte harmonische Nebeneinander der beiden Religionen und damit auch das friedliche Zusammenleben der Nepalesen auf dem »Dach der Welt«. Die einzelnen Bauteile des Pavillons bestehen aus Holz, Stein und Metall und wurden von 800 nepalesischen Familien in Handarbeit nach alter Tradition vorgefertigt. Eine Rahmenkonstruktion aus Hartholz trägt ein hölzernes Dach mit handgemachten Dachziegeln und bossierten Messingplatten. Eine wie ein Baum gestaltete Treppe erschließt die obere Ebene der halbrunden Stupa. Die religiösen Elemente werden ergänzt durch eine Art umlaufenden Laubengang, der ebenfalls in Handarbeit erstellt wurde. Alle Gebäudebereiche sind mit Terrakottafliesen und Originalsteinen aus Nepal gepflastert. Besucher betreten die Anlage über eine begehbare Mauer und gelangen in einen großzügigen Hof. Hier reflektiert das klare Wasser in einem Becken die Formen von Stupa und Pagode. Eine Wiesenfläche und ein Garten mit einheimischen blühenden Pflanzen und Sträuchern sorgen für eine ruhige Atmosphäre.

The Himalaya Pavilion of the Kingdom of Nepal unites two traditional currents of Asian architecture. It combines elements of the Buddhist stupa with those of the Hindu pagoda. The round form of the stupa's floor plan symbolizes nature, the earth and the cosmos, while the square shape of the floor ground plan stands for mankind and its creative potential. The theme of the exhibition is the harmonious coexistence of the two religions, whose Nepalese followers have lived together in peace on the "roof of the world" for more than 2,500 years. The individual parts of the pavilion are made of wood, stone and metal and were prefabricated by members of 800 Nepalese families in accordance with long-standing handcrafting traditions. A hardwood framework construction supports a wooden roof covered by hand-made roofing tiles and hammered brass plates. A stairway in the shape of a tree leads to the upper level of the semicircular stupa. The religious elements are complemented by a kind of circular arbor which was also built by hand. All areas within the buildings are paved with terracotta tiles and original Nepalese stones. Visitors enter the complex on an elevated walkway which brings them to an expansive courtyard. The clear water of a pool in the courtyard reflects the images of the stupa and the pagoda. A small meadow and a garden featuring native blooming plants and shrubbery provide for a quiet and relaxing atmosphere.

**Architekt: Amrit Ratna Shakya, Homemaker**
**Implementing Experts Group, Kathmandu**
**Kontaktarchitekten: Jabusch + Schneider Architektur,**
**Hannover**
**Grundstücksgröße: 2.500 Quadratmeter**
**Bebaute Fläche: 760 Quadratmeter**
Architect: Amrit Ratna Shakya, Homemaker
Implementing Experts Group, Kathmandu
Contact architects: Jabusch + Schneider Architektur,
Hanover
Lot size: 2,500 square meters
Constructed area: 760 square meters

**Die Gebäudeteile umschließen einen**
**Innenhof.**
The buildings enclose an inner courtyard.

**Der schlanke Turm der Stupa überragt den gesamten Pavillon.**
The slim stupa tower rises high above the entire pavilion.

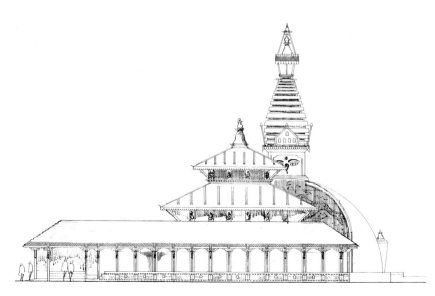

**Ansicht von Süden**
View from the south

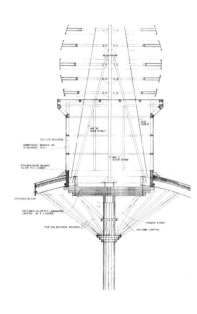

**Detail der Stupa-Konstruktion**
Detail of the stupa construction

**Konstruktionsdetail**
Construction detail

# Singapur
## Singapore

Architekt: Pico Art International Pte Ltd., Singapur
Kontaktarchitekten: MAR Architekten, Düsseldorf
Grundstücksgröße: 2.000 Quadratmeter
Bebaute Fläche: 1.268 Quadratmeter
Architect: Pico Art International Pte Ltd., Singapore
Contact architects: MAR Architekten, Dusseldorf
Lot size:2,000 square meters
Constructed area: 1,268 square meters

**Der tropische Dachgarten lädt zum Ausruhen ein.**
The tropical rooftop garden is a setting for rest and relaxation.

Der zweigeschossige Pavillon Singapurs, der zu 70 Prozent aus recycelbaren Materialien wie Glas, Stahl, Holz und Stein besteht, ist in seiner Gestaltung geprägt durch eine Mischung aus traditioneller und High-Tech-Architektur. Der tropische Dachgarten, der als eine Oase der Ruhe auf dem Gebäude angelegt ist, zeigt, warum Singapur den Ruf einer »Garden City« genießt. Gleichzeitig werden Besucher hier über ökologisch sinnvolle Landschaftsplanung, verbunden mit moderner Umwelttechnologie, informiert. Wesentlich für das Erscheinungsbild des aus einem vorgefertigten Stahlrahmen konstruierten Gebäudes ist zudem die Gestaltung der Außenfassade: Über eine Länge von 21 Metern erstrecken sich Singapurs traditionelle farbenfrohe Shophouses mit Läden und Restaurants. Sie wurden als originalgetreue Nachbildung zunächst in Singapur aufgebaut und dann nach Deutschland verschifft.
Der Ausstellungsbereich mit zwei Multimedia-Theatern ist so angelegt, dass sich Besucher auf umlaufenden Rampen durch den Pavillon bewegen. Dadurch eröffnet der Weg immer wieder Rück- und Ausblicke aus verschiedenen Perspektiven. Teile des Pavillons sollen nach der EXPO 2000 zu Ausstellungszwecken in Singapur wieder aufgebaut werden.

Seventy percent of the two-story pavilion representing Singapore comprises such recyclable materials as glass, steel, wood and stone. One of the most prominent design features is the combination of traditional and high-tech architecture. The building's tropical rooftop garden, conceived as an oasis of peace and quiet, shows why Singapore has gained its reputation as a "Garden City." At the same time, the garden exhibit acquaints visitors with the possibilities for achieving ecologically sound landscape planning in conjunction with modern environmental technology. One of the most striking aspects of the outward appearance of the building, which is erected on a prefabricated steel framework, is the design of the exterior facade: a 21-meter-long row of replicas of Singapore's traditional multicolored shophouses with their stores and restaurants. They were constructed as true-to-life models of the originals in Singapore and then shipped to Germany.
The exhibition area, with its two multimedia theaters, is designed to allow visitors to move through the pavilion on circular ramps, offering a range of different views of the exhibitions from changing perspectives. Parts of the pavilion are to be rebuilt in Singapore for exhibition purposes after EXPO 2000.

**Blick von Nordwesten auf den Pavillon Singapurs**
View of Singapore's pavilion from the northwest

# Sri Lanka
# Sri Lanka

**Architekt: Prof. Nimal da Silva, Colombo**
**Kontaktarchitekten: Jabusch + Schneider Architektur,**
**Hannover**
**Grundstücksgröße: 3.600 Quadratmeter**
**Bebaute Fläche: 2.160 Quadratmeter**
**Architect: Prof. Nimal da Silva, Colombo**
**Contact architects: Jabusch + Schneider Architektur,**
**Hanover**
**Lot size: 3,600 square meters**
**Constructed area: 2,160 square meters**

**Nachbildung eines buddhistischen Felsen-**
**tempels in der Ausstellung**
Replica of a Buddhist stone temple in the
exhibition

Sri Lanka präsentiert sich in einem Ausstellungsgebäude mit einer Grundfläche von 33 x 60 Metern und einer Höhe von 10,5 Metern. Der Wandaufbau der Stahlbaukonstruktion besteht innen und außen aus sichtbaren Trapezprofil- tafeln, die großzügig mit landestypischen Ornamenten verziert sind. Zwischen dem Ein- und Ausgang an der Südseite des Geländes heißt eine 6 Meter hohe Buddha-Statue die Besucher des Pavillons willkommen. Die meisten Ein- wohner Sri Lankas sind Buddhisten, ihre Religion prägt die Ausstellung im Innern des Gebäudes. Im Mittelpunkt steht der Nachbau eines Felsentempels, und Malereien aus dem »Tempel des heiligen Zahns von Kandy« schmücken die Decke. Für Besucher stehen auch ein Restaurant sowie eine Veranstaltungs- und Showfläche mit 150 Sitzplätzen zur Verfügung.

Sri Lanka makes its presentation in a 10.5-meter-tall exposition building cover- ing a plot of ground measuring 33 x 60 meters. The inside and outside walls of the steel construction consist of visible trapezoid profile panels decorated lavishly with typical Sri Lankan ornamentation. A six-meter-high statue of Buddha welcomes visitors to the pavilion between the entrance and the exit on the south side of the building. Most Sri Lankans are Buddhists, and their religion figures significantly in the exhibitions inside the pavilion. A replica of a stone temple is a major focal point, and the ceiling is decorated with paint- ings from the "Temple of the Holy Tooth of Kandy." Visitors will also find a restaurant and an auditorium with a seating capacity of 150 in the pavilion.

**Eingangsbereich des Pavillons**
Pavilion entrance area

# Thailand
## Thailand

**Die Gestaltung der Grünflächen symbolisiert thailändische Landschaften.**
The design of the green areas symbolizes typical Thai landscapes.

Der thailändische Ausstellungspavillon besteht größtenteils aus vorgefertigten Bauelementen, die von einer leichten Stahlkonstruktion getragen werden. Das Dach besitzt eine Metalleindeckung. Seine Form erinnert an Berge und steht damit in Verbindung zu den Außenräumen, die den größten Teil der Pavillonfläche einnehmen und in Anlehnung an typische thailändische Landschaften gestaltet sind. Wasser als Ursprung allen Lebens nimmt in der Ausstellung des landwirtschaftlich geprägten Thailand eine zentrale Rolle ein: Ein Teich symbolisiert Flüsse und das Meer, Reisfelder erinnern an die zentrale Ebene, und Berge repräsentieren den Norden des Landes. Thailand gilt als die »Reisschüssel Asiens« und hat seinen Ausstellungsbeitrag unter das Motto »Essen für die Welt durch Artenvielfalt« gestellt. Die moderne Lebensmittelproduktion ist neben den Bereichen »Leben und Arbeiten«, »Bildung und Kultur«, »Umwelt und Entwicklung« sowie »Freizeit und Mobilität« eines der zentralen Themen der Präsentation in dem pyramidenförmigen Pavillon.

The Thai Pavilion is built for the most part of prefabricated elements supported by a lightweight steel structure. The roof covering is metal. The shape of the building suggests mountains and thus relates to the outdoor spaces which occupy most of the pavilion site and are designed to reflect the character of the Thai landscape. As the source of all life, water plays an important role in the presentation of this largely agricultural country. A pond symbolizes rivers and the sea, rice fields call to mind the central plains, and mountains represent the northern region of Thailand. Thailand is known as the "Rice Bowl of Asia" and the theme of its contribution to EXPO 2000 is "Food for the World through Species Diversity." In addition to "Living and Working," "Education and Culture," "Environment and Development," "Leisure and Mobility," modern food production is one of the central topics featured in the presentation in the pyramid-shaped Thai Pavilion.

**Architekt: C. A. Willemse, Design 103 International Ltd., Bangkok**
**Grundstücksgröße: 4.200 Quadratmeter**
**Bebaute Fläche: 1.325 Quadratmeter**
Architect: C. A. Willemse, Design 103 International Ltd., Bangkok
Lot size: 4,200 square meters
Constructed area: 1,325 square meters

**Blick von Nordwesten auf den Pavillon**
View of the pavilion from the northwest

# Venezuela
# Venezuela

Venezuelas Pavillon ist charakterisiert durch Tausende tropischer Pflanzen und trägt den Namen: »Eine Blume Venezuelas für die Welt«. Als Dach des offen gestalteten, gläsernen Gebäudes in Form eines abgeschnittenen Kegels dient eine riesige, künstliche Blüte, die sich öffnen und schließen kann. Insgesamt 16 rund 10 Meter lange Blätter in »Mönch und Nonne«-Form, die sich in geschlossenem Zustand überlappen, sind an einem Tragmast in der Gebäudemitte befestigt. Die Erschließung der einzelnen Ausstellungsebenen des 18 Meter hohen Pavillons erfolgt über eine spiralförmige Treppe in der Mitte des Gebäudes oder per Aufzug. Über Rampen werden Besucher wieder nach unten geleitet und zum Ausgang geführt. Das gesamte Erdgeschoss ist mit terrakottafarbenen Dreieckziegeln ausgelegt, die Böden der Obergeschosse sind aus Schiffsbodenparkett. Die Fassaden bestehen aus Glas und Lochblech in Metallrahmen und sind mit Pflanzkübeln und Fischbecken dekoriert. Blumenkübel stehen auf dem Abschluss der Außenwände und versprühen Wasser, das an den Scheiben herunterfließt. Aus den ringförmig angeordneten Aquarien im ersten Obergeschoss ergießt sich Wasser kaskadenförmig über die Pflanzterrassen. Es fließt über einen Kanalring ab, wird in unterschiedlichen Kreisläufen gereinigt und schließlich wieder in den Zyklus eingespeist.

One of the most noteworthy features of Venezuela's pavilion is the presence of thousand of tropical plants which reflect the theme of "A Flower from Venezuela for the World." The roof of the glass building with its open configuration, designed in the shape of a flat-topped cone, is a huge artificial flower with petals that open and close. A total of 16 "monk-and-nun" petals, each ten meters long, which overlap when the blossom is closed, are attached to the supporting mast in the middle of the building. Visitors access the individual exhibition levels in the 18-meter-high pavilion from a central spiral stairway or from an elevator. Ramps lead from the upper levels to the building exit. The entire ground floor is covered with terracotta-colored triangular tiles, while the floors of the upper stories are surfaced with wooden strip flooring. The facades are constructed of framed glass and perforated sheet metal segments and decorated with planters and small pools with fish. Flower pots positioned along the bottom of the outside walls spray water that runs down the faces of the panes. Cascading water streams down over the planted terraces from the ring-shaped arrangement of aquariums on the second floor. It flows into a circular drainage canal, is cleaned in a series of purification phases and eventually returned to the circulation system.

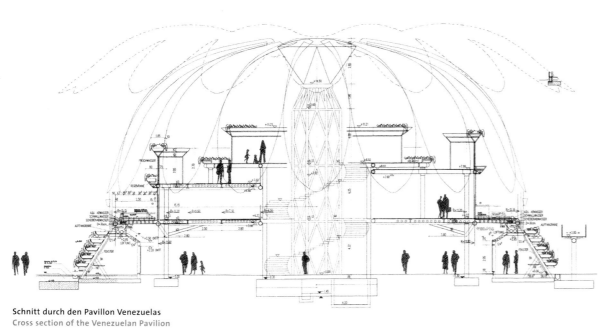

**Schnitt durch den Pavillon Venezuelas**
Cross section of the Venezuelan Pavilion

Architekt: Fruto Vivas Arquitecto, Caracas
Kontaktarchitekten: Haack, Krüger und Partner, Hannover
Grundstücksgröße: 2.725 Quadratmeter
Bebaute Fläche: 1.480 Quadratmeter
Architect: Fruto Vivas Arquitecto, Caracas
Contact architects: Haack, Krüger und Partner, Hanover
Lot size: 2,725 square meters
Constructed area: 1,480 square meters

Pflanzen dominieren das Erscheinungsbild des Gebäudes.
Plants dominate the outward appearance of the building.

# Nicht-offizielle Teilnehmer
## Non-Official Participants

# Big Tipi
## Big Teepee

Das Big Tipi ist ein überdimensionaler Nachbau eines traditionellen Sioux-Zeltes und dient als Treffpunkt für Jugendliche. Es besteht aus zwölf ungeschälten Douglasienstämmen, die aus Sulzburg im Schwarzwald stammen. Sie mussten als Sondertransport nachts nach Hannover gebracht werden, denn jeder dieser Stämme ist 33 Meter lang, wiegt über 8 Tonnen, hat an der Basis einen Durchmesser von 100 Zentimetern und am oberen Ende noch einen Durchmesser von 50 Zentimetern. Entsprechend den Kriterien der Nachhaltigkeit wurden nur Bäume ausgewählt, die im Forstbewirtschaftungsplan bereits zur Fällung vorgesehen waren.

Die Stämme lagern auf zwölf Betonfertigteilfundamenten und werden durch einen Zug- und zwei Druckringe gehalten. Der obere Zugring hat einen Durchmesser von 2,5 Metern, der untere Druckring einen Durchmesser von knapp 14 Metern. Die Außenhaut des Zeltes besteht aus einer Stoffmembran mit Kunststoffbeschichtung, die mit Gurten auf einer Unterkonstruktion aus Stahlrohren befestigt ist. Der Boden ist mit einer 5 Zentimeter starken Rindenmulchdeckung belegt.

Als feste Einrichtung ist in der Spitze des Big Tipi ab 4 Metern Höhe ein Hochseil-Klettergarten, der so genannte High Ropes Course, installiert. Seile sind in unterschiedlichen Höhen und Richtungen so an den Baumstämmen befestigt, dass sie ein dichtes Netz bilden für Geschicklichkeitsübungen.

The Big Teepee is a larger-than-life replica of a traditional Sioux shelter and serves as a meeting place for youth. It consists of twelve bark-covered Douglas fir trunks harvested in Sulzburg in the Black Forest. The trunks had to be shipped to Hanover by special night transport, as each of them is 33 meters long, weighs over eight tons and measures 100 centimeters in diameter at its base and 50 centimeters at its top. In keeping with principles of conservation, all of trees selected had already been designated for cutting in the forest management plan.

The trunks are footed on twelve prefabricated concrete foundation pads and are held in place by one pull ring and two pressure rings. The upper pressure ring has a diameter of 2.5 meters, while the lower ring measures nearly 14 meters across. The outer skin of the tent consists of a fabric membrane with a plastic coating fastened with belts to a framework of steel pipes. The floor is covered with layer of bark mulch five centimeters thick.

A climber's exercise course known as the "High Ropes Course" is permanently installed in the upper section of the teepee, beginning at four meters above ground level. Ropes fastened to the tree trunks at different levels and running in different directions form a dense net in which climbers can test and practice their skills.

**Der Hochseil-Klettergarten in der Zeltspitze**
The High Ropes Course in the top of the teepee

Architekten: planungsgruppe Schröder, Schulte-Ladbeck, Strothmann – Architekten BDA + Assoziierte, Dortmund
Idee: Agentur Bildwerk, Expo und Event GmbH, Dortmund
Bauherr: Kinder- und Jugendplattform Expo 2000, Hannover
Grundstücksgröße: 1.750 Quadratmeter
Architects: Planungsgruppe Schröder, Schulte-Ladbeck, Strothmann – Architekten BDA + Assoziierte, Dortmund
Concept: Agentur Bildwerk, Expo und Event GmbH, Dortmund
Client: Kinder- und Jugendplattform EXPO 2000, Hanover
Lot size: 1,750 square meters

**Mit seiner Höhe von fast 30 Metern ist das Big Tipi das größte Indianerzelt der Welt.**
Thirty meters from base to top, the Big Teepee is the tallest Indian tent in the world.

# cyclebowl – Duales System Deutschland AG
cyclebowl – Duales System Deutschland AG

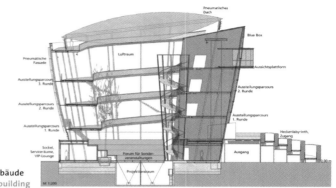

**Schnitt durch das Gebäude**
Cross section of the building

Der Ausstellungsbeitrag der Duales System Deutschland AG ist ein Pavillon der Kreisläufe. Die Gestaltungsprinzipien der cyclebowl orientieren sich an dem schonenden und nachhaltigen Umgang mit Ressourcen. Das demontierbare, leichte und wieder verwendbare Gebäude wurde im Wesentlichen aus Stahl, Kunststoffen, Glas und Aluminium hergestellt. Das Grundgerüst der knapp 25 Meter hohen cyclebowl besteht aus einem Stahltragwerk. Die Außenhülle wird aus insgesamt 28 pneumatisch gestützten »Luftkissen« gebildet. Sie bestehen aus lichtdurchlässigen, transparenten Kunststofffolien, die in Aluminiumrahmen eingefasst und mit der Stahlkonstruktion verschraubt sind. Durch den Luftdruck in diesen Elementen erhält die Fassade des Pavillons ihre Stabilität. Die Klimatisierung der cyclebowl erfolgt energiesparend über eine natürliche Be- und Entlüftung, ein Verschattungssystem bei starker Sonneneinstrahlung und die Kühlung durch einen Wasserkreislauf. Tagsüber zirkuliert Wasser durch das Gebäude und sorgt für ein angenehmes Raumklima. Nachts wird das Wasser an der Fassade versprüht, läuft hinunter, wird aufgefangen und auf natürliche Weise gekühlt. Am nächsten Morgen beginnt der Kreislauf erneut.

Im Innern des Pavillons führt eine spiralförmige, leicht ansteigende Rampe (6 Prozent) Besucher durch die drei Ebenen der Ausstellung, in der die Entstehung, die Gegenwart und mögliche Zukunftsperspektiven der Kreislaufwirtschaft dargestellt werden. Spiegelgänge, Projektionen oder Simulationen und ein Labor zum Experimentieren vermitteln den Besuchern vielschichtige Eindrücke und Informationen.

**Architekt: Atelier Brückner, Labor für Architekturen und Szenografie, Stuttgart**
**Grundstücksgröße: 2.462 Quadratmeter**
**Bebaute Fläche: 1.150 Quadratmeter**
Architect: Atelier Brückner, Labor für Architekturen und Szenografie, Stuttgart
Lot size: 2,462 square meters
Constructed area: 1,150 square meters

The contribution of the Duales System Deutschland AG to EXPO 2000 is a pavilion of circulation systems. The design principles underlying the configuration of the cyclebowl reflect a concern for thoughtful and conservative use of resources. The building, which can be easily disassembled and made available for further use is constructed primarily of steel, plastics, glass and aluminum. The framework for the cyclebowl, which measures nearly 25 meters in height, is a steel construction. The outer shell consists of 28 pneumatically filled "air pillows" made of translucent and transparent plastic sheeting and mounted in aluminum frames bolted to the steel framework. The constant air pressure in these elements gives the pavilion facade its stability. The climate in the cyclebowl is controlled by a natural, energy-saving ventilation and exhaust system, a shade system activated during periods of strong sunlight and a circulating-water cooling system. During the day, water circulating through the building maintains pleasant inside temperatures. At night, water is sprayed on the facade and runs down the faces of the building to a collection basin in a natural cooling process. The circulation system is activated again the next morning.

Inside the pavilion, a spiral ramp leads visitors on a moderate incline (six percent) to the different levels and exhibits designed to inform them about the origins, the current state and the future perspectives of resource-circulation and recycling. Mirrored hallways, projections, simulations and an experimental laboratory offer visitors a diverse range of impressions and information.

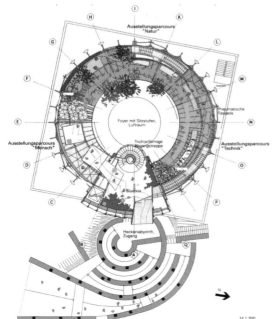

**Grundriss der cyclebowl**
Floor plan of the cyclebowl

**Blick von Südosten**
View from the southeast

# Zero Emissions Research Initiative (ZERI)
## Zero Emissions Research Initiative (ZERI)

Die ZERI-Foundation (Zero Emissions Research Initiative) beschäftigt sich seit Jahren mit der sinnvollen Verwendung von Produktionsrückständen. In ihrem Beitrag zur EXPO 2000 zeigt sie, dass nachwachsende Rohstoffe problemlos für den Hausbau geeignet sind. Entsprechend ist ihr 14 Meter hoher und 40 Meter breiter offener Pavillon eine Konstruktion aus Bambus, der in Kolumbien verbreiteten Riesensonnenblume Arbocolo, natürlichem Zement, Kupfer sowie einem Gemisch aus Terrakotta, Zement und Bambusfaserplatten. Das Tragwerk des Pavillons wurde aus rund 4.000 Bambusstäben mit einer Länge von 9 Metern gebaut. Ihre Knotenpunkte sind mit natürlichem Zement ausgegossen und dadurch stabilisiert. Die Wände bestehen aus Bambusstäben, die mit Beton verstärkt wurden. Sie erreichen fast die Tragfähigkeit von Stahl, sind dabei aber wesentlich flexibler und leichter. Erste Bewährungsproben hat diese Konstruktion bereits in den kolumbianischen Erdbebengebieten bestanden. In Kolumbien wurde 1999 ein Prototyp des Gebäudes errichtet, sodass sich die deutschen Behörden vor Erteilung der Baugenehmigung ein Bild von der Standfestigkeit des ZERI-Pavillons machen konnten.
Ausführliche Informationen über die ungewöhnliche Bauweise bietet die Publikation des Vitra Design Museums *Grow your own house – Simon Velez und die Bambusarchitektur*. Sie entstand in Kooperation mit der ZERI-Foundation und C.I.R.E.C.A. und ist unter ISBN 3-931936-25-2 zu beziehen.

The ZERI Foundation (Zero Emissions Research Initiative) has focused its activities for many years on the effective use of production waste and residues. In its presentation for EXPO 2000, the foundation demonstrates the suitability of renewable raw materials for housing construction. In keeping with that objective, ZERI's open pavilion (14 meters high and 40 meters wide) is a structure made of bamboo, the giant sunflower arbocolo found widely in Colombia, natural cement, copper and a mixture of terracotta, cement and bamboo-fiber panels.
The supporting framework for the pavilion was constructed of some 4,000 stalks of bamboo measuring nine meters in length. Joints connecting the elements were packed with natural cement to enhance stability. The walls consist of bamboo rods reinforced with concrete. They have nearly the same load-bearing capacity as steel, yet are considerably lighter and more flexible. This construction underwent initial testing in regions of Colombia known for their susceptibility to earthquakes. A prototype of the building was erected in Colombia in 1999, providing the German authorities evidence of the stability of the ZERI Pavilion prior to the award of a building permit.
The publication of the Vitra Design Museum entitled *Grow Your Own House – Simon Velez und die Bambusarchitektur* offers detailed information on the unusual construction of this pavilion. It was produced in cooperation with the ZERI Foundation and C.I.R.E.C.A., and can be ordered with the code ISBN 3-931936-25-2.

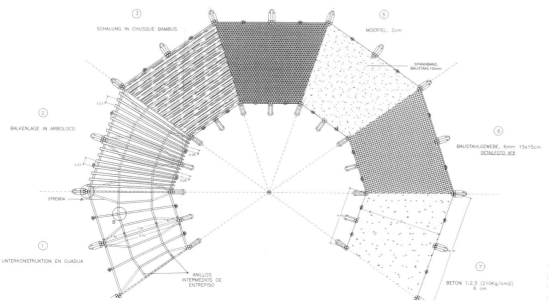

Draufsicht des Bodenaufbaus in der oberen Ebene
View of the floor structure in the upper level from above

**Architekt: Simon Velez, Bogotá**
**Kontaktarchitekt: Büro Masswerk, Hannover**
**Bauherr: ZERI-Foundation, Genf**
**Grundstücksgröße: 2.150 Quadratmeter**
**Bebaute Fläche: 1.300 Quadratmeter**
Architect: Simon Velez, Bogotá
Contact architect: Büro Masswerk, Hanover
Client: ZERI-Foundation, Geneva
Lot size: 2,150 square meters
Constructed area: 1,300 square meters

Der ZERI-Pavillon erinnert in seiner Form an einen Pilz.
The mushroom-shaped ZERI Pavilion

**Prototyp des ZERI-Pavillons in Manizales, Kolumbien**
Prototype of the ZERI Pavilion in Manizales, Columbia

**Konstruktionsdetails**
Construction details

**Das Bauteam erhält die Nachricht, dass der Pavillon in Deutschland gebaut werden kann.**
The construction team receives the announcement that the pavilion can be built in Germany.

**Blick in die Dachkonstruktion**
View of the roof construction

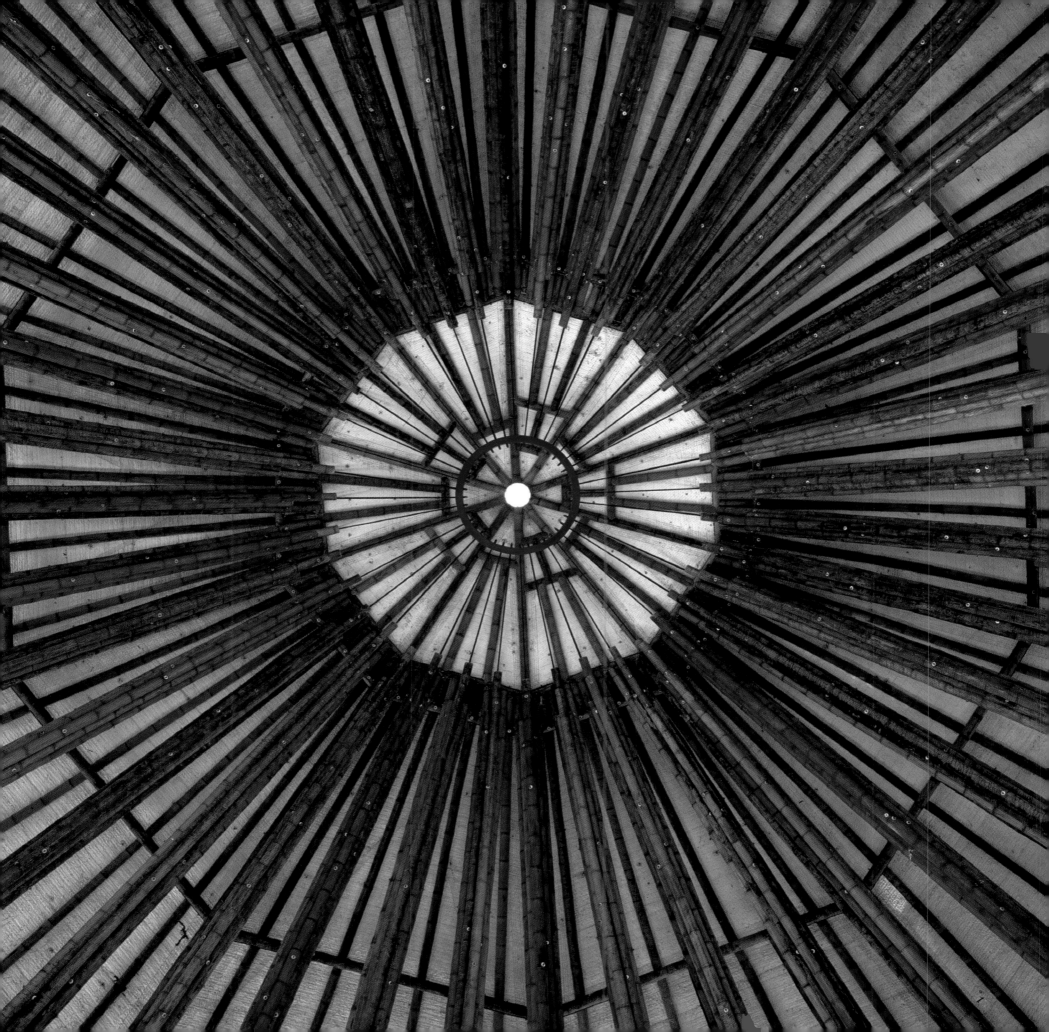

# B. Pavillongelände Ost · Offizielle Teilnehmer
## B. East Pavilion Site · Official Participants

# Äthiopien
## Ethiopia

Der äthiopische Pavillon stellt einen Querschnitt durch eine Bergsiedlung dar. Besucher können diese Siedlung auf einem Rundgang von der Steinzeit bis zur Gegenwart erleben. Dabei können sie ebenso das Aufrichten eines riesigen Obelisken beobachten wie etwas über die gegenwärtigen Bemühungen erfahren, mit moderner landwirtschaftlicher Nutzung das ökologische Gleichgewicht im Hochland zu bewahren.

In Äthiopien haben sich uralte Techniken zur ökologischen Nutzung erhalten, während gleichzeitig moderne Technologien eingeführt werden. Das schwierige Leben im gebirgigen Hochland und die Bemühungen um eine nachhaltige Entwicklung werden so dargestellt, dass Länder und Regionen mit ähnlichen Bedingungen die Erfahrungen der Äthiopier nutzen können. Inszenierungen mit Licht und moderner Multimedia-Technik informieren über das Leben unterschiedlicher Bevölkerungsschichten, von jungen und alten Menschen, von Geschäftsleuten und Bauern. Als zentrale Anlaufstelle der Besucher dient der traditionelle Ort für Erzählungen, der »Baum der Geschichten«.

Das ostafrikanische Land gilt wegen des Fundes von 3,2 Millionen Jahre alten menschlichen Gebeinen als die Wiege der Menschheit. So zählt auch das berühmte Skelett »Lucy« (Australopithecus afarensis) zu den Ausstellungsstücken. Im Innern des Pavillons erinnert die Präsentation der 2000 Jahre alten Stadt Axum und des für seine Felsenkirchen berühmten Orts Lalibela an die Ursprünge der drei großen monotheistischen Weltreligionen.

The Ethiopian Pavilion represents a chronological cross-section view of a mountain village. Visitors can experience the settlement on a tour that takes them from the Stone Age to the present, observing the process of erecting a huge obelisk as well as present-day efforts to preserve the ecological balance of the highland ecosystem through modern approaches to agriculture.

Ancient techniques for the ecological use of resources have survived in Ethiopia despite the introduction of modern technologies. The hard life in the mountain highlands and the measures undertaken to ensure sustainable development are presented in such a way as to enable countries and regions faced with similar conditions to benefit from the experience of the Ethiopian people. Staged presentations with light and modern multimedia technology provide information about life among the different segments of the population – the young and the old, business people and farmers. A central point of attraction and encounter for visitors is the traditional setting for storytelling, the "Tree of Stories."

The site of the discovery of human bones believed to be 3.2 million years old, this East African country is regarded as the "Cradle of Humanity." The famous skeleton of "Lucy" (Australopithecus afarensis) is one of the exhibits at the pavilion. Inside the pavilion, a presentation devoted to the 2000-year-old city of Axum and the town of Lalibela, famous for its churches in the cliffs, recalls the origins of the three great monotheistic religions of the world.

Architekt: Arthesia Themenwelten und Kommunikationsarchitektur GmbH, Berlin
Grundstücksgröße: 1.225 Quadratmeter
Bebaute Fläche: 800 Quadratmeter
Architect: Arthesia Themenwelten und Kommunikationsarchitektur GmbH, Berlin
Lot size: 1,225 square meters
Constructed area: 800 square meters

Im Zentrum des äthiopischen Pavillons steht der »Baum der Geschichten«.
The "Tree of Stories" stands in the center of the Ethiopian Pavilion.

Die Ausstellung im Innern informiert über die Geschichte des Landes.
The exhibition inside the building informs visitors about the country's history.

# Belgien
## Belgium

Der belgische Pavillon ist ein komplett demontierbares und somit flexibel aufstellbares Gebäude mit einem stützenfreien Innenraum von circa 50 x 38 Metern. Das konstruktive Konzept basiert auf einer außen installierten Stahlkonstruktion, bestehend aus acht Fachwerkträgern mit einer Länge von 37,8 Metern, die auf 16 Stützen im Abstand von 7,2 Metern aufgelagert sind. Die Primärkonstruktion nimmt die Lasten der Deckenkonstruktion des ersten Obergeschosses und die der Fassadenkonstruktion auf, wodurch eine geringere Dimensionierung der Fassade möglich wurde. Diese Idee des Loslösens von der Grundstruktur zieht sich durch das gesamte Konzept des Pavillons.

Seine Aufteilung wird hauptsächlich durch das Atrium, den zentralen Erschließungskern, strukturiert, der das Gebäude linear durchschneidet und eine getrennte Führung der Besucherströme im Ober- und Erdgeschoss ermöglicht. Einen spannungsreichen Kontrast ergeben die geschlossene »Blackbox« im Erdgeschoss und das offene und transparente Obergeschoss.

Im Erdgeschoss liegt der 1.800 Quadratmeter große Ausstellungsbereich, der sich der Präsentation der unterschiedlichen Regionen des Landes widmet. Die Wände in diesem Ausstellungstrakt bestehen aus Stahlrahmen mit einer Füllung aus Holzpaneelen. Im Obergeschoss dominiert Glas, das Dach besteht aus einer Art Gitterrost und Lamellen. In dieser Ebene befinden sich ein Restaurant und der VIP-Bereich. Durch verschiebbare Wände lässt sich das Obergeschoss bei Bedarf in einen großen, durchgehenden Empfangsbereich verwandeln. Eine überdachte Terrasse kann auch für das Restaurant genutzt werden.

**Architekt: Karsten Riedel, Groep Planning, Brüssel**
**Grundstücksgröße: 3.013 Quadratmeter**
**Bebaute Fläche: 1.905 Quadratmeter**
Architect: Karsten Riedel, Groep Planning, Brussels
Lot size: 3,013 square meters
Constructed area: 1,905 square meters

**Empfangsbereich im Obergeschoss**
Reception area on the upper level

The Belgian Pavilion has a completely column-free interior and can be dismantled completely. Measuring 50 x 38 meters, the structure can thus be rebuilt in virtually any setting. The structural concept is based upon an outer steel framework consisting of eight girders, each 37.8 meters long, resting on 16 vertical supports positioned at intervals of 7.2 meters. The primary structure supports the weight of the floor and ceiling of the second floor and the facade, making it possible to reduce the dimensions of the facade. This idea of independence from the base structure is evident in every visible aspect of the pavilion concept.

The spatial configuration inside the pavilion is structured primarily by the atrium, the central access area, which makes a linear cut through the building and provides for separate routes for visitor movements on the ground and second floors. The enclosed "Black Box" on the ground floor and the open, transparent second floor present a tension-laden contrast.

The exhibition area (covering 1,800 square meters of floor space) on the ground floor is devoted to presentations focused on the different regions of Belgium. The walls in the exhibition tract are made of steel frames filled with wooden panels. Glass is the dominant material on the upper level. The roof consists of a grid construction covered with slats. A restaurant and VIP lounge are located on this floor. Sliding walls make it possible to convert the upper level into a large, open reception area. The canopied patio can also be used as a restaurant dining section.

**Modell des belgischen Pavillons**
Model of the Belgian Pavilion

**Eingangsfront**
Entrance facade

# China
## China

**Vor dem Pavillon bilden chinesische Skulpturen einen Blickfang.**
Chinese sculptures outside the pavilion are an eye-catching attraction.

The Chinese Pavilion consists of two separate buildings, each designed for a different purpose. The focal point is a cube set on a square ground plan and surrounded on three sides by a U-shaped exhibition and service building. The cube, which houses a 360-degree movie theater, measures 22.5 meters on each side and is 8.5 meters tall. The different heights of the second building and the installation of roof elements connecting certain segments made it possible to create an exhibition area comprising spaces of different sizes and heights. The dominant feature of the pavilion's overall appearance is the design of its facade. Images of the Great Wall of China are printed on a gauze curtain, lending the geometrically configured edifice a unique expressive character. A piece of the original Great Wall was buried in the earth when the cornerstone was laid.

Visitors may enter the building through any of several different entrances, from which they are guided along upward and downward routes through the various thematic sections of the exhibition. Topics addressed in the exhibition range from space exploration to dam-building and forestry projects to traditional Chinese medicine. A souvenir shop and a restaurant await visitors at the end of their tour.

Plans for the use of the pavilion after EXPO 2000 were made early on. Following the close of the World Exposition, a center for traditional Chinese medicine will occupy two levels of the building. The structure will also house the China Center – the only institution of its kind in Europe – which is devoted to the development of economic, cultural and scientific exchange between Germany and the People's Republic of China.

Entsprechend seiner unterschiedlichen Nutzungsbereiche ist der chinesische Pavillon in zwei Baukörper gegliedert. Im Mittelpunkt steht ein Kubus mit quadratischem Grundriss, der von einem U-förmigen Ausstellungs- und Servicegebäude umgeben ist. Das Quadrat, in dem ein 360-Grad-Kino eingerichtet wurde, hat eine Kantenlänge von 22,5 Metern und eine Gesamthöhe von 8,4 Metern. Durch unterschiedliche Höhen des zweiten Baukörpers und das partielle Einziehen einer Zwischendecke entstand ein Ausstellungsbereich mit variierenden Raumgrößen und -höhen. Geprägt ist das Erscheinungsbild des Pavillons durch seine Fassadengestaltung. Auf einen Gazebehang sind Abbilder der Chinesischen Mauer gedruckt, die dem streng geometrischen Bau seinen unverwechselbaren Ausdruck geben. Bei der Grundsteinlegung wurde ein Originalstück aus der Chinesischen Mauer in den Boden eingelassen.

Besucher können das Gebäude durch mehrere Eingänge betreten und werden auf einem auf und ab führenden Weg durch die unterschiedlichen Themenbereiche der Ausstellung geleitet. Deren Bandbreite reicht von Weltraumforschung über Staudamm- und Aufforstungsprojekte bis zu chinesischer Heilkunst. Am Ende des Rundgangs warten ein Souvenirshop und ein Restaurant auf die Besucher.

Die Nachnutzung des Pavillons stand bereits frühzeitig fest. Auf zwei Ebenen wird nach der Weltausstellung ein Zentrum für traditionelle chinesische Medizin entstehen. Des Weiteren wird hier das Chinesische Zentrum einziehen, eine in Europa einmalige Institution zum Ausbau wirtschaftlicher, kultureller und wissenschaftlicher Kontakte zwischen Deutschland und der Volksrepublik China.

**Architekt:** GVI Gesellschaft zur Verwaltung von Immobilien mbH, Hannover
**Bauherr:** Building Technologies Company GmbH, Hannover
**Grundstücksgröße:** 3.600 Quadratmeter
**Bebaute Fläche:** 1.875 Quadratmeter
Architect: GVI Gesellschaft zur Verwaltung von Immobilien mbH, Hanover
Client: Building Technologies Company GmbH, Hanover
Lot size: 3,600 square meters
Constructed area: 1,875 square meters

**Die Fassade ist geprägt durch Darstellungen der Chinesischen Mauer.**
The facade is decorated with images of the Great Wall of China.

# Dänemark
## Denmark

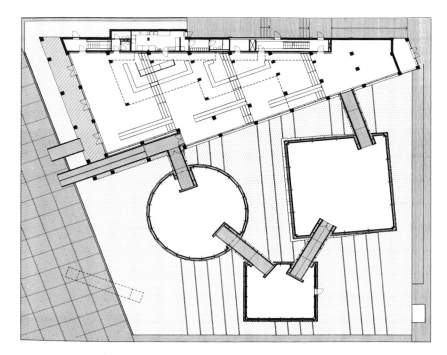

*Grundriss des dänischen Pavillons*
*Floor plan of the Danish Pavilion*

Das Erscheinungsbild des dänischen Pavillonkomplexes ist gekennzeichnet durch geometrische Baukörper und Wasser. Neben einem zweigeschossigen Hauptgebäude stehen für Ausstellungen drei eingeschossige Themenpavillons in Form einer Halbkugel, eines Würfels und einer Pyramide bereit. Alle Baukörper sind in einem terrassierten Wasserbecken angeordnet und untereinander mit Stegen verbunden. Das Hauptgebäude besteht aus einer tragenden Stahlkonstruktion mit Betonfertigteilen. Für das Dach wurden Holz-Fertigteilkassetten verwendet. Die drei Themenpavillons basieren auf einer Stahlkonstruktion mit Glaspaneelen als Außenverkleidung. Am Haupteingang zum Europa Boulevard bietet eine fast 400 Quadratmeter große Holzplattform Platz für wartende Besucher. Der Pavillon ist so angelegt, dass er nach der Weltausstellung abgebaut und an anderer Stelle weitergenutzt werden kann. Ausstellungsschwerpunkt im Zentralgebäude ist »Kreativität durch Spielen«. Des Weiteren erhalten Besucher hier touristische Informationen und können im Restaurant dänische Spezialitäten kosten. An die Wände der Halbkugel werden Filme über Windkraft projiziert, im Würfel befindet sich eine Ausstellung zum Thema Wasser. In der Pyramide beschäftigt sich eine Ausstellung mit dem Zusammenhang zwischen Lebensmitteln und Gesundheit.

The overall impression evoked by the Danish Pavilion complex is dominated by its geometrically designed buildings and by the presence of water. In addition to a two-story main building, exhibition space is provided in three one-story theme pavilions in the shapes of a hemisphere, a cube and a pyramid. All of the buildings are positioned within a terraced pool of water and connected by elevated walkways. The main building consists of a supporting steel construction and prefabricated concrete components. Prefabricated wooden sections were used for the roof. The three theme pavilions are based upon steel frameworks with outside walls made of glass panels. The main entrance facing Europa Boulevard is fronted by a wooden platform with nearly 400 square meters of space for waiting visitors. The pavilion is designed to be dismantled and rebuilt at another location following the close of the World Exposition.

The focal point of the exhibits in the main building is the theme of "Creativity through Play." Visitors to this building can also obtain tourist information or enjoy Danish specialties in the pavilion restaurant. Films on the subject of wind power are projected on the walls of the hemisphere, and an exhibit devoted to the subject of water is presented in the cube. The exhibition in the pyramid deals with the relationship between nutrition and health.

**Architekt: Peter Bysted, Bysted A/S, Hellerup**
**Kontaktarchitekt: Architekturbüro pk nord, Hannover**
**Grundstücksgröße: 3.015 Quadratmeter**
**Bebaute Fläche: 1.225 Quadratmeter**
**Grundfläche Wasserbecken: 1.346 Quadratmeter**
Architect: Peter Bysted, Bysted A/S, Hellerup
Contact architect: Architekturbüro pk nord, Hanover
Lot size: 3,015 square meters
Constructed area: 1,225 square meters
Pool area: 1,346 square meters

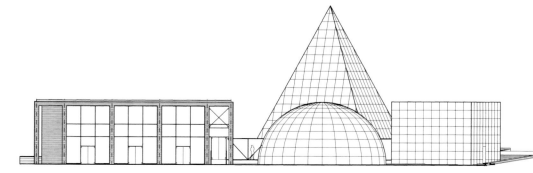

Westansicht
View from the west

Blick vom Europa Boulevard
View from Europa Boulevard

# Estland
## Estonia

**Modell des estnischen Pavillons**
Model of the Estonian Pavilion

Der estnische Pavillon wirkt leicht und durchsichtig mit seiner Außenhülle aus Rauchglas, das 25 Prozent Licht durchlässt. Die tragende Konstruktion besteht aus schwarzen Metallrahmen, die durch Bolzen miteinander verbunden sind. Die architektonischen Besonderheiten finden sich in der Fußboden- und der Dachkonstruktion des Gebäudes. Zwei Glasschichten mit einem Abstand von 50 Zentimetern bilden einen doppelten Boden. Der Raum unter der ersten, bläulichen Glasschicht und der zweiten aus Rauchglas wird als Ausstellungsfläche für Objekte traditioneller estnischer Schmiedekunst genutzt. Je nach Bedarf werden die Exponate unter der ersten oder der zweiten Glasschicht beleuchtet. Auf diese Weise sind sie den Besuchern nahe – und bleiben doch unerreichbar.

Auf dem Dach sind im Abstand von 2 Metern schlanke Kunstfichten mit einer Höhe von 2,5 Metern befestigt. Dieser Fichtenpark wird wellenförmig auf und ab bewegt. Diese Bewegung, die das Meer um Estland, den schaukelnden sumpfigen Erdboden und den vom Wind zerzausten Wald symbolisieren soll, ist durch das Glasdach auch im Innern des Pavillons erlebbar. Von den kegelförmigen Behältern, in denen die Bäume verankert sind, hängen an Drahtseilen Kalksteine herab. Sie greifen den Rhythmus der Wellen auf und bewegen sich durch eine aus fest montierten Steinen gebildete Ebene hindurch. Diese so genannte Wolkenebene wird durch Lichteffekte als Winterhimmel inszeniert. Der gesamte Pavillon ist von einem von West nach Ost ansteigenden Weg umgeben, von dem aus Besucher die Wolkenebene das eine Mal von unten, das andere Mal von oben sehen können. Betreten wird der Pavillon über eine breite Treppe und zwei Durchgänge, durch die die Besucherströme am Haupteingang verteilt werden. Der Ausstellungsbereich im Erdgeschoss des 18 Meter hohen Pavillons ist durch verschiebbare Trennwände in drei Räume unterteilt; bei speziellen Veranstaltungen kann daraus ein großer Raum gebildet werden. Durch einen Hintereingang an der Ostseite des Pavillons werden Gäste in den VIP-Raum im ersten Stock geleitet.

The Estonian Pavilion evokes an impression of lightness and transparency with its outside shell of tinted glass, which allows 25 percent of available sunlight to pass into the interior. The framework structure consists of metal girders and supports bolted together. Unique architectural features are found in the building's floors and roof. Two layers of glass spaced 50 centimeters apart form a double floor. The space beneath the first layer of bluish glass and the gray-tinted layer is devoted to an exhibition of objects of the traditional Estonian art of blacksmithing. The exhibits beneath the first or the second layer of glass are illuminated as needed. In this way, they can be viewed from close up by visitors – yet they remain inaccessible.

Slim artificial firs, each 2.5 meters tall, are positioned at two-meter intervals on the roof. This park of fir trees moves up and down in a wavelike pattern. This motion, intended to symbolize the sea surrounding Estonia, the unsteady, swampy ground and the wind-swept Estonian forest, can be also observed from inside the pavilion through the glass roof. Limestone boulders are suspended from wires attached to the cone-shaped containers in which the trees are rooted. They take up the rhythm of the waves as they move through a plane formed by a number of fixed stones. Lighting effects give this so-called "cloud level" the appearance of a winter sky. The entire pavilion is encircled by a rising walkway leading from west to east, from which visitors can view the cloud level from below and from above. The pavilion is entered from a broad stairway through two doorways that divide the stream of incoming visitors at the main entrance. The exhibition area on the ground floor of the 18-meter-high pavilion building is subdivided by sliding partitions into three rooms. On special occasions, the partitions can be shifted to create a single large room. Guests are guided to the VIP lounge through a rear entrance on the eastern side of the pavilion.

Architekt: Andrus Köresaar, Coolbars, Tallinn
Kontaktarchitekten: KSP Engel und Zimmermann
Architekten BDA, Berlin und Braunschweig
Grundstücksgröße: 1.500 Quadratmeter
Bebaute Fläche: 750 Quadratmeter
Architect: Andrus Köresaar, Coolbars, Tallinn
Contact architects: KSP Engel und Zimmermann
Architekten BDA, Berlin and Braunschweig
Lot size: 1,500 square meters
Constructed area: 750 square meters

Gläserne Transparenz bestimmt das
Erscheinungsbild.
Glassy transparency is the prevailing
impression evoked by the pavilion.

# Finnland
## Finland

Finnland hat seinem Pavillon einen Namen gegeben: »Windnest« heißt das Ensemble aus zwei viergeschossigen Gebäuderiegeln und einem eingefassten dichten Birkenwald, durch den man über hölzerne Brücken von einem Gebäudeteil in den anderen gehen kann.

Der Birkenhain, in dem rund 100 eigens nach Hannover geflogene Bäume ihren typischen Duft verbreiten, symbolisiert die große Bedeutung des Waldes für die finnische Gesellschaft. Neben Ausstellungen zum Thema Kommunikation und Informationsgesellschaft gibt es im finnischen Pavillon daher auch den Ausstellungsbereich »Forstcluster«, der verschiedene Aspekte des Waldes beleuchtet.

Die Außenfassaden der beiden geschlossenen, 16 Meter hohen Gebäuderiegel bestehen aus wärmebehandeltem Birkenholz; auch auf der Dachhaut liegt ein Holzrost aus wärmebehandelter Birke. Der Bereich des Birkenwäldchens ist nicht überdacht. Die dem Wald zugewandten Fassaden der Pavillonflügel bestehen ganz aus Glas, und auch die den Wald nach außen abgrenzenden Flächen sind Glaswände mit Tragwerken aus Stahl. Entlang der Südseite des Gebäudes verläuft ein Holzsteg, der teilweise von einem Segeldach in Stahl-Leichtbaukonstruktion überspannt ist. Der Haupteingang befindet sich an der Westseite des Pavillons am Europa Boulevard.

Die natürliche Belichtung und Belüftung sowie die Verwendung naturbelassener Materialien entsprechen dem Gedanken der Nachhaltigkeit: Auch nach der EXPO 2000 wird der finnische Pavillon auf dem Pavillongelände Ost als Multifunktionsgebäude weitergenutzt werden.

Finland has given its pavilion a name. The "Windnest" is an ensemble of two four-story building wings framing a dense grove of birches, through which visitors move from one building to the other over wooden bridges.

The birch grove, where some 100 trees flown to Hanover especially for EXPO 2000 emit their characteristic scent, symbolizes the significant role the forest plays in Finnish society. In addition to exhibits on the themes of communication and the Information Society, the Finnish Pavilion features an exhibition area known as the "Forstcluster," in which various aspects of forestry are illuminated.

The outside walls of the two closed, 16-meter-high building tracts consist of heat-treated birchwood. The surface of the roof is also covered by a latticework made of heat-treated birch. The birch grove itself is not covered. The facades of the pavilion wings facing the grove consist entirely of glass, and the grove is also bordered by glass walls with steel frames. A wooden walkway runs along the southern face of the building and is partially covered by a canvas roof installed as a lightweight-steel construction. The main entrance is located on the western side of the pavilion facing Europa Boulevard.

The natural lighting and ventilation, combined with the use of natural building materials, are in full conformity with the concept of sustainability. The Finnish Pavilion will remain in use even after EXPO 2000 as a multipurpose facility on the East Pavilion Site.

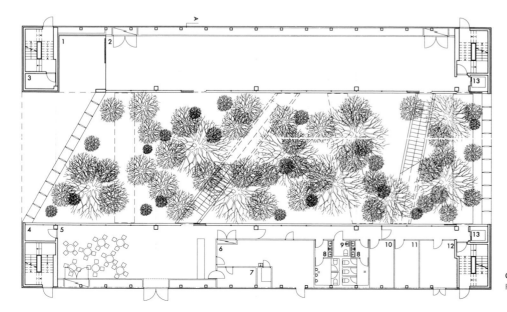

Grundriss des Gebäudes
Floor plan of the Pavilion building

Architekten: Sarlotta Narjus und Antti-Matti Siikala, SARC Architects Ltd., Helsinki
Kontaktarchitekten: Dietz + Joppien Architekten, Frankfurt am Main
Grundstücksgröße: 3.015 Quadratmeter
Bebaute Fläche: 1.875 Quadratmeter

Architects: Sarlotta Narjus and Antti-Matti Siikala, SARC Architects Ltd., Helsinki
Contact architects: Dietz + Joppien Architekten, Frankfurt am Main
Lot size: 3,015 square meters
Constructed area: 1,875 square meters

Blick von Südwesten auf den Pavillon
View of the pavilion from the southwest

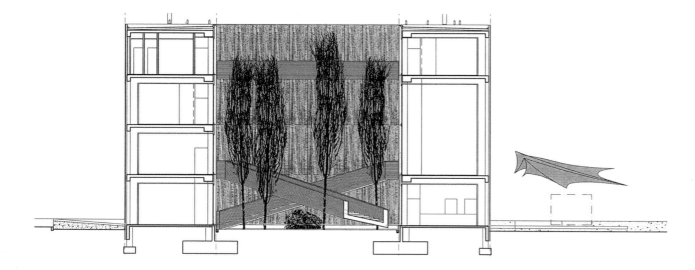

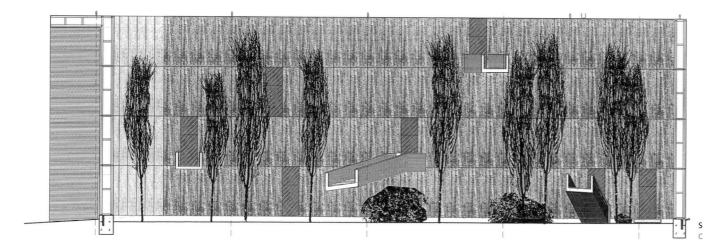

Schnitte durch den finnischen Pavillon
Cross sections of the Finnish Pavilion

Durch den Birkenwald verbinden hölzerne
Brücken die beiden Gebäuderiegel.
Wooden bridges connect the two building
wings through the birch grove.

# Frankreich
## France

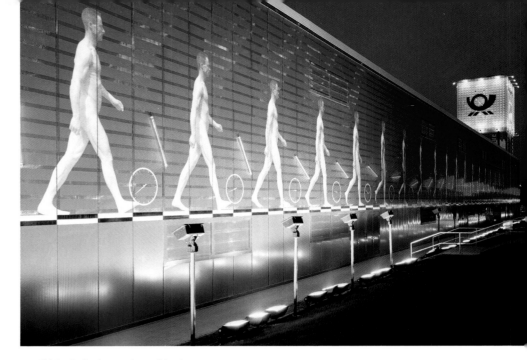

Das Bild *Der laufende Mann* kennzeichnet
die Eingangsfront.
Photograph of *The Running Man* on the
front entrance facade

Als größtes Bauwerk auf dem Pavillongelände Ost liegt das französische Aus-stellungsgebäude direkt gegenüber dem Deutschen Pavillon. Bauherr des Pavillons ist die französische Sportartikelfirma Decathlon, die das Gebäude während der Weltausstellung an das Land vermietet hat und anschließend selbst als Fachmarkt nutzen wird. Diese spätere Nutzung war bereits Grund-lage des Architekturwettbewerbs, in dem die Ansprüche des Großunterneh-mens in Form eines schlichten, unauffälligen Quaders umgesetzt wurden. Das Gebäude präsentiert sich in Glas mit einem Trag-werk aus Stahl und gewachsenen Baumstämmen. Das Glas der Fassade ist im oberen Drittel so bedruckt, dass im Zusammenhang mit den Holzstämmen von außen der Eindruck eines Waldes mit dichtem Blätterwerk entsteht. Geneigte Rundholz-stützen weiten sich astartig zur Decke aus und tragen einen Holzträgerrost mit geringer Spannweite. Die teilbedruckte und thermisch regulierbare Fassade schafft zusammen mit dem Material Holz einen lichtdurchfluteten und natür-lich wirkenden Innenraum mit vielen Nutzungsmöglichkeiten.
Die Eingangsfront des französischen Pavillons unterscheidet sich in ihrer Ge-staltung von den drei anderen Fassaden. Sie ist bedeckt von der großen Reproduktion eines Fotos von Etienne-Jules Marey mit dem Titel *Der laufende Mann*. Das Foto stammt aus dem Jahr 1888, also aus der Zeit, als die Bilder laufen lernten. Lichtbündel, die in einem bestimmten Rhythmus auf die Fassa-de geworfen werden, vermitteln den Eindruck von Bewegung. Eine leicht auf-wärts führende Fußgängerbrücke zieht sich bis in den Pavillon hinein. Besucher betreten das Gebäude durch das Bild und werden, wenn sie die Brücke über-queren und sich dem Eingang nähern, selbst zur Widerspiegelung dieses Bil-des. Die Präsentation des französischen Beitrags ist so gestaltet, dass Besucher über einen Ausstellungsweg durch das »Laboratoire de France« geführt wer-den. Es reicht vom »Weltall« über einen »Körperraum« bis zum »Universum der Maschinen«.

1. Preis Architekturwettbewerb:
Françoise-Hélène Jourda, Paris
Ausstellungsdesign: C. A. P. Productions, Paris
Grundstücksgröße: 11.300 Quadratmeter
Bebaute Fläche: 7.500 Quadratmeter
First prize in architectural competition:
Françoise-Hélène Jourda, Paris
Exhibition design: C. A. P. Productions, Paris
Lot size: 11,300 square meters
Constructed area: 7,500 square meters

The largest edifice on the East Pavilion Site, the French Exposition building stands directly opposite the German Pavilion. The pavilion client is the French sportswear company Decathlon, which has leased the building to the national government for the duration of the World Exposition and plans to use it as a shopping outlet afterwards. These plans for subsequent utilization were taken into consideration during the architectural competition in which the require-ments of the corporation were implemented with the design for a simple, unpretentious cube-shaped structure. The office of Françoise-Hélène Jourda responded to the requirements of the corporation with the design for a simple, unpretentious cube-shaped structure. The building appears as a glass edifice on a framework of steel and mature tree trunks. The glass panes in the facade are decorated in such a way that they join the wooden trunks in evoking the impression of a forest with thick foliage when viewed from the outside. Bowed wooden poles spread outward like branches and support a small latticed struc-ture of wooden beams. In combination with the wooden elements, the partial-ly decorated facade with its thermal control system creates an interior space bathed in light which presents an entirely natural look and can be used for a variety of different purposes.
The entrance facade of the French Pavilion presents a design that is quite dif-ferent from that of the other three facades. It is covered with a large-scale re-production of a photograph by Etienne-Jules Marey entitled *The Running Man*. The photo was taken in 1888 and thus dates from the infancy of moving pic-tures. Bundled rays of light projected on the facade at specific intervals evoke the impression of motion. A pedestrian bridge with a slight rising incline leads into the pavilion. Visitors enter the building through the photograph and, as they cross the bridge and approach the entrance, become reflections of the image themselves. The French presentation at EXPO 2000 is designed in such a way that visitors are guided along an exhibition tour through the "Laboratoire de France," which contains exhibits ranging from "Space" and "Body Space" to the "Universe of Machines."

Baumartige Holzstützen prägen das
Erscheinungsbild im Innern des Pavillons.
A "forest" of wooden pillars is a prominent
feature of the interior of the pavilion.

# Griechenland
## Greece

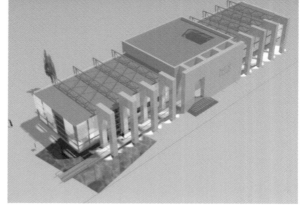

Der griechische Pavillon mit seinem rechteckigen Grundriss ist eine Konstruktion aus Betonbögen und demontierbaren Stahlfachwerkträgern, die mit perforierten Metallplatten verkleidet sind. Das Gebäude präsentiert sich mit einer Kombination aus offener Gestaltung und geschlossenen Rückzugsbereichen. Besucher betreten den Pavillon über eine ansteigende Rampe aus Holzbrettern auf einer Stahlunterkonstruktion. Sie führt entlang der nördlichen, transparenten Fassade über ein Wasserbecken zum Eingang. Der mittige, fast 11 Meter hohe Eingangskubus, in dem eine Ausstellung über den Stand der Vorbereitungen für die Olympischen Spiele 2004 in Athen informiert, ist mit Marmor verkleidet. Thema der zu beiden Seiten anschließenden, rund 8 Meter hohen Ausstellungsbereiche ist das Zusammenspiel zwischen Mensch und Natur. Anhand von moderner Multimedia-Technik zeigt Griechenland, wie zukunftsweisende Technologien und traditionelle Werte gleichberechtigt nebeneinander stehen. Die Grundrissgestaltung, die Besuchern den Weg durch das Gebäude vorgibt, ist in ihrer klassische Raumaufteilung teilweise der antiken griechischen Tempelarchitektur entlehnt.

The Greek Pavilion with its rectangular ground plan is a structure consisting of concrete arches and steel girders covered with perforated metal plates. The framework is designed for easy dismantling. The building presents a combination of open-space design and enclosed areas for retreat. Visitors enter the pavilion from a rising board ramp mounted on a steel supporting framework. The ramp runs along the northern, transparent facade over a pool of water to the entrance. The central, nearly 11-meter-high entrance cube, in which an exhibit informs visitors about the progress of preparation for 2004 Olympic Games in Athens, is covered in marble. The theme presented in the roughly eight-meter-high exhibition area located on both sides of the entrance is the interaction of mankind and nature. With the aid of modern multimedia technology, Greece demonstrates how future-oriented technologies and traditional values can coexist as equal partners. The design of the ground plan, which guides visitors along their way through the building, is based upon a classical room configuration adapted in part from ancient Greek temple architecture.

**Architekt: Marios M. Angelopoulos, Doxiadis Associates, Athen**
**Kontaktarchitekt: Büro Masswerk, Hannover**
**Grundstücksgröße: 2.000 Quadratmeter**
**Bebaute Fläche: 1.260 Quadratmeter**
Architect: Marios M. Angelopoulos, Doxiadis Associates, Athens
Contact architect: Büro Masswerk, Hanover
Lot size: 2,000 square meters
Constructed area: 1,260 square meters

Blick in den Eingangskubus
View into the entrance cube

Ein Holzsteg führt zum Eingang des griechischen Pavillons.
A wooden walkway leads to the pavilion entrance.

# Vereinigtes Königreich
## United Kingdom

Eine moderne Aluminiumfassade in Kombination mit Glaselementen verleiht dem britischen Pavillon seinen filigranen Charakter. Die transluzente Vorhangfassade an den beiden Stirnseiten des zweigeschossigen Gebäudes bildet einen besonderen Blickfang. Das Vereinigte Königreich hat den Pavillon während der Weltausstellung für seine Präsentation angemietet. Auf einer Grundfläche von 2.730 Quadratmetern stehen hierfür unterschiedliche Ausstellungsbereiche sowie Büro- und Funktionsräume in zwei Ebenen zur Verfügung. Die gesamte Konzeption des Gebäudes beruht auf einer äußerst flexiblen Bauweise. Im Hinblick auf geänderte Anforderungen bei der Nachnutzung, zum Beispiel als Gewerbe- oder Büroflächen, ist der nachträgliche Einbau von Zwischendecken oder versetzbaren Raumtrennwänden von vornherein bedacht worden. Das Ausstellungskonzept des Londoner Architekturbüros HP:ICM steht unter dem Motto »No Man is an Island«. In einer Art »Blackbox« präsentiert sich das Land auf vier unterschiedlichen Themeninseln, die in einer Wasserfläche liegen und durch Brücken miteinander verbunden sind. Hier können Besucher Eindrücke aus dem Alltag und der kulturellen Vielfalt des Vereinigten Königreichs sowie seiner Auseinandersetzung mit der Umwelt gewinnen.

A modern aluminum facade is combined with glass elements to give the British Pavilion a filigree character. The translucent curtained faces of the two ends of the two-story building are particularly eye-catching features. The United Kingdom has leased the pavilion for the duration of the World Exposition. Several different exhibition areas, along with office space and engineering rooms, are available for use on two levels. The total building concept is based on an extremely flexible construction model. With an eye to the different building-utilization requirements (conversion to commercial or office space, for example) that will arise following the end of EXPO 2000, the architects included options for the installation of suspended ceilings and moveable room partitions in their original plans.
The exhibition concept developed by the London architects' office HP:ICM is based on the theme "No Man Is an Island." Great Britain makes its presentation in a kind of "black box" on four different theme islands surrounded by water and connected by bridges. Visitors to the pavilion have an opportunity to gain impressions of everyday life in United Kingdom, the kingdom's broad cultural diversity and its efforts to come to grips with environmental issues.

**Architekt:** Ingo Krümmel, Goldbeckbau GmbH, Hamburg
**Ausstellungskonzept:** HP:ICM, London
**Bauherr:** Goldbeck Projekt GmbH, Bielefeld
**Grundstücksgröße:** 4.037 Quadratmeter
**Bebaute Fläche:** 2.730 Quadratmeter
**Architect:** Ingo Krümmel, Goldbeckbau GmbH, Hamburg
**Exhibition concept:** HP:ICM, London
**Client:** Goldbeck Projekt GmbH, Bielefeld
**Lot size:** 4,037 square meters
**Constructed area:** 2,730 square meters

**Blick von Nordosten auf den britischen Pavillon**
View of the British Pavilion from the northeast

**Eine Ausstellungsinsel**
An exhibition island

balance for t
Im Gleic
committed to ou
for our land
– unser Weg in di
nnt mit Engagement für Stadt u
Eisen
Thatch
Reet
Wood
Holz
Grass
Gras

# Irland
## Ireland

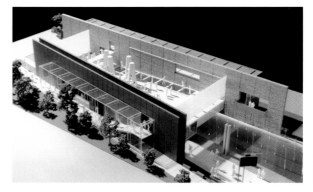

Bei ihrem Entwurf ließen sich die Architekten von der irischen Landschaft anregen. Der irische Pavillon ist eine Synthese aus typischen Elementen, die die Insel zu bieten hat: grüne Hügel, Wasser, große Feldsteine, Steinbrüche und die sich überall durch die Landschaft ziehenden Steinmauern, die errichtet werden, um den Wind abzuhalten und die Äcker zu säubern. Der dreigeschossige irische Pavillon, eine Stahlrahmen- und Glaskonstruktion, ist eingefasst von zwei unterschiedlichen, über 10 Meter hohen Steinmauern, die das Erscheinungsbild des Gebäudes prägen. Die eine besteht aus Metallgitterkörben, die mit Feldsteinen gefüllt sind, die andere aus dunkelgrauem, poliertem Kilkenny-Kalkstein. Zwischen diesen Mauern liegt der Ausstellungsbereich, in dem ein Pfad zu fünf verschiedenen Stationen führt. Besuchern wird hier eine interaktive Reise von der prähistorischen Vergangenheit Irlands bis in die Zukunft geboten. Höhepunkt des Ausstellungsparcours ist die »Sensory Wall«, die mit Wind, Regen, Sprache und Musik alle Sinne der Besucher anspricht. Der Pavillon demonstriert den verantwortungsvollen Umgang mit Ressourcen, denn das Gebäude ist komplett rückbaubar und kann an anderer Stelle weitergenutzt werden.

The architects drew inspiration from the Irish landscape for their design of the pavilion. The Irish Pavilion presents a synthesis of elements typical of the island: green hills, water, massive rocks, quarries and the stone walls that mark the face of the landscape everywhere in Ireland, barriers erected to resist the wind and keep the fields free of debris. The three-story pavilion, a steel-frame-and-glass construction, is framed by two different stone walls, each ten meters high, which dominate the overall impression evoked by the complex. One wall is made of metal wire baskets filled with field stones, the other of dark-gray, polished Kilkenny limestone. The exhibition area is located between these two walls and is accessible from a path that leads to five different stations. Visitors are offered an interactive tour from Ireland's prehistoric past to its future. The most spectacular point on the exhibition tour is the "Sensory Wall," which appeals to all of the visitors' senses with wind, rain, spoken language and music. The pavilion is a living demonstration of a responsible approach to the use of resources, as the building can be completely dismantled and rebuilt for further use at a different location.

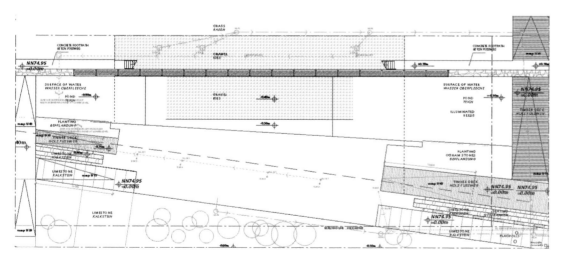

**Grundriss des irischen Pavillons**
Floor plan of the Irish Pavilion

Architekten: Murray & Laoire Architects, Dublin
Kontaktarchitekten: Planungsgemeinschaft Garriock & Associates, Uetze
Auftraggeber: Department of Enterprise, Trade and Employment
Projektmanager: The Office of Public Works
Grundstücksgröße: 2.390 Quadratmeter
Bebaute Fläche: 956 Quadratmeter
Architects: Murray & Laoire Architects, Dublin
Contact architects: Planungsgemeinschaft Garriock & Associates, Uetze
Contracting agency: Department of Enterprise, Trade and Employment
Project Manager: The Office of Public Works
Lot size: 2,390 square meters
Constructed area: 956 square meters

**Detail der Feldsteinwand**
Detail of the field-stone wall

**Blick vom Europa Boulevard**
View from Europa Boulevard

**Die »Sensory Wall«**
The "Sensory Wall"

# Italien
## Italy

Der italienische Beitrag ist inspiriert vom Werk des Universalgenies Leonardo da Vinci, der bereits vor 500 Jahren visionäre Ideen rund um den Themenkomplex Mensch, Natur und Technik entwickelte. Der 26 Meter hohe und 60 Meter breite Pavillon erinnert in seiner Form an die Kuppel eines Doms von da Vinci. Die Halbkugel ist von einer Kunststoffmembran überspannt, schlanke Stahlträger bilden das Gerüst der modernen Traglufthalle. Die »Penna«, ein 50 Meter hoher Mast aus poliertem Metall, stellt einen besonderen Blickfang dar. Auf einer Piazza vor dem Gebäude werden Eindrücke italienischer Lebensart, Landschaften und Küche vermittelt. Von diesem Platz aus führen zwei umlaufende rechteckige Rampen die Besucher in den Ausstellungsbereich in rund 10 Metern Höhe. Zur Präsentation im Innern gehören Originalstudien Leonardo da Vincis ebenso wie ein Fluggerät, das der Meister im Rahmen seiner Studien über den Vogelflug entworfen hat. Die Brücke zur Gegenwart wird durch italienische Weltfirmen beispielsweise aus der Automobilbranche geschlagen, die aus einigen Entwürfen da Vincis konkrete Produkte entwickelt haben.

The Italian Pavilion is inspired by the work of Leonardo da Vinci, the universal genius who developed a number of visionary ideas relating to the thematic complex of mankind, nature and technology some 500 years ago. Twenty-six meters high and 60 meters wide, the pavilion calls to mind the shape of a cathedral dome by da Vinci. The cupola is covered by a plastic membrane. Slim steel girders form the supporting framework for the modern air-bubble construction. The "Penna," a polished metal mast rising to a height of 50 meters, is an especially prominent attraction.
Impressions of Italian lifestyles, landscapes and cuisine are presented on a square outside the building. Two rectangular ramps leading around the building provide visitors access to the exhibition area, which is elevated about ten meters above ground level. The exhibits inside the pavilion building include original studies by da Vinci, among them his flying machine, drawn by the great master within the context of his studies of the flight of birds. The link to the future is forged by global giants of Italian industry, including representatives of the automobile industry, in the form of specific products developed on the basis of several of da Vinci's ideas.

Architekten: Sturchio Architects & Designers, Rom
Grundstücksgröße: 4.395 Quadratmeter
Bebaute Fläche: 3.260 Quadratmeter
Architects: Sturchio Architects & Designers, Rome
Lot size: 4,395 square meters
Constructed area: 3,260 square meters

**Blick in die Kuppel**
View into the dome

**Die »Penna« ragt hoch über den kuppelförmigen Pavillon hinaus.**
The "Penna" towers high above the domeshaped pavilion

# Jemen
## Yemen

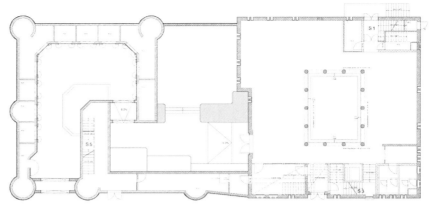

**Grundriss des jemenitischen Pavillons**
Floor plan of the Yemenite Pavilion

Der Pavillon des Jemen besteht im Wesentlichen aus zwei Bereichen, dem der Stadtmauer mit marktähnlicher Atmosphäre und dem des Ausstellungsgebäudes. Die Stadtmauer wurde nach traditioneller Bauweise aus lehmverputzten Ziegeln errichtet. Sie beinhaltet mehrere kleine Räume, in denen jemenitische Produkte, Techniken und Handwerke präsentiert werden. Eine terrassenförmig angelegte Freiluftausstellung zeigt die landestypische Agrarstruktur. Zusätzlich befindet sich hier ein Platz für Aufführungen. Besucher, die den Pavillon betreten, werden über diesen »Marktplatz« zum Hauptgebäude geführt. Diese dreigeschossige »Samsara« entspricht in ihrer Gestaltung öffentlichen Gebäuden der Stadt Sanaa und repräsentiert damit verschiedene soziale und kulturelle Aspekte des Landes. Bildtafeln, Modelle und Objekte stellen jemenitische Architektur, Bauweisen und Planungskonzepte vor.

Über alle drei Geschosse umschließt der Bau einen nach oben offenen Luftraum. Die Ausstellung ist so konzipiert, dass Besucher durch den gesamten Komplex geleitet werden. Im zweiten Obergeschoss führt dieser Weg auch auf die Stadtmauer hinaus, wo man einen guten Überblick über die Ausstellung im Freien erhält. Für VIP-Veranstaltungen steht im zweiten Obergeschoss ein spezieller Raum, der so genannte »Mafraj«, zur Verfügung. Traditionell diente er dem Zusammentreffen jemenitischer Männer.

The pavilion of the state of Yemen comprises two major sections, that of the city wall with its street-market flair and that of the exhibition building. The city wall was built using the traditional construction method of clay and bricks. It comprises a number of small rooms where products, techniques and handicrafts from Yemen are exhibited to visitors. A terraced open-air exhibit offers a view of agricultural structures typical of the country and also provides space for performances. Visitors entering the pavilion are led across the "marketplace" to the main building. This three-story *Samsara* is constructed in the style of public buildings in the city of Sanaa and thus represents a number of important aspects of social and cultural life in Yemen. Pictures, models and objects present examples of Yemenite architecture, building methods and planning concepts.

The building completely encloses a central space that remains open to the sky. The exhibition is conceived in such a way that visitors are guided through the entire complex. On the third floor, the route leads out to the city wall, where visitors enjoy a view of the whole exhibition from the outside. A special room on the third floor, the so-called *Mafraj*, is available for VIP events. Such rooms traditionally served as meeting places for Yemenite men.

**Fassadendetail**
Detail of the pavilion facade

**Architekt: Dar-Almohandis Mohamed Kassim Alarikey, Sanaa**
**Kontaktarchitekten: Anderhalten Veauthier Architekten, Berlin**
**Grundstücksgröße: 1.500 Quadratmeter**
**Bebaute Fläche: 937 Quadratmeter**
Architect: Dar-Almohandis Mohamed Kassim Alarikey, Sanaa
Contact architects: Anderhalten Veauthier Architekten, Berlin
Lot size: 1,500 square meters
Constructed area: 937 square meters

**Der Jemen präsentiert sich mit landestypischer Architektur.**
A presentation of typical Yemenite architecture

# Jordanien
## Jordan

**Modellaufnahme**
Photo of a model of pavilion

Im Königreich Jordanien gibt es mehr als 13.000 eingetragene Ausgrabungs-stätten. Dementsprechend erinnert der Pavillon an eine moderne Ausgrabungs-stätte und präsentiert ein Mosaik, das Besucher zu einer Entdeckungsreise einlädt. Nach Betreten des Pavillons gelangt man zunächst auf eine Art Galerie, die als Bühne für traditionelle Darbietungen dient und einen Überblick über die tiefer gelegene Ausstellung ermöglicht. Ein Aufzug und zwei breite, gerüst-artige Treppen an den beiden Schmalseiten des Pavillons führen in die untere Ebene, 2,7 Meter unter dem Geländeniveau. Der Pavillon liegt größtenteils im Freien, an der östlichen Längsseite befinden sich einige Räume, die von der unteren Ebene aus betreten werden können. Dazu zählen Serviceeinrichtun-gen, eine VIP-Lounge und ein arabischer Imbiss.

Zentrales Element des jordanischen Beitrags ist das Mosaik. Es besteht aus fast 100 unterschiedlich hohen Blöcken aus witterungsbeständigen Materialien, die jeweils eine einheitliche Grundfläche von 90 x 90 Zentimetern aufweisen. Rasterartig auf gleicher Ebene mit der Fußbodenoberfläche angeordnet, sind viele der Mosaikblöcke zum Betreten gedacht, auf anderen befinden sich Ex-ponate, die alle Bereiche des jordanischen Lebens repräsentieren. Für die Expo-nate, die von Künstlern, Handwerkern und Studenten des Landes hergestellt wurden, war ein spezieller Wettbewerb durch die jordanische Nationalgalerie und das Bildungsministerium ausgelobt worden. Die Exponate fügen sich zu einer Art Skulpturengarten, in dem unter anderem Nachbildungen bedeu-tender archäologischer Fundstücke zu sehen sind. Nach der Weltausstellung soll der Pavillon im Zentrum der jordanischen Hauptstadt Amman als Touris-tenattraktion wieder aufgebaut werden.

There are more than 13,000 registered archaeological excavation sites in the Kingdom of Jordan. Accordingly, the pavilion is designed as a replica of a modern excavation site featuring a mosaic floor inviting visitors to undertake a journey of discovery. Upon entering the pavilion, visitors find themselves in a kind of gallery which serves as a stage for traditional performances and offers a view of the exhibition on the lower level. An elevator and two wide, scaffold-style stairways along the two narrow sides of the pavilion lead down to the lower level 2.7 meters below ground. Most of the pavilion is outdoors, and there are several rooms on the long eastern side of the building that can be entered from the lower level. These include service facilities, a VIP lounge and a snack bar featuring Arab specialties.

Perhaps the most striking feature of the Jordanian pavilion is the mosaic floor. It consists of nearly 100 blocks of different heights made of weather-resistant materials, each set in a section of the floor measuring 90 x 90 centimeters. Arranged in a grid pattern flush with the surface of the floor, many of the mosaic blocks are intended to be walked on. Others bear scenes representing virtually every aspect of Jordanian life. Commissions for the pieces done by Jordanian artists, artisans and students were awarded on the basis of a special competition by the Jordanian National Gallery and the Ministry of Education. These pieces combine to form a kind of sculpture garden in which, among other things, replicas of significant archaeological finds are exhibited. After the end of EXPO 2000, the pavilion is to be dismantled and re-erected in down-town Amman, the capital of Jordan, as a tourist attraction.

Architekt: Expo Design Team based at Akram Abu
Hamdan Associates, Amman
Generalplanung: Atelier Wolfgang Rang,
Frankfurt am Main mit
Office of Modern Buildings, Amman
Hock + Reinke, Haibach
GM Planen und Beraten, Griesheim
Grundstücksgröße: 2.040 Quadratmeter
Bebaute Fläche: 1.500 Quadratmeter

Architect: Expo Design Team based at Akram Abu
Hamdan Associates, Amman
General planning: Atelier Wolfgang Rang,
Frankfurt am Main in cooperation with the
Office of Modern Buildings, Amman
Hock + Reinke, Haibach
GM Planen und Beraten, Griesheim
Lot size: 2,040 square meters
Constructed area: 1,500 square meters

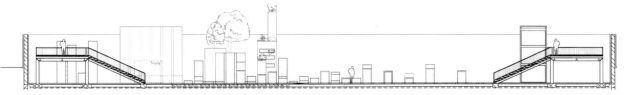

**Längsschnitt durch den jordanischen Pavillon**
Longitudinal section of the Jordanian Pavilion

**Blick von der Galerie auf den Ausstellungs-bereich**
View of the exhibition area from the gallery

# Kroatien
## Croatia

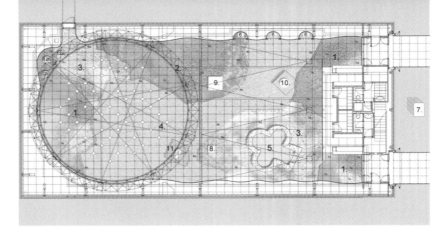

**Grundriss des kroatischen Pavillons**
Floor plan of the Croatian Pavilion

Umgeben von Wasser, kann der kroatische Pavillon mit seiner Konstruktion aus verkleideten Fachwerkträgern nur über Brücken erreicht werden. Ein über 4 Meter hoher Monolith aus poliertem Stahl markiert inmitten der Wasserlandschaft den Eingang in das rechteckige Gebäude, das über ein Erdgeschoss und eine Galerie verfügt. Der geschlossene, rund 10 Meter hohe Pavillon simuliert einen Wasserfall, in dem sich der Himmel spiegelt. Die Fassaden sind dazu mit einer leicht gewellten Plastikfolie versehen, über die ständig Wasser läuft. Die Gebäudehülle wird in erster Linie als Notwendigkeit für die Gestaltung eines geschlossenen Ausstellungsraums betrachtet. Das Wasser als Gestaltungsmaterial wechselt nach innen in klassische Baumaterialien.
Im Ausstellungsbereich des Pavillons gehen Besucher über einen gläsernen Boden, unter dem vielfältige Landschaften, Kulturdenkmäler und auch der Grundriss einer alten kroatischen Kirche dargestellt sind. Zahlreiche künstlerische Artefakte verweisen symbolisch auf die kulturelle Tradition Kroatiens, Werke von Künstlern des 20. Jahrhunderts geben Einblicke in die heutige Zeit. Die Präsentation der kroatischen Landschaften, Geschichte und Kultur sowie technischer Entwicklungen zum Umwelt- und Naturschutz werden durch ständige Diaprojektionen und eine Rundum-Videoprojektion ergänzt. Musik und Lichtinszenierungen runden die erlebnisorientierte Gesamtdarstellung ab, die bei den Besuchern Interesse für Kroatien wecken möchte und in ihrer Art eine Weiterentwicklung der Präsentation des Landes auf der EXPO '98 in Lissabon darstellt.

Completely surrounded by water, the Croatian Pavilion, a paneled framework structure, is accessible only across bridges. A polished steel monolith measuring four meters in height stands in the midst of the watery landscape at the entrance to the rectangular building, which has a ground floor and a gallery level. The enclosed, ten-meter-high pavilion simulates a waterfall in which the sky is reflected. The facades are covered with corrugated plastic foil, over which water runs continuously. The building shell is intended primarily to serve the function of providing the necessary sheltered exhibition space. Used outside as an element of design, water gives way in the interior to conventional building materials.
Visitors inside the exhibition area of the pavilion walk across a glass floor beneath which representations of diverse landscapes, cultural monuments and the floor plan of an old Croatian church can be seen. A large collection of art artifacts bears symbolic witness to the cultural tradition of Croatia, while 20th-century works offer insights into more recent times. The presentation of Croatian landscapes, history and culture along with demonstrations of technological developments in the fields of environmental protection and nature conservation are accompanied by a non-stop slide show and a surround-view video projection. Music and light shows round out the total event-oriented program designed to awaken an interest in Croatia on the part of pavilion visitors. In its own way, the presentation takes up where the country's contribution to EXPO '98 in Lisbon left off.

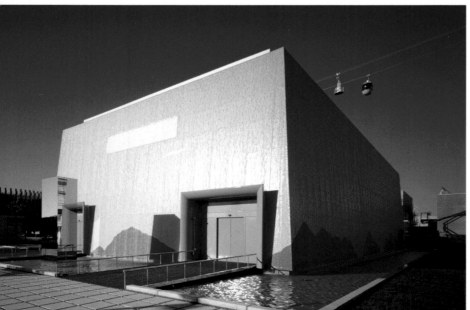

**Eingangsfront**
Entrance facade

**Architekt: Branko Siladin, Odak i Siladin arhitekti, Zagreb**
**Kontaktarchitekt: Büro Ivan Kozjak, Hannover**
**Grundstücksgröße: 2.400 Quadratmeter**
**Bebaute Fläche: 640 Quadratmeter**
Architect: Branko Siladin, Odak i Siladin arhitekti, Zagreb
Contact architect: Büro Ivan Kozjak, Hanover
Lot size: 2,400 square meters
Constructed area: 640 square meters

**Der gläserne Boden im Innern des Gebäudes**
The glass floor inside the pavilion

# Lettland
# Latvia

Der Pavillon Lettlands besteht aus zwei unterschiedlichen Baukörpern. Der höhere bildet den Eingangsbereich und umschließt die Form eines umgekehrten »Kegelstumpfes«, der einen nach oben offenen, ruhigen Innenhof bildet. Die Materialien dieses Bereichs sind typisch für die Landschaften der Ostsee: Holz, Sand und Reet. In diesem Hof und in dem angrenzenden eingeschossigen Gebäudeteil befindet sich die Ausstellungsfläche des Pavillons mit einem kleinen Shop. Besprechungs-, Büro- und Serviceräume liegen im hinteren Teil des Gebäudes. Die Cafeteria auf dem begehbaren Dach wird über die Galerie im Eingangsgebäude erschlossen. Der Pavillon basiert auf einer reinen Holzkonstruktion. Sie ruht auf einer Bodenplatte, die im Bereich des Innenhofs ausgespart ist.

The Latvian pavilion comprises two separate buildings. The taller of the two is the entrance area which surrounds an upside-down "conical stump" that forms a quiet inner courtyard open toward its top. The materials used in this section of the pavilion are typical of Baltic Sea landscapes: wood, sand and reed thatch. Located in the courtyard and in the adjacent one-story building are the pavilion exhibition areas and a small shop. Consultation, office and service rooms are found in the rear section of the building. The cafeteria on the penthouse roof can be entered through the gallery in the entrance building. The pavilion is constructed entirely of wood and rests on a slab which is left open in the area of the inner courtyard.

**Architekt: Andrejs Gelzis, Briniskigo Projektu Birojs, Riga**
**Kontaktarchitekten: KSP Engel und Zimmermann**
**Architekten BDA, Berlin und Braunschweig**
**Grundstücksgröße: 1.500 Quadratmeter**
**Bebaute Fläche: 800 Quadratmeter**
**Architect: Andrejs Gelzis, Briniskigo Projektu Birojs, Riga**
**Contact architects: KSP Engel und Zimmermann**
**Architekten BDA, Berlin and Braunschweig**
**Lot size: 1,500 square meters**
**Constructed area: 800 square meters**

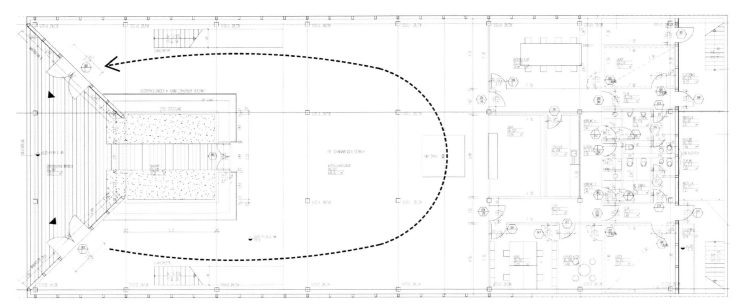

**Grundriss des lettischen Pavillons**
Floor plan of the pavilion

**Eingangsbereich**
View of the entrance area

# Litauen
## Lithuania

Für die Präsentation ihres Landes entwarfen die Architekten aus Litauen eher ein Designobjekt als einen klassischen Pavillon. Das auffällige gelbe Gebäude, zu dem sich die Planer nach eigenen Angaben durch das World Wide Web inspirieren ließen, symbolisiert das Streben der Gesellschaft nach mehr Dynamik, Kommunikation und Offenheit. Die Rahmenkonstruktion des über 12 Meter hohen Gebäudes bildet ein Metallgerüst, für die Fassadenverkleidung wurden Sandwichplatten gewählt. Hinter diesen geschlossenen Fassaden informiert der junge Staat mit modernen multimedialen Mitteln über Kultur, Land und Leute. Präsentiert werden auch Beispiele wissenschaftlicher Kreativität und technologischer Leistungsfähigkeit. Der Pavillon selbst ist ein Beweis dafür, denn für seinen Bau wurden weitgehend Materialien »Made in Lithuania« verwendet. Nach der Weltausstellung wird er in Litauen als Ausstellungspavillon genutzt werden.

The edifice conceived by the Lithuanian architects resembles a design object rather than a classical pavilion. The eye-catching yellow building, whose planners cite the World Wide Web as a source of inspiration for their design concept, symbolizes Lithuanian society's commitment to greater dynamism, better communication and increased openness. The skeleton of the 12-meter-high building is formed by a metal framework. Sandwich panels were selected for the outer lining of the facades. Behind these closed walls, the young nation informs visitors about its culture, its geography and its people with the aid of modern multimedia resources. The presentations include examples of scientific creativity and technological productivity. The pavilion itself offers eloquent testimony to both, as it was built for the most part with materials made in Lithuania. The structure is to be used in Lithuania as an exhibition pavilion following the end of EXPO 2000.

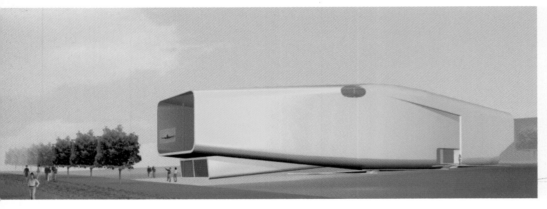

Computeranimation
Computer animation

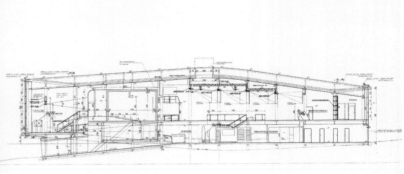

Schnitt durch den litauischen Pavillon
Cross section of the Lithuanian pavilion

Architekten: Audrius Bucas und Gintaras Kuginys, Vilnius
Kontaktarchitekten: Ingenieurbüro V. Merkewitsch und Partner, Seelze
Grundstücksgröße: 1.500 Quadratmeter
Bebaute Fläche: 1.200 Quadratmeter
Architects: Audrius Bucas and Gintaras Kuginys, Vilna
Contact architects: Ingenieurbüro V. Merkewitsch und Partner, Seelze
Lot size: 1,500 square meters
Constructed area: 1,200 square meters

Blick vom Europa Boulevard
View from Europa Boulevard

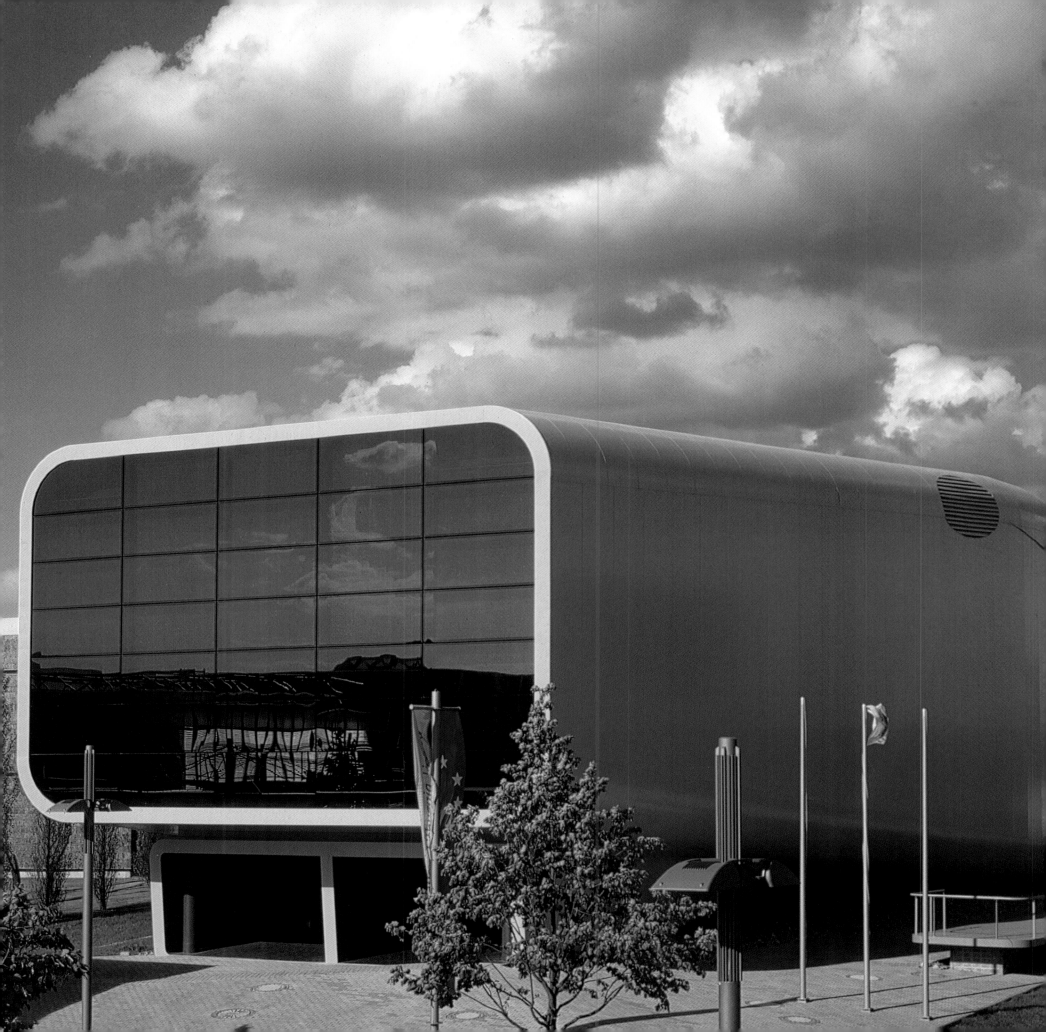

# Monaco
## Monaco

Monaco präsentiert sich in einem offen gestalteten Pavillon aus Glas, Aluminium und Holz in fast mediterranem Ambiente, umgeben von großen Wasserflächen und einem Jachthafen mit Bootsstegen. Vom Eingang im Osten des Grundstücks werden Besucher auf Holzstegen über das Wasser in den Empfangsbereich des Pavillons geführt. Hier finden sich eine Bar, ein VIP- sowie ein Merchandising-Bereich. In einer Pre-Show wird die enge Verbindung des Fürstentums mit dem Wasser thematisiert. Jede der insgesamt vier oberen Ebenen ist unterschiedlichen Nutzungen vorbehalten, alle verfügen jedoch über Gastronomieflächen mit vorgelagerten Terrassen in verschiedenen Himmelsrichtungen. Im zweiten Stockwerk, zu dem eine großzügige Freitreppe hinaufführt, ist das Herzstück des Pavillons angesiedelt, ein 360-Grad-Kino für vielfältige Präsentationen des Landes. Im dritten und vierten Obergeschoss stehen VIP-Lounges, Business- und Präsentationsbereiche für Empfänge und unterschiedliche Veranstaltungen bereit. Die Dachterrasse ist als mediterrane Garteninsel im Stil eines »Jardin Exotique« gestaltet und bietet eine gute Aussicht über das Expo-Gelände.

Monaco makes its presentation in a pavilion featuring an open design consisting of glass, aluminum and wood in an almost Mediterranean setting surrounded by large bodies of water and a yacht harbor with docks. Visitors are led from the entrance in the eastern part of the lot on wooden walkways over the water to the pavilion reception area. A bar, a VIP lounge and a merchandising center are located here. A preview show highlights the principality's close ties with the sea and water. Each of the four upper levels is reserved for different purposes, but all have their own restaurant areas, which include outdoor terraces facing north, south, east and west. Located on the third floor, accessible from a broad, open stairway, is the centerpiece of the pavilion, a 360-degree surround-view theater for a variety of presentations relating to Monaco. The fourth and fifth floors contain VIP lounges, settings for business functions and presentation areas for receptions and events of all kinds. The rooftop terrace is designed as a Mediterranean garden island in the style of a *jardin exotique* and offers a fine view of the Expo grounds.

**Grundriss des Erdgeschosses**
Plan of the ground-floor level

**Architekt: Hans Degraeuwe, Degraeuwe Consulting N. V., Heidergem / Belgien**
**Kontaktarchitekt: artemedia ag, Chemnitz**
**Grundstücksgröße: 3.900 Quadratmeter**
**Bebaute Fläche: 1.400 Quadratmeter**
Architect: Hans Degraeuwe, Degraeuwe Consulting N. V., Heidergem / Belgium
Contact architect: artemedia ag, Chemnitz
Lot size: 3,900 square meters
Constructed area: 1,400 square meters

**Blick von Südosten auf den monegassischen Pavillon**
View of the Monegasque Pavilion from the southeast

# Niederlande
## The Netherlands

»Holland schafft Raum« ist das Motto des niederländischen Ausstellungsbeitrags. Die Architekten nahmen es wörtlich und stapelten in dem rund
40 Meter hohen Pavillon typische holländische Landschaften übereinander.
Fast 90 Prozent der Grundstücksfläche blieben dadurch unbebaut und werden
als Garten genutzt. Der Entwurf thematisiert die Fähigkeit der Niederländer,
den ihnen zur Verfügung stehenden Raum optimal zu nutzen, und erinnert an
die Gegenden, die durch künstliche Landgewinnung entstanden sind.
Der Pavillon besteht aus sechs Ausstellungsebenen mit je 1.000 Quadratmetern
Fläche und kommt ganz ohne Fassade aus. Er ist so aufgebaut, dass Besucher
mit einem Aufzug auf das Dach fahren und sich von dort langsam durch oder
um die verschiedenen Bereiche herum nach unten begeben. In der oberen
Ebene erwartet sie eine Wasserlandschaft mit einer Insel und Windrädern als
Symbole für alternative Formen der Energiegewinnung. In der darunter liegenden Etage befinden sich Theater- und Vortragsräume, in denen sich die Niederlande ihren Besuchern multimedial präsentieren. Ein Wasservorhang schirmt
diesen Bereich nach außen ab und vermittelt den Eindruck, als regne es auf die
anschließende Waldebene herab. Die Bäume, die in einer dicken Erdschicht ein-
gepflanzt sind, wurden schon Monate vor der Weltausstellung nach Hannover
gebracht, damit sie sich akklimatisieren. Auch konstruktiv spielen Bäume eine
bedeutende Rolle für den niederländischen Pavillon, denn eingespannte Baum-
stämme tragen die Last der oberen Ebenen. Die folgenden Bereiche zeigen eine
Wurzellandschaft mit großen Pflanztöpfen sowie eine Ebene mit Gewächs-
häusern und den für Holland typischen Blumen. In der untersten Ebene durch-
wandern Besucher eine Dünenlandschaft und Nachbildungen von Grotten.
Im Untergeschoss schließlich stehen Räume für VIPs und für die Bewirtung der
Gäste sowie weitere Serviceeinrichtungen zur Verfügung. Mit dieser effizien-
ten und Platz sparenden Bauweise ist es den Niederländern gelungen, auf
engstem Raum alle Facetten ihres Landes darzustellen und gleichzeitig das
Expo-Motto »Mensch – Natur – Technik: Eine neue Welt entsteht« sinnfällig
umzusetzen.

"Holland Creates Space" is the theme of the Dutch presentation at EXPO 2000.
Taking the idea literally, the architects stacked landscapes typical of the
Dutch countryside one on top of the other in the pavilion, a structure nearly
40 meters high. This left nearly 90 percent of the grounds free for a garden.
The design concept emphasizes the capacity of the Dutch for making optimum
use of the space available to them and serves as a reminder of the regions
recovered from the sea.
The pavilion comprises six exhibition levels, each with 1,000 square meters of
floor space, and has no facade. It is built in such a way that visitors can take an
elevator up to the roof and then gradually work their way down through or
around the various exhibition areas. The upper level features an aquatic landscape with an island and windmills symbolizing alternative forms of energy
production. The next level down contains theater and lecture rooms where
viewers are treated to a multimedia presentation about the Netherlands. A curtain of water isolates this section from the outside, creating the impression of
rain falling on the forested level below. The trees, which are planted in a thick
layer of soil, were shipped to Hanover months before the opening of the World
Exposition in order to give them sufficient time to adjust to the climate. Trees
also play a significant role in the construction of the pavilion, as a framework
of tree trunks bears the weight of the upper levels. The next lower levels feature a root-culture landscape with large planters and a floor with hothouses
and flowers typical of Holland. Having arrived at the lowest level, visitors
wander through a landscape of dunes and replicas of grottoes. The basement
floor has rooms for VIPs, places to eat and drink and other service facilities.
With this highly efficient, space-saving style of construction, the Dutch have
succeeded in presenting virtually every facet of life in their country while
offering a revealing practical demonstration of the Expotheme "Humankind –
Nature – Technology" in a very limited space.

Architekten: MVRDV Architekten, Rotterdam
Kontaktarchitekten: grbv GbR mbH
Beratende Ingenieure im Bauwesen, Hannover
Grundstücksgröße: 9.015 Quadratmeter
Bebaute Fläche: 1.024 Quadratmeter
Architects: MVRDV Architekten, Rotterdam
Contact architects: grbv GbR mbH
Beratende Ingenieure im Bauwesen, Hanover
Lot size: 9,015 square meters
Constructed area: 1,024 square meters

Gestapelte Landschaften
Stacked landscapes

**Die Waldebene**
The forest level

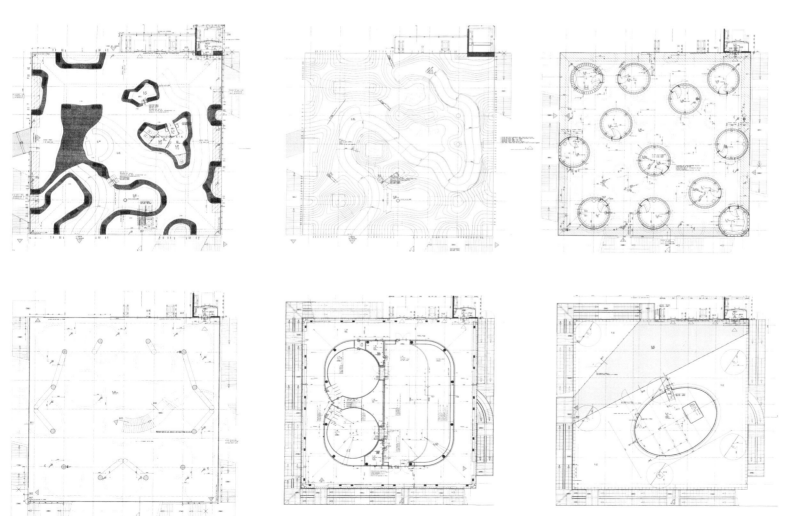

**Grundrissabfolge**
Floor plans of the six levels

**Auf dem Dach des niederländischen Pavillons**
On the roof of the Dutch Pavilion

# Norwegen
## Norway

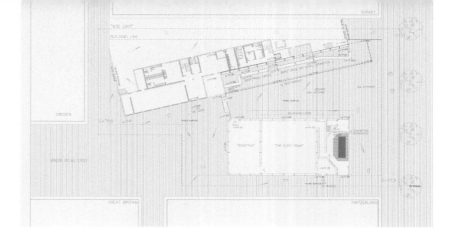

**Grundriss des Pavillons**
Floor plan of the pavilion

**Im »Raum der Stille«**
In the "Quiet Room"

Der Pavillonkomplex Norwegens besteht aus zwei voneinander unabhängigen Gebäudekörpern, einem Ausstellungs- und einem Servicegebäude. Zu den Besonderheiten des Ausstellungsbereichs gehören ein donnernder, 15 Meter hoher Wasserfall und der so genannte »Raum der Stille«. Der Wasserfall ist die Kopie eines echten Wasserfalls aus einem norwegischen Fjord, einem der wenigen, hinter denen man hindurchgehen kann. Genau dies wird auch im Pavillon ermöglicht. Als Land voller Kontraste überrascht Norwegen seine Besucher im Innern mit dem »Raum der Stille«. Diesen Kubus konzipierte die norwegische Künstlerin Marianne Heske mit Videosequenzen aus der Natur als einen Ort der Reflexion.

Gegensätze prägen auch die Gestaltung der beiden Bauteile. Der Ausstellungspavillon mit seiner Grundfläche von 15 x 33 Metern ist ausgeführt in geleimten Holzelementen mit einer Außenverkleidung aus Aluminium. Neben dem Wasserfall und dem »Raum der Stille« enthält dieses 15 Meter hohe Gebäude auch einen Bereich, in dem das Hauptthema Norwegens »Umwelt – Energie – Technologie« umfassend dargestellt wird. Als Kontrast zur Aluminiumfassade des Hauptgebäudes ist das niedrigere Servicegebäude ausschließlich in Holz ausgeführt. Auf zwei Etagen und einer Grundfläche von 12 x 70 Metern beherbergt es unter anderem ein Konferenzzentrum und ein Fischrestaurant der Spitzenklasse. Bei der Planung wurde eine eventuelle Nachnutzung von vornherein mitbedacht. Beide Gebäude sind aus Einzelelementen zusammengesetzt, die leicht demontiert werden können. Voraussichtlich werden sie als Hotel in Norwegen weitergenutzt werden.

The Norwegian pavilion complex comprises two separate buildings: an exhibition hall and a service center. The most remarkable highlights of the exhibition include a thundering 15-meter waterfall and the so-called "Quiet Room." The waterfall is modeled after a real waterfall in a Norwegian fjord, one of the few that people can walk behind, and the pavilion makes this adventure possible for its visitors. A country of many contrasts, Norway surprises its visitors inside the pavilion with the "Quiet Room." This cube-shaped space was designed by the Norwegian artist Marianne Heske as a place of peace and reflection featuring video clips of nature scenes.

The design of the two buildings incorporates a number of opposites. The exhibition pavilion, which occupies a space of 15 x 33 meters, is constructed of glued wooden elements with aluminum siding. In addition to the waterfall and the "Quiet Room," this 15-meter-high building also houses the area in which the main Norwegian theme of "Environment – Energy – Technology" is presented in an extensive range of exhibits. As a contrast to the aluminum facade of the main building, the lower service building is executed entirely in wood. Distributed over two floors and encompassing 12 x 70 meters of floor space, it contains, among other things, a conference center and a top-class seafood restaurant. The architects anticipated the possible reuse of the complex after the end of EXPO 2000 from the outset. Both buildings are assembled from individual elements which can be easily dismantled. They will presumably be used as hotel facilities in Norway.

Architekt: Wilhelm Munthe-Kaas, LPO arkitektur & design as, Oslo
Kontaktarchitekt: Akzente Architektur & Landschaftsplanung GbR, Hannover
Grundstücksgröße: 3.381 Quadratmeter
Bebaute Fläche: 1.426 Quadratmeter
Architect: Wilhelm Munthe-Kaas, LPO arkitektur & design as, Oslo
Contact architect: Akzente Architektur & Landschaftsplanung GbR, Hanover
Lot size: 3,381 square meters
Constructed area: 1,426 square meters

**Der rauschende Wasserfall prägt das Erscheinungsbild des Pavillons.**
The rushing waterfall is the most prominent attraction in the pavilion.

# Polen
## Poland

Architekt: Studio Architektoniczne, Krakau
Kontaktarchitekten: HLW + Partner Architekten +
Ingenieure, Hannover
Grundstücksgröße: 2.300 Quadratmeter
Bebaute Fläche: 1.316 Quadratmeter
Architect: Studio Architektoniczne, Krakow
Contact architects: HLW + Partner Architekten +
Ingenieure, Hanover
Lot size: 2,300 square meters
Constructed area: 1,316 square meters

In der Ausstellung
Inside the exhibition

Polen hat sich für eine offene Form seines Pavillons entschieden, um die Öffnung des Landes nach Westen zu symbolisieren. Das Gebäude ist bestimmt durch große Transparenz und seine außen liegende Tragstruktur. Das statische Grundgerüst des Pavillons basiert auf fünf Stahlrahmen mit einer Spannweite von 28 Metern. Das Dachtragwerk besteht aus vier Raumfachwerkträgern, von denen das Dach senkrecht abgehängt ist. Alle Außenwände ebenso wie das transparente Dach bestehen aus Fiberglas mit Stahlrahmen. Die durchsichtigen und beweglichen Wände des Ausstellungsbereichs können je nach Bedarf flexibel zur Seite geschoben werden.

Das Restaurant im östlichen, geschlossenen Gebäudeteil ist als typisch polnisches Familienrestaurant eingerichtet. Zu den Ausstellungsschwerpunkten zählen eine virtuelle Reise durch die Landschaften Polens und seine Architektur sowie ein regelmäßig veranstaltetes Diskussionsforum mit führenden Vertretern aus Wirtschaft, Gesellschaft, Politik und Kultur. Die 16 einzelnen Regionen des Landes stellen sich in »Regionalen Wochen« mit eigenen Präsentationen vor.

Poland has opted for an open pavilion design as a symbol of its opening to the West. Characteristic features of the building are its great transparency and its exposed framework structure. The pavilion's basic structural framework consists of five steel framing elements with a width of 28 meters. The roof support system comprises four beams from which the roof is suspended vertically. All of the outside walls and the transparent roof are made of fiberglass panels in steel frames. The transparent, moveable walls in the exhibition area can be shifted to one side as needed.

The dining room in the building section closed off to the east is furnished as a typical family-style restaurant. The focal points of the exhibition include a virtual journey through Polish landscapes and architectural settings and a regularly scheduled discussion forum featuring leading figures from the fields of business, social affairs, politics and culture. The 16 individual regions of the country offer their own presentation during the "Regional Weeks."

Blick vom Europa Boulevard
View from Europa Boulevard

# Portugal
## Portugal

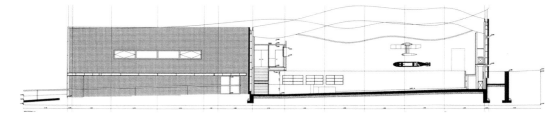

Der Schnitt verdeutlicht die wellenförmige
Dachform.
The cross section shows the undulating
form of the roof.

Der portugiesische Pavillon vereint in seiner Gestaltung moderne Architektur-elemente mit dem Respekt vor der Tradition, der sich in der Wahl der Materia-lien ausdrückt. Kork wurde als Baustoff verwendet, nicht nur, weil Portugal eines der führenden Länder in der Korkproduktion ist, sondern auch, weil das natürliche Material absolut umweltverträglich verarbeitet und wieder recycelt werden kann. In Form von 15 Zentimeter starken gepressten Korksteinen ist es auf die tragende Stahlkonstruktion aufgebracht.

Weiterhin ist der Pavillon durch den spannungsreichen Dialog zwischen der rechtwinkligen Form des Grundrisses und der geschwungenen Dachform charakterisiert. Das Dach besteht aus einem räumlichen Tragwerk, das in zwei Ebenen wie eine Hügellandschaft geschwungen und auf der Ober- und Unter-seite mit einer vorgespannten Teflon-Membran bedeckt ist. Diese Membran ist lichtdurchlässig; tagsüber gewährleistet sie eine natürliche Grundbeleuch-tung, und nachts zeichnet sich der Innenraum ab.

Die rechteckige Grundform des Gebäudes wird an einer Seite durch einen schmalen Schenkel ergänzt, sodass sich ein Hof bildet. Die farbigen Außen-flächen der Hoffassaden sind mit handgefertigten keramischen Fliesen gestal-tet, einem ebenfalls bekannten portugiesischen Produkt. Die Fassade zum Europa Boulevard ist mit Kalksandstein belegt. Der eingravierte Schriftzug »Portugal« sowie die Stützen des Vordachs auf der Hoffläche sind aus Marmor und Granit gefertigt. Zwei große Korkeichen in der Mitte des Platzes markieren den Haupteingang in den zweigeschossigen Pavillon. Besucher betreten direkt den zentralen, fensterlosen Ausstellungsraum, der durch die Hügellandschaft des Dachs und den Korkestrich am Boden eingefasst wird. Im Obergeschoss stehen ein Konferenzraum und ein VIP-Bereich zur Verfügung. Im Erdgeschoss befinden sich ein Buchladen, ein Shop und eine Cafeteria. Nach der Weltaus-stellung wird der Pavillon demontiert und in Portugal weitergenutzt werden.

The design of the Portuguese Pavilion joins aspects of modern architecture with a gesture of respect for tradition, which is expressed in the choice of building materials. Cork was used here, not only because Portugal is one of the world's leading producers of cork but also because it is a natural material that can be processed and recycled without any risk whatsoever to the envi-ronment. It is applied to the steel framework in the form of pressed cork bricks with a thickness of 15 centimeters.

Another remarkable aspect of the pavilion is the tension that emerges from the dialogue between the rectangular form of the foundation and the curving configuration of the roof. The roof consists of a three-dimensional framework that undulates in two planes like a hilly landscape. It is covered on its upper and lower surfaces with a translucent Teflon membrane. During the daylight hours it provides natural basic illumination; at night it highlights the interior space.

The rectangular ground plan of the building is supplemented by a narrow wing on one side, which forms a small courtyard. The colored outer surfaces of the facades facing the courtyard are decorated with ceramic tiles, also a well-known product of Portugal. The facade facing Europa Boulevard is lined with chalky sandstone. The engraved plaque with the word "Portugal" and the pillars supporting the canopy above the courtyard are made of marble and granite. Two large cork trees in the middle of the square mark the location of the main entrance to the two-story pavilion. Visitors enter directly into the central, windowless exhibition room, which is framed above and below by the hilly landscape of the roof and the cork flooring. A conference room and a VIP lounge are located on the upper floor. The ground floor contains a book shop, small store and a cafeteria. The pavilion will be dismantled after the World Exposition and reconstructed for further use in Portugal.

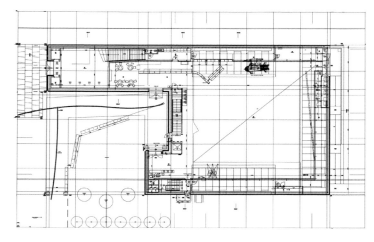

Grundriss des portugiesischen Pavillons
Floor plan of the Portuguese pavilion

**Architekten:** Álvaro Siza und Eduardo Souto de Moura, Porto
**Kontaktarchitekten:** Anderhalten Veauthier Architekten, Berlin
**Grundstücksgröße:** 2.325 Quadratmeter
**Bebaute Fläche:** 967 Quadratmeter
**Architects:** Álvaro Siza and Eduardo Souto de Moura, Porto
**Contact architects:** Anderhalten Veauthier Architekten, Berlin
**Lot size:** 2,325 square meters
**Constructed area:** 967 square meters

**Über den offenen Hof betreten Besucher
den Pavillon.**
Visitors enter the pavilion through the
open courtyard.

# Rumänien
## Romania

Klangkörper aus unterschiedlichen
Holzsorten
Musical instrument made of various types
of wood

Der rumänische Pavillon hat bereits im Vorfeld der Weltausstellung Beachtung gefunden. Der Entwurf für das Projekt »Reticula Verde«, »Grünes Netzwerk« auf Rumänisch, wurde im Dezember 1999 an der Accademia di Arte in Mailand als neue beispielhafte Architektur ausgezeichnet. Der Anspruch der Nachhaltigkeit charakterisiert das Konzept des temporären Pavillons: So wird der gesamte Energiebedarf durch alternative Energien gedeckt, die entsprechende Menge wird aus Rumänien ins europäische Stromnetz eingespeist.

Die Wände des Ausstellungsgebäudes bestehen aus einer membranbespannten zweifachen Gerüstbaukonstruktion mit einer Tiefe von 2 und einer Höhe von 9 Metern. Die feingliedrige, silberne Metallstruktur bildet den Rahmen für Pflanzen – den eigentlichen Bedeutungsträger des Pavillons. Sie weben ein grünes, fast textiles Netzwerk und vermitteln zwischen Innen und Außen. Die Pflanzen filtern Licht und Sonnenwärme und schaffen eine angenehm halbschattige Atmosphäre für die Ausstellung, die unter dem Motto »Natur und Kultur« steht. Die Dachkonstruktion bilden linsenförmige Fachwerkträger aus Brettschichtholz im Abstand von 4 Metern sowie eingehängte Einfeld-Pfetten und eine dünne Dachschalung. Für den Innenausbau wurde eine Skelettkonstruktion in Holztafelbauweise gewählt.

Besucher des Pavillons betreten zunächst einen großzügigen, hellen Erschließungs- und Ausstellungsbereich mit einer Bühne, einem »horizontalen Wald« und einem Klangkörper aus unzähligen Holzsorten, für den eigens eine europäische Rhapsodie komponiert wurde. Im hinteren Bereich des Pavillons liegen ruhig und abgeschieden thematische Ausstellungsräume, winkelförmig in die Tiefe des Raums gestellt. In der oberen Ebene stehen eine Lounge und weitere Räume beispielsweise für Präsentationen bereit.

Architekt: studio a architekten, Chur und Zürich
Grundstücksgröße: 2.744 Quadratmeter
Bebaute Fläche: 1.800 Quadratmeter
Architect: studio a architekten, Chur and Zurich
Lot size: 2,744 square meters
Constructed area: 1,800 square meters

The Romanian Pavilion drew acclaim even in advance of the World Exposition. The proposal for the project entitled "Reticula Verde," which means "Green Network" in Romanian, was awarded a prize for exemplary architecture at the Accademia di Arte in Milan in December 1999. The concept for the temporary pavilion reflects the principles of resource conservation. All energy required for the complex will be supplied from alternative energy sources, and a corresponding quantity of electricity will be fed into the European power network from Romania.

The walls of the exhibition building consists of a double framework construction with a depth of two meters and a height of nine meters covered with a membrane. The delicate-membered, silver-colored, metal structure provides a frame for plants – the most significant elements in the pavilion presentation. They weave a green, almost textile network and mediate between inside and outside space. The plants filter light and heat from the sun, creating a pleasant, semi-shaded atmosphere for the exhibition, the theme of which is "Nature and Culture." The roof construction comprises lens-shaped lattice beams of laminated boards placed four meters apart with single-span panels and a thin layer of roof planking. A wood-panel skeleton construction was selected for the interior.

Visitors to the pavilion enter through a spacious, well-lit entrance and exhibition area containing a stage, a "horizontal forest" and a musical instrument made of many different types of wood, for which a European Rhapsody was especially composed. Located in the quiet, somewhat remote rear section of the pavilion are thematic exhibition areas with angular configurations leading into the depth of the room. A lounge and rooms for presentations and other events are found on the upper level.

Pflanzen in einer Metallstruktur bilden die
Hülle des rumänischen Pavillons.
Plants set in a metal framework form the
shell of the Romanian Pavilion.

# Schweden
## Sweden

Schnitt durch das Gebäude
Cross section of the building

Das Erscheinungsbild des schwedischen Pavillons ist durch seine streng kubische Form gekennzeichnet. Typisch für das gesamte Gebäude ist die Verwendung von Holz an Decken, Wänden und Böden. Drei Außenwände des aus Stahlbetonfertigteilen errichteten Pavillons sind nahezu vollständig geschlossen und mit einer mattschwarz beschichteten Holzschalung bekleidet. Hingegen besteht die vierte Fassade, dem nach Norden ausgerichteten zentralen Innenhof zugewandt, aus einer Stahl-Glas-Konstruktion mit den Abmessungen 42 x 11,2 Meter. Das dreigeschossige Gebäude wird durch eine temporäre Außenbühne ergänzt. Die Bühnenrückwand an der Nordostseite des Grundstücks hat eine raumbildende Wirkung auf den Innenhof.

Die Ausstellung im schwedischen Pavillon, der nach der Weltausstellung in Hannover weitergenutzt wird, steht unter dem Motto »Brücken zum Wissen«. Dies spiegelt sich auch in seiner Gestaltung wider: Als Blickfang schon von außen durch die Glasfassade sichtbar, erstreckt sich eine große Brückenskulptur quer über die gesamte Hallenfläche. Die einfache, klassische Bogenform versinnbildlicht das Streben des Menschen, immer neue Wege zu finden. Auf der einen Seite des Brückenwiderlagers wird ihr Verhältnis zur Natur, auf der anderen Seite ihr Verhältnis zur Technik dargestellt. Neben diesem zentralen Ausstellungsbereich befinden sich im Erdgeschoss des Pavillons eine zusätzliche kleine Ausstellungsfläche für wechselnde Präsentationen, ein Auditorium für Konzerte sowie ein Foyer mit VIP-Zugang. Ein großer Konferenzraum mit einem vorgelagerten Foyer und einer Snackbar im ersten Obergeschoss sowie Service- und Büroräume im dritten Stock vervollständigen das Angebot. Die einzelnen Ebenen sind über einen Aufzug und eine zentrale Treppe verbunden.

The most prominent visual feature of the Swedish pavilion is its perfect cubic form. Typical of the building as a whole is the use of wood in ceilings, walls and floors. Three outside walls of the pavilion, which is constructed of prefabricated reinforced concrete elements, are almost completely closed and covered with wood paneling coated dull black. The fourth facade, which faces the central inner courtyard toward the north, presents a steel-and-glass structure measuring 42 x 11.2 meters. A temporary outdoor stage is erected outside the three-story building. The rear wall of the stage on the northeastern side of the lot gives shape to the space comprised by the inner courtyard.

The exhibition in the Swedish Pavilion, which is to be used for other purposes following the World Exposition, revolves around the theme of "Bridges to Knowledge." This idea is reflected in the pavilion's design as well. A point of attraction visible from outside through the glass facade is a large bridge sculpture spanning the entire length of the hall. The simple, classic arch configuration symbolizes the constant striving of humankind to discover new paths. On one side of the bridge abutment is an exhibit devoted to the relationship between people and nature; the exhibit on the other side deals with that of people and technology. In addition to this central exhibition space, there is another small exhibition area for temporary exhibits on the ground floor of the pavilion, a concert auditorium and a lobby with VIP access. A large conference room with an outside foyer and a snack bar on the second floor and service and office spaces on the top floor complete the program of pavilion services and facilities. The different levels are connected by an elevator and a central stairway.

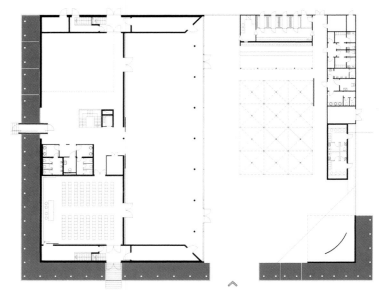

Grundriss des schwedischen Pavillons
Floor plan of the Swedish Pavilion

Architekt: Greger Dahlström, FOJAB arkitekter, Malmö
Gesamtplanung: KBA Architekten und Ingenieure GmbH, Berlin
Bauherr: Ncc Siab
Grundstücksgröße: 2.509 Quadratmeter
Bebaute Fläche: 1.706 Quadratmeter
Architect: Greger Dahlström, FOJAB arkitekter, Malmö
Project planning: KBA Architekten und Ingenieure GmbH, Berlin
Client: Ncc Siab
Lot size: 2,509 square meters
Constructed area: 1,706 square meters

Die Glasfassade ermöglicht schon von außen einen Blick in den Ausstellungsbereich.
The glass facade offers a view of the exhibition area from outside.

# Schweiz
# Switzerland

Die Schweiz präsentiert sich in einem 50 x 60 Meter großen Pavillon aus ge-stapelten Holzbalken. Wie in einem Holzlager sind 3.000 Kubikmeter frisch geschnittenes Lärchen- und Föhrenholz zu 9 Meter hohen Stapeln geschichtet und bilden ein verwinkeltes System aus Gängen und Höfen. Die riesigen Stapel werden von Stahlstäben und Stahlfedern niedergehalten und zusammen-gepresst. Mit seiner labyrinthischen Raumstruktur soll der nach allen Seiten offene Pavillon die Offenheit der Schweizer symbolisieren.

Die Freiluftarchitektur, in die Wind und stellenweise auch Regen und Sonne eindringen kann, gibt den Besuchern keine festgelegten Wege vor. Klang- und Lichtinstallationen bieten immer neue Anreize und sprechen zusammen mit der Architektur, dem Duft des Holzes und speziellen gastronomischen Angeboten alle Sinne der Besucher an. Der »Klangkörper Schweiz« versteht sich als Gesamtereignis. Nach der Weltausstellung kann der Pavillon abgebaut, die Balken können als Konstruktionsholz weitergenutzt werden.

Switzerland makes its presentation in a pavilion built of stacked wooden beams measuring 50 x 60 meters. Three thousand cubic meters of freshly cut larchwood and Scots pine are arranged in nine-meter-high stacks forming an intricate system of corridors and courtyards. The huge stacks are compacted and held together by steel rods and springs. With its labyrinthine spatial structure, the pavilion, which is open to all sides, is meant to symbolize the openness of the Swiss people.

The open-air architecture, penetrated by wind and, in some places, by sun and rain, offers visitors no prescribed route. Sound and light installations provide a series of different stimuli and appeal in concert with the architecture, the scent of the wood and the specialties of Swiss cuisine to all of the senses. The "Resonance of Switzerland" is conceived as a total event. After the end of the World Exposition, the pavilion can be dismantled and the beams used for other construction projects.

**Architekt: Peter Zumthor, Haldenstein**
**Grundstücksgröße: 3.977 Quadratmeter**
**Bebaute Fläche: 3.019 Quadratmeter**
Architect: Peter Zumthor, Haldenstein
Lot size: 3,977 square meters
Constructed area: 3,019 square meters

**Ein »Klangkörper« aus Bauholz**
A "resonant body" made of wooden beams

**Die labyrinthische Struktur schafft interes-sante Innenräume.**
The labyrinthine structure creates fascinat-ing interior spaces.

# Spanien
## Spain

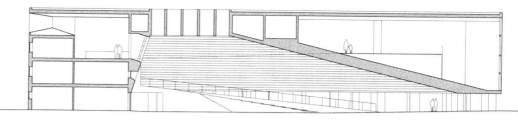

**Schnitt durch das Gebäude**
Cross section of the building

Der spanische Pavillon präsentiert sich von außen als großer Korkblock, in den tiefe Zäsuren eindringen. Die zerklüftete äußere Geometrie des Gebäudes steht im Gegensatz zu der präzisen Form und Strenge der Innenräume. Der eindrucksvolle Ort, der sich im Innern verbirgt, soll beim Besucher eine bleibende Erinnerung hinterlassen.

Der öffentliche Platz wird von der Außenwelt durch eine Vielzahl unregelmäßiger und willkürlich angeordneter Pfeiler abgeschirmt. Diese Pfeiler tragen die tief heruntergezogene Deckenkonstruktion in der Form eines Pyramidenstumpfes. Der natürliche zentrale Lichteinfall sowie die ausgewogene Akustik tragen maßgeblich zu der angenehmen Atmosphäre bei.

Obwohl der Platz nach drei Seiten offen ist, bildet er dennoch einen ruhigen, klar definierten Raum. Er bietet den Rahmen für unterschiedliche Aktivitäten und ist zugleich der Zugang zu der Ausstellung im Obergeschoss. In der natürlich belichteten Ausstellungsebene entdeckt der Besucher die Innenhöfe, die durch die tiefen Einschnitte in den Baukörper geformt werden und die er von außen nur erahnen kann.

Viewed from outside, the Spanish Pavilion appears as a huge block of cork with deep incisions. The fissured external geometry of the building stands in stark contrast to the precise form and austerity of the inside spaces. It is hoped that the awe-inspiring setting concealed within the building will remain a lasting memory for visitors.

The public square is isolated from the outside world by a large number of large pillars positioned in a random arrangement. These pillars support the downward-sloping roof construction in the form of a pyramid stump. The natural light that enters the central area and the well-balanced acoustics contribute significantly to the creation of a pleasant atmosphere.

Although the square is open on three sides, it nevertheless forms a peaceful, clearly defined space. It provides the spatial context for a variety of different activities and offers access to the exhibition on the upper level as well. In the naturally illuminated exhibition area, visitors discover the interior courtyards formed by the deep cuts in the building shell, places of which the view from outside provides only vague hints.

**Architekt: Cruz y Ortiz, Sevilla**
**Kontaktarchitekt: OHM mit Carmina Schmick, Hamburg**
**Grundstücksgröße: 4.000 Quadratmeter**
**Bebaute Fläche: 2.987 Quadratmeter**
Architect: Cruz y Ortiz, Seville
Contact architect: OHM with Carmina Schmick, Hamburg
Lot size: 4,000 square meters
Constructed area: 2,987 square meters

**Grundriss des spanischen Pavillons**
Floor plan of the Spanish Pavilion

**Tiefe Einschnitte zerklüften die geschlossene Korkfassade.**
Deep incisions form fissures in the smooth surface of the cork facade.

**Der zentrale Platz im Innern**
The central square inside the pavilion

# Tschechische Republik
## Czech Republic

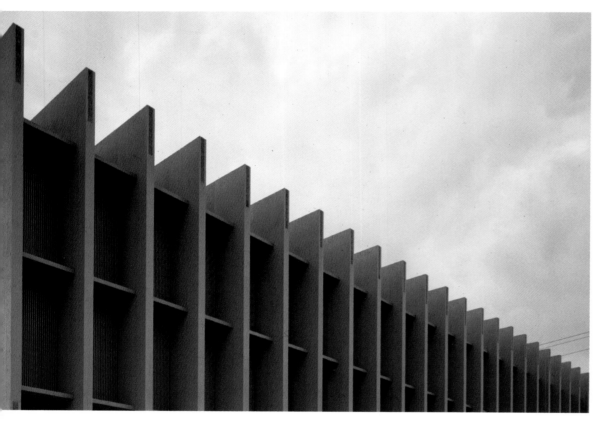

**Architekt: Marek Chalupa, D. U. M. architekti, Prag**
**Kontaktarchitekt: Akzente Architektur & Landschafts-**
**planung GbR, Hannover**
**Grundstücksgröße: 2.500 Quadratmeter**
**Bebaute Fläche: 997 Quadratmeter**
Architect: Marek Chalupa, D. U. M. architekti, Prague
Contact architect: Akzente Architektur & Landschafts-
planung GbR, Hanover
Lot size: 2,500 square meters
Constructed area: 997 square meters

**Seitenansicht des tschechischen Pavillons**
Side view of the Czech Pavilion

Der tschechische Pavillon besteht aus einer aufgeständerten Holzkonstruktion. Der untere Bereich zwischen den Stützen ist offen, nur der Restaurant- und Servicebereich im hinteren Teil ist verglast. Auf diesem Stützenwald ruht das eigentliche Ausstellungsgebäude. Besucher des Pavillons gelangen durch diese Stützen hindurch zu den Rolltreppen, die nach oben in den Pavillon führen. Über dem Restaurant sind auf zwei Ebenen Büroräume untergebracht. Der Ausstellungsbereich ist eingeschossig und nutzt die gesamte Höhe des Raumes. Die Stirnseite des lang gestreckten Baukörpers ist verglast, ziehharmonikaartige Fassaden charakterisieren das Erscheinungsbild der Längsseiten. Hier sind die Holzrahmen mit Holzwerkstoffen verkleidet. Der Pavillon nutzt nur einen geringen Teil des Grundstücks, sodass an den Längsseiten zwei begrünte Erdwälle angelegt werden konnten.

The Czech Pavilion is an elevated wooden structure. The lower level between the pile supports is open – only the restaurant and service area in the rear is glassed in. The actual exhibition building rests on top of this forest of piles. Visitors to the pavilion pass among the piles to an escalator which takes them up into the pavilion. Office rooms are located on two levels above the restaurant. The exhibition area occupies a single level and makes use of the full height of the room. The front face of the elongated building is glass, while accordion-like facades characterize the look of the long sides, on which the wooden frames are covered with wood paneling materials. The pavilion occupies only a small portion of the lot, allowing space for two long earthen mounds decorated with greenery along the side facades.

Eingangsfront am Europa Boulevard
Entrance facade on Europa Boulevard

# Türkei
## Turkey

**Architekten: Dipl.-Ing. Murat Tabanlioğlu und Melkan Gürsel Tabanlioğlu, Tabanlioğlu Architecture & Consulting LTD. CO., Istanbul**
**Grundstücksgröße: 2.490 Quadratmeter**
**Bebaute Fläche: 1.848 Quadratmeter**
Architects: Dipl.-Ing. Murat Tabanlioğlu and Melkan Gürsel Tabanlioğlu, Tabanlioğlu Architecture & Consulting LTD. CO., Istanbul
Lot size: 2,490 square meters
Constructed area: 1,848 square meters

**In der Ausstellung**
Inside the exhibition

Der über 12 Meter hohe türkische Pavillon basiert auf einer Stahlkonstruktion. Das Dach des Gebäudes, das sich in fünf Würfel gliedert, besteht aus Glaskuppeln. Um zu verdeutlichen, dass die Türkei an drei unterschiedliche Meere angrenzt, ist der Pavillon von Wasser umgeben. Seine Vorderfront besteht aus Glas und ist zur Steuerung des Lichteinfalls mit einem Holzgitter, einem typischen Merkmal der türkischen Architektur, versehen. Dieses Gitter wurde gespalten, um Besuchern schon von außen den Blick auf eine Brücke als Hauptsymbol der türkischen Präsentation freizugeben.

Die Brücke ist ein Sinnbild für den großen kulturellen Reichtum, den die verschiedenen Zivilisationen im Laufe der vergangenen 9.000 Jahre hinterlassen haben. In den unterschiedlichen Ausstellungsbereichen werden die Geschichte, die Kultur, der landschaftliche Reichtum und das moderne Gesicht der Türkei vorgestellt, unterstützt durch Computertechnik und Projektionen auf eine riesige, aus dem Wasser aufragende Leinwand.

Lichtinszenierungen erinnern an die südliche Sonne des Landes, und auch zahlreiche heimische Pflanzen tragen zu der lebendigen Atmosphäre des Pavillons bei. Musikdarbietungen und mystische Düfte runden diese Präsentation ab, die alle Sinne der Besucher anspricht.

More than 12 meters high, the Turkish Pavilion is based upon a steel-frame construction. The roof of the building, which is comprised of five cubic elements, consists of glass domes. In order to emphasize that Turkey is bordered by three different seas, the pavilion is surrounded by water. Its front facade is glass over which a wooden lattice – a typical feature of Turkish architecture – has been placed to regulate incoming sunlight. A gap was left in the lattice so that visitors would have a view of a bridge, the main symbol of the Turkish presentation, from the outside.

The bridge is a symbol of the great cultural wealth left behind by the different civilizations in the course of the past 9,000 years. A number of different exhibits present the history, the culture, the agricultural abundance and the modern face of Turkey with the aid of computer technology and projections on a huge screen that rises up from the water's surface.

Light shows call to mind the sunlight of southern Turkey, and numerous native plants give a sense of life and vitality to the atmosphere in the pavilion. Musical performances and mystical scents round out this presentation, which appeals to all of the five senses.

**Eingangsfront des türkischen Pavillons**
Entrance facade of the Turkish Pavilion

# Ungarn
## Hungary

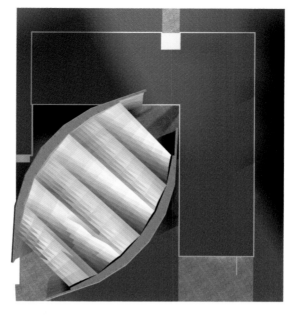

**Computeranimation**
Computer animation

Der ungarische Pavillon besteht aus einem 20 Meter hohen, organisch geform-
ten Baukörper, der von einem niedrigen L-förmigen Bau umgeben ist. Entsprechend seiner Gestaltung steht das große, statuenartige Gebäude als Ausstellungsbereich im Mittelpunkt, der angegliederte Serviceteil ordnet sich
unter.

Die beiden bogenförmigen Schalen des Hauptpavillons öffnen sich als Eingang
nach Nordosten. Betont wird dieser Bereich durch das Statuenpaar *Das Tor
der Liebe* von dem Künstler Pál Kö. Die Konstruktion der doppelschichtigen
Schalen besteht aus einer Stahlrippenstruktur mit einer Rotfichtenbekleidung.
Zwischen den beiden Schichten verbergen sich Gänge, Treppen und technische
Ausrüstungen. Die beiden Schalen umschließen den Ausstellungsbereich,
den so genannten »Spektakelraum«. An einigen Stellen sind die Schalen nach
innen geöffnet beziehungsweise aufgeklappt und werden für Inszenierungen
genutzt. Der offene Raum wird durch ein an Seilen gespanntes Leinwand-
system vor Regen geschützt. Besucher werden durch den Pavillon geleitet: Über
eine breite Treppe gelangen sie zunächst in den Ausstellungsraum im Untergeschoss, einen dunklen Raum, inszeniert mit Musik- und Lichteffekten. Erst
danach kehren sie wieder nach oben zurück in den Spektakelraum, in dem sie
die »Spektakelshow« mit projizierten Riesenbildern erleben können.

Das zum Teil unterkellerte Servicegebäude hat ein grünes, bepflanztes Dach.
Im Nordflügel befindet sich unter anderem der VIP-Bereich, der mit einem
schmiedeeisernen, verschiebbaren Tor verschlossen ist, eine Arbeit des ungarischen Schmiedemeisters János Lehoczky. VIP-Gäste können den Ausstellungsbereich direkt durch das Kellergeschoss betreten. In der Ecke des Winkelbaus
liegen ein Informationsstand und ein Souvenirladen; im zweiten Flügel laden
ein Café und ein Restaurant zu ungarischen Spezialitäten ein.

The Hungarian Pavilion comprises a 20-meter-high, organically configured
main building surrounded in part by a low, L-shaped structure. The large,
statuesque exhibition building is designed as the focal point of the presentation, while the adjacent service wing plays a background role.

The two arch-shaped shells of the main pavilion building open to the northwest, forming the entrance. Attention is drawn to this area by a pair of statues,
*The Gateway of Love*, by artist Pál Kö. The double-layered shells consist of a
steel-rib construction covered with red fir. Concealed between the two layers
are hallways, stairs and technical equipment. The two shells enclose the exhibition area, identified as the "Room of Spectacles." The shells open or fold
out towards the inside in several places, providing space for exhibits and
performances. The open space is protected against rain by a system of tarpau-
lins and cables. Visitors are led through the pavilion, arriving initially from a
broad stairway in the exhibition area in the basement, a dark room animated
by musical and light effects. From there they are guided upward into the
Rooms of Spectacles where they can watch the huge projected images of the
"Spectacle Show."

The service building, with its partial basement, has a green roof covered with
vegetation. Located along with other functional spaces in the north wing is
the VIP area, which is closed off by a forged-iron sliding gate, a work realized
by the Hungarian master smith János Lehoczky. VIPs may enter the exhibition
area directly from the basement level. The corner of the L-shaped building
accommodates an information booth and a souvenir shop; a café and a restaurant in the other wing invite visitors to sample Hungarian specialties.

Architekt: György Vadász, Vadász & Partners
Architectural Co., Budapest
Kontaktarchitekt: Architekturbüro Norbert Jokiel,
Düsseldorf
Grundstücksgröße: 3.015 Quadratmeter
Bebaute Fläche: 1.788 Quadratmeter
Architect: György Vadász, Vadász & Partners
Architectural Co., Budapest
Contact architect: Architekturbüro Norbert Jokiel,
Düsseldorf
Lot size: 3,015 square meters
Constructed area: 1,788 square meters

**Eingangsbereich**
Entrance area

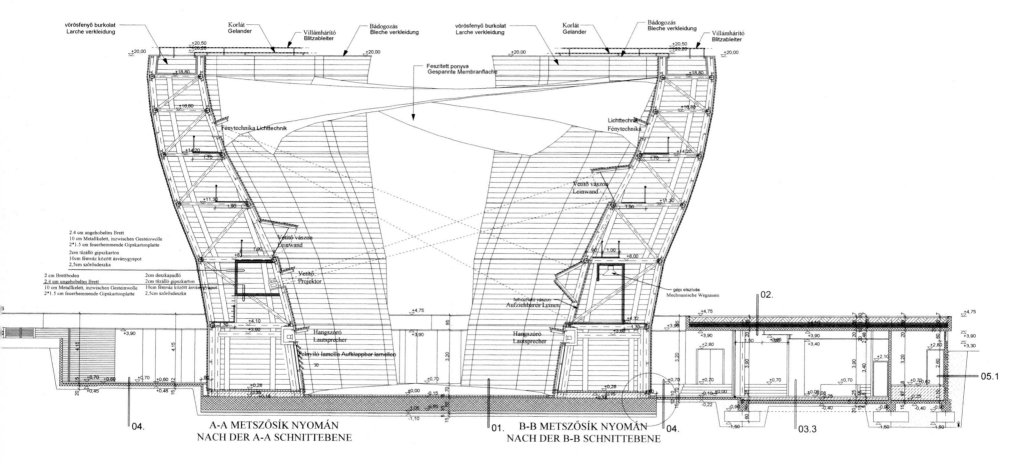

A-A METSZŐSÍK NYOMÁN
NACH DER A-A SCHNITTEBENE

B-B METSZŐSÍK NYOMÁN
NACH DER B-B SCHNITTEBENE

**Schnitt durch den ungarischen Pavillon**
Cross section view of the pavilion

**Im Spektakelraum**
In the Room of Spectacles

# Vereinigte Arabische Emirate
## United Arab Emirates

Die Vereinigten Arabischen Emirate laden in den Nachbau eines großen Wüstenforts ein. Durch eine Pforte zwischen 18 Meter hohen Türmen betreten Besucher den aus drei Elementen bestehenden Gebäudekomplex, der komplett aus recycelbarem Fiberglas hergestellt wurde. Der Weg führt zunächst zu dem eingeschossigen, U-förmigen Ausstellungsgebäude. In einem zurückgesetzten, zweigeschossigen Gebäude liegen Büro- und Serviceräume. Das dritte, 23 Meter hohe, runde Pavillonelement enthält ein 360-Grad-Kino, in dem ein Film über die Pläne des Landes, die natürlichen Ressourcen zu schützen und die Abhängigkeit der Wirtschaft vom Öl abzubauen, informiert.

Unter dem Motto »Von der Tradition zur Moderne« präsentieren die Vereinigten Arabischen Emirate ihre kulturellen Wurzeln und geben zugleich Einblicke in ihre Zukunftspläne. Im Mittelpunkt der Anlage steht ein Marktplatz, auf dem traditionell gekleidete Handwerker alltäglichen Arbeiten des alten Arabien nachgehen. Unzählige Palmen, roter Wüstensand, Kamele und Araberpferde wurden eingeflogen, um möglichst authentisches Leben zu inszenieren. Die Palmen versinnbildlichen auch die Veränderung des Landes: Durch das Pflanzen von 28 Millionen Palmen verwandelte sich die karge Wüstengegend nach und nach in den so genannten »Garten der Golfregion«.

The United Arab Emirates invite visitors into a replica of a large desert fort. Visitors enter the three-part building complex through a gateway formed by two 18-meter towers. The entire complex is constructed of recyclable fiberglass. The tour leads first to the U-shaped, one-story exhibition building. Office and service areas are housed in a two-story building set back somewhat from the main visitors' route. The third part of the pavilion is a 23-meter-high structure featuring a 360-degree surround-view movie theater in which a film informs visitors about the country's plans for protecting and preserving its natural resources and reducing its economy's dependence on oil.

Focusing on the theme "From Tradition to Modernism," the United Arab Emirates present their cultural roots and provide insights into their plans for the future. At the heart of the complex is a marketplace where craftsmen dressed in traditional garb pursue the routines of daily work in ancient Arabia. Countless palm trees, red desert sand, camels and Arabian horses were flown to Hanover to present an authentic picture of life in the Emirates. The palm trees also symbolize the current of change in the country. The planting of 28 million palm trees has transformed the once barren desert terrain into what is now known as the "Garden of the Gulf Region."

Architekt: Alain Durand-Henriot, Abu Dhabi
Kontaktarchitekt: Obermeyer Planen + Beraten, Hannover
Grundstücksgröße: 8.100 Quadratmeter
Bebaute Fläche: 2.960 Quadratmeter
Architect: Alain Durand-Henriot, Abu Dhabi
Contact architect: Obermeyer Planen + Beraten, Hannover
Lot size: 8,100 square meters
Constructed area: 2,960 square meters

Grundriss des Pavillons
Floor plan of the pavilion

Eingangstor
Entrance gateway

**Blick auf das Kinogebäude**
View of the movie theater

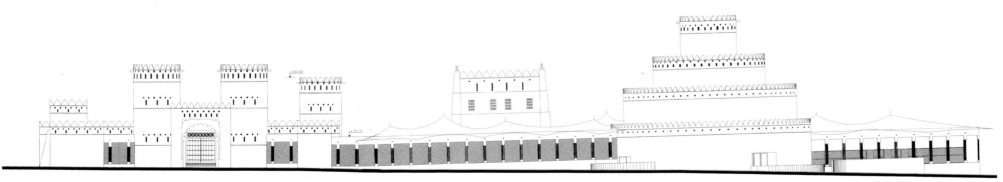

**Ansicht**
View of the pavilion

**Auf dem Marktplatz**
At the marketplace

# Nicht-offizielle Teilnehmer
## Non-Official Participants

# Pavillon der Hoffnung
## Pavilion of Hope

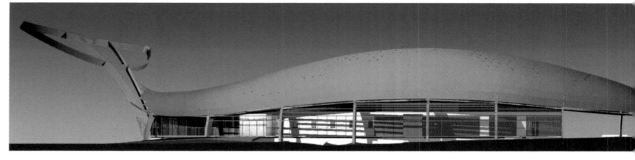

Seitenansicht des Pavillons
Side view of the pavilion

Als Jugendeinrichtung liegt der Pavillon der Hoffnung im Süden des Weltausstellungsgeländes in exponierter Lage direkt am Wasser. Das Gebäude hat die Form eines Wals und erinnert damit an die Geschichte des Propheten Jonas, der im Bauch eines Wal gerettet wurde und ein neues Leben beginnen konnte. Hintergrund dieses Entwurfs ist das Ausstellungskonzept der Bauherrengruppe, zu der auch der CVJM und World Vision gehören: Die Besucher werden im Bauch des Wals auf eine »Reise der Hoffnung« geschickt.

Die Form des Wals wurde weitgehend der natürlichen Anatomie des Meeressäugers nachempfunden. Große Leimbinder aus Brettschichtholz überspannen eine Grundfläche von 35 x 87 Metern und bilden damit die Rippen und das Rückgrat des Wals. Seine »Haut« besteht aus einer grau schimmernden Dacheindeckung aus Zink. Die Ausrichtung des Tragwerks orientiert sich an der natürlichen Bewegung des Tieres; zusätzlich unterstützt die Lage am Wasser den Eindruck, der Wal, dessen Fluke 19,5 Meter hoch aufragt, würde gerade aus seinem natürlichen Element auftauchen.

Der eigentliche Baukörper liegt unter der rund 13 Meter hohen formbildenden Konstruktion. Seine transparente Fassade hebt die Trennung von Innen und Außen auf und macht Besucher neugierig auf das Geschehen im Gebäude. Wie für den Propheten beginnt für die Besucher die »Reise der Hoffnung« im Schlund des Wals. Von diesem Eingangsbereich in der unteren Ebene des Gebäudes werden sie entlang eines roten Fadens in einen Kinosaal, einen Ausstellungs- und Kommunikationsbereich und in Zonen der Ruhe und Besinnung geführt. Vor dem Verlassen des Gebäudes markiert der entspannende Aufenthalt im Bistro schließlich das Ende der Reise.

The youth pavilion named the Pavilion of Hope stands at a prominent waterside location in the southern section of the grounds of EXPO 2000. The building is shaped like a whale and thus calls to mind the biblical story of the prophet Jonah, who was rescued in the belly of a whale and given a new lease on life. The basis for this design is the exhibition concept drafted by the client group, to which the CVJM (the German chapter of the YMCA) and World Vision also belong. Visitors are dispatched on a "Journey of Hope" in the belly of the whale.

The whale shape was based for the most part on the natural anatomy of this aquatic mammal. Large laminated glued beams span a space of ground measuring 35 x 87 meters, forming the whale's ribs and backbone. Its "skin" consists of a gray, shimmering zinc roof-covering. The configuration of the framework structure is oriented toward the animal's natural patterns of movement. Its position in the water enhances the impression that the whale, whose fluke rises 19.5 meters into the air, is about to break the surface of its natural element.

The actual building structure lies beneath the 13-meter-high shape-giving construction. Its transparent facade blurs the distinction between inside and outside and arouses the viewers' curiosity about what is happening inside the building. Like the prophet, visitors begin their "Journey of Hope" in the throat of the whale. From this entrance area on the lower level of the building they are led along a red rope to a small movie theater, an exhibition and communication area and to areas for quiet contemplation. Before leaving the building they end their journey with a relaxing stop in the bistro.

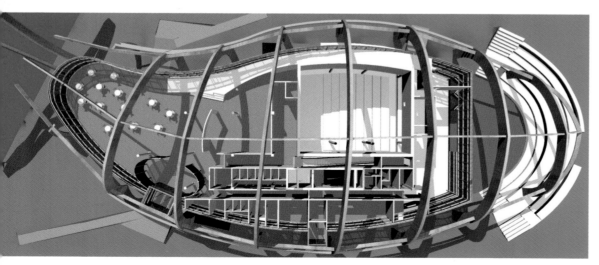

Architekten: Buchhalla + Partner, Hannover
Bauherr: Pavillon der Hoffnung e.V., Kassel
Grundstücksgröße: 3.180 Quadratmeter
Bebaute Fläche: 1.300 Quadratmeter
Architects: Buchhalla + Partner, Hanover
Client: Pavillon der Hoffnung e.V., Kassel
Lot size: 3,180 square meters
Constructed area: 1,300 square meters

Die Aufsicht verdeutlicht den Aufbau des Gebäudes.
A view from above reveals the configuration of the building.

Am Wasser ist der »Wal« in seinem Element.
The "whale" in its watery element

# Postbox
## Postbox

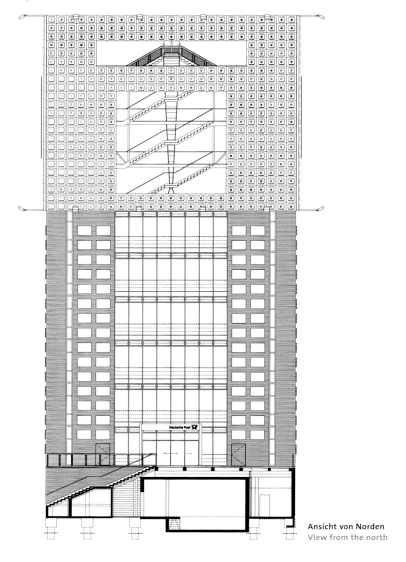

**Ansicht von Norden**
View from the north

Seit seiner Fertigstellung Ende 1999 dient der »größte Briefkasten der Welt« als Informations- und Aussichtsplattform für Besucher. Die Postbox ist schon von weitem sichtbar – ihre obere Aussichtsebene in 43 Metern Höhe ist der höchste begehbare Punkt auf dem östlichen Weltausstellungsgelände. Die zehngeschossige Postbox gliedert sich in zwei unterschiedlich gestaltete Teile. Die sechs Basisgeschosse mit ihren Fassaden aus Aluminium und Glas beinhalten Räume für Ausstellungen, Konferenzen, Tagungen und Events sowie ein Café und einen Service Point. Deutlich hebt sich das viergeschossige Top des Gebäudes in Form eines überdimensionalen gelben Briefkastens ab, das aus 1.587 originalgroßen Briefkastennachbildungen zusammengesetzt ist. Die zehn Geschosse ruhen auf einem Sockelgeschoss, auf dem während der EXPO 2000 eine Sammlung von Briefkästen aus aller Welt zu sehen ist. Zusammen mit den auf allen Fassaden angebrachten Logos der Mitglieder des Weltpostvereins symbolisieren sie das globale Kommunikations- und Transportnetz.

Das Gebäude ruht auf insgesamt 36 Bohrpfählen mit einer Länge von 12 Metern. Die Stahlkonstruktion des Briefkasten mit seinen vier Ebenen und der sechs Basisgeschosse besteht aus einem räumlichen Fachwerksystem. Für alle Träger und Stahlkonstruktionen wurden handelsübliche Walzprofile oder Rundstahl verwendet. Das räumliche Fachwerk ist aus rund 2.400 Einzelstäben mit Schraubverbindungen gebildet. Da die Postbox nach der Weltausstellung voraussichtlich abgebaut wird, ermöglicht diese Konstruktion eine einfache und zerstörungsfreie Demontage des Gebäudes.

**Architekten: Tschorz & Tschorz, Köln**
**Bauherr: Deutsche Post Unternehmenskommunikation**
**Grundstücksgröße: 1.304 Quadratmeter**
**Bebaute Fläche: 598 Quadratmeter**
Architects: Tschorz & Tschorz, Cologne
Client: Deutsche Post Unternehmenskommunikation
Lot size: 1,304 square meters
Constructed area: 598 square meters

Since its completion in late 1999, the "largest mailbox in the world" has served as an information and viewing platform for visitors. The Postbox is visible from a distance – at 43 meters, its uppermost outlook is the highest accessible point on the East Pavilion Site. The ten-story Postbox is divided into two parts featuring different designs. The six lower levels with their aluminum-and-glass facades contain spaces for exhibitions, conferences, meetings and events as well as a café and a service point. The four-story top section of the building presents an entirely different face in the form of a gigantic yellow mailbox constructed out of 1,587 original-sized mailbox replicas. These ten stories rest on a foundation floor on which a collection of mailboxes from all over the world is exhibited during EXPO 2000. Together with the logos of the members of the World Post Club affixed to all of the facades, they symbolize the global communication and transportation network.

The building stands on a total of 36 sunken piles, each 12 meters long. The steel construction of the mailbox on four levels and the six lower floors consists of a three-dimensional latticed beam system. Standard rolled and rod steel elements were used for all load-bearing and connecting components. The three-dimensional lattice construction comprises some 2,400 individual beams with bolt connections. As the Postbox is scheduled for removal from the site after EXPO 2000, this construction favors the simple and non-destructive dismantling of the building.

Die Postbox markiert einen Eckpunkt des
Pavillongeländes Ost.
The Postbox stands at one corner of the
East Pavilion Site.

**Auf der höchsten Aussichtsplattform**
On the highest viewing platform

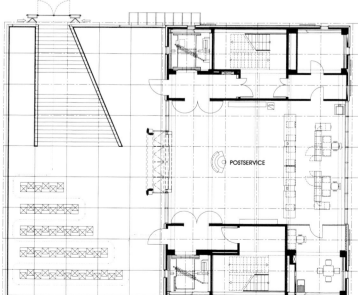

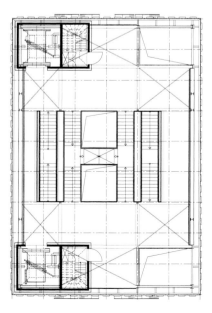

POSTSERVICE

**Grundriss des
Erdgeschosses**
Floor plan of
the first floor

**Grundriss des
9. Obergeschosses**
Floor plan of the
tenth floor

**»Briefkasten«-Ebenen**
The "mailbox" element

# Ausstellungsarchitektur
## Exposition Architecture

Durch das Konzept der Weltausstellung, das bestehende Messegelände als Teil des Expo-Areals mitzunutzen und weiterzuentwickeln, stehen zahlreiche moderne Ausstellungshallen für unterschiedliche Präsentationen zur Verfügung. Als eigener Beitrag der EXPO 2000 nutzt der Themenpark die gesamte Ostschiene des Messegeländes mit fünf nebeneinander liegenden Hallen und einer Gesamtfläche von 100.000 Quadratmetern. Darin werden in beeindruckenden Erlebniswelten insgesamt elf Leitthemen präsentiert. Exemplarisch werden hier die Themen »Zukunft der Arbeit«, »Mobilität«, »Zukunft Gesundheit« und »Energie« vorgestellt.

Des Weiteren nutzten zahlreiche internationale Teilnehmer und Organisationen das Angebot und mieteten eine Präsentationsfläche in einer der sechs dazu bereitgestellten Ausstellungshallen an. Ohne einen eigenen aufwändigeren Pavillon bauen zu müssen, fanden sie so einen ansprechenden Rahmen für ihre Beiträge. Dokumentiert werden im Folgenden einige Beispiele der vielgestaltigen Ausstellungsarchitektur.

Thanks to the planning concept for EXPO 2000, which calls for the use and development of the existing trade fair facilities as a part of the World Exposition grounds, a number of modern exhibition halls are available for a variety of different presentations. The Thematic Area, the contribution of the EXPO 2000 Committee, occupies the entire eastern sector of the trade fair grounds, comprising a row of five halls and a total area of 100,000 square meters. The Thematic Area presents eleven major themes in fascinating microcosmic realms of experience. By way of example, brief descriptions of the themes "The Future of Work," "Mobility," "Health Futures" and "Energy" are provided in the following sections.

Many international participants and organizations have taken advantage of this opportunity and leased presentation areas in one of the six available exhibition halls. In this way, they have acquired an attractive setting for their presentations without the need to erect a much more costly pavilion of their own. Several examples of this diverse exposition architecture are documented below.

# A. Themenpark
## A. Thematic Area

# Zukunft der Arbeit
# The Future of Work

Die Arbeitswelt befindet sich derzeit in einem rasanten Umwälzungsprozess, der die Lebensverhältnisse der Menschen in allen Ländern und Regionen radikal verändern wird. Fragen nach zukünftigen Arbeitsbedingungen besitzen daher eine besondere Aktualität. Die Ausstellung »Zukunft der Arbeit« präsentiert eine Vielzahl von Projekten mit Partnern aus aller Welt, die konkrete Lösungen, Ideen und Visionen für die Arbeitswelt des 21. Jahrhunderts aufzeigen.

Stararchitekt Jean Nouvel hat als Szenograf für diese Ausstellung ein Welttheater der Arbeit entworfen: eine ellipsenförmige Theaterarena, die Besucher über eine lange Rampe betreten. Auf dem Weg in die Arena sind hinter halbdurchlässigen Wänden erste schattenhafte Aktionen wahrzunehmen. Im Theater selbst zeigen Hunderte von Darstellern mit modernem Tanztheater unterschiedliche Szenarien aus neuen Arbeitswelten. Sie agieren dabei nach der Regie des belgischen Choreografen Frédéric Flameands, der diese »Tableaux vivants« entworfen hat. Der Besucher ist von allen Seiten von Live-Aktionen umgeben. In die einzelnen Inszenierungen sind Videokunst, Filme sowie Licht- und Toneffekte einbezogen. Der Zuschauer kann die Bandbreite der Gesamtdarstellung nur erfassen, wenn er sich durch den Raum bewegt, sich um die eigene Achse dreht, wenn er also selbst handelt. Besucher werden zu Akteuren, und die Szenografie verschmilzt mit der Botschaft der Ausstellung, sich neuen Herausforderungen zu stellen, Chancen wahrzunehmen und die Zukunft aktiv mitzugestalten.

The world of work is presently undergoing rapid , radical change that is certain to have a significant impact on the lives and living conditions of people in every country and region of the world. Thus questions about future working conditions are high on the lists of concerns for practically all of us today. The exhibition entitled "The Future of Work" presents a wide range of projects in cooperation with partners from all over the world. Focal points of the exhibitions are ideas, visions and concrete solutions for the world of work in the 21st century.

Star architect and scenographer Jean Nouvel has designed a world theater of work for this exhibition: an elliptical theater arena which visitors enter on a long ramp. On their way into the arena, they glimpse the first shadowy images of dramatized activities through semi-transparent walls. Inside the theater, hundreds of performers play out various scenes from new worlds of work in modern dance-theater sequences under the direction of choreographer Frédéric Flameands, creator of these *tableaux vivants*. Visitors are virtually surrounded by live performances incorporating a range of media including video clips, films and light and sound effects. Theatergoers are able to grasp the full bandwidth of the whole presentation only by moving about inside the arena, turning on their own axes — in other words, by taking action themselves. They become actors, and the scenography becomes an expression of the exhibition's appeal to all to accept new challenges, grasp new opportunities and play an active part in shaping the future.

Szenograf: Jean Nouvel, Paris
Scenographer: Jean Nouvel, Paris

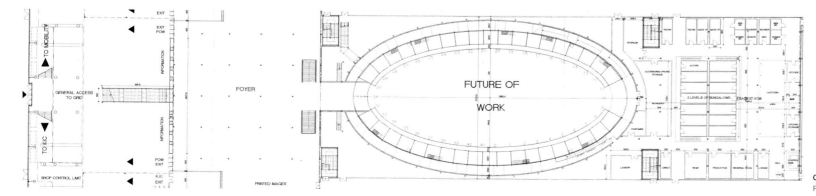

**Grundriss des Ausstellungsbereichs**
Floor plan of the exhibition area

**Die Rampe führt Besucher
in die Theaterarena.**
Visitors enter the theater
arena from a ramp.

**Eindrücke aus der Arena**
Impressions from inside
the arena

# Mobilität
# Mobility

Mobilität ist ein Ausdruck menschlicher Freiheit, ein Motor des Fortschritts und die Voraussetzung für Handel und Versorgung; zahlreiche Entwicklungen sind nur auf das menschliche Grundbedürfnis der Fortbewegung zurückzuführen. Doch die heutigen Erscheinungsformen der Mobilität werfen zunehmend Probleme auf. Eine zentrale Herausforderung des 21. Jahrhunderts ist es, die Mobilität zu erhalten und sie zukünftig intelligenter, sicherer und ökologisch vertretbar zu gestalten.

Für die Ausstellung »Mobilität« hat Jean Nouvel ein »Panorama der Mobilität« entworfen, ein Szenario, in dem großformatige Bildprojektionen Geschichten erzählen. In der Wartezone oberhalb der Ausstellungsfläche werden Besucher wie im Kino mit kurzen Trailern neugierig gemacht auf den »Hauptfilm«. Eine Spirale führt in den Ausstellungsbereich hinab; darüber werden in »Morphing«-Technik zahlreiche radbetriebene Maschinen gezeigt – einige Tausend Jahre Geschichte, komprimiert auf wenige Minuten. Der Ausstellungsraum ist 40 Meter breit. Er erscheint endlos, da die 80 Meter langen seitlichen Projektionsflächen durch Spiegelreflexionen optisch gestreckt werden. Im Deckenbereich, über den Köpfen der Besucher, befinden sich Darstellungen des Universums, Bilder von Galaxien und Planeten. Sie veranschaulichen eine langsame, quasi »zeitlose« Bewegung und bilden damit einen Kontrast zu den turbulenten Bildsequenzen an den Seitenwänden.

Hauptthema der Ausstellung ist die Vernetzung und Integration der Verkehrssysteme, denn die Verkehrsknotenpunkte zwischen Luft, Schiene, Straße und Wasser ermöglichen täglich den Ortswechsel einer schier unendlichen Zahl von Menschen und Gütern. Großformatige Filmcollagen fragen in eindringlicher Bildsprache nach Motiven, Zielen und Hintergründen der Mobilität. Die Filme variieren stark: Collagen wechseln sich ab mit Sequenzen sich wiederholender Bilder, es gibt stehende Bilder und Phasen, in denen das Bild verschwindet und nur Geräusche die Bewegung wiedergeben. Geführt von dieser Dynamik der Bilder folgt der Besucher schließlich einem leichten Bodengefälle und verlässt die Ausstellung.

Mobility is an expression of human freedom, a motor of progress and a fundamental prerequisite for trade and the supply of goods and services. Many historical developments are the direct fruits of the human need for movement. Yet modern-day manifestations of mobility have given rise to an increasing number of problems. Preserving mobility and making it more intelligent, safer and more benign from an environmental perspective is one of the most crucial challenges of the 21st century.

Jean Nouvel has designed a "Panorama of Mobility" for the "Mobility" exhibition, a scenario of stories narrated in large-scale visual projections. Visitors in the waiting area above the exhibition room are shown previews of the "main feature," as in a movie theater, to arouse their curiosity. A spiral stairway leads down into the exhibition area. Above it is a presentation of numerous wheel-driven machines, shown in a high-speed time-lapse technique – several thousand years of history compressed into just a few minutes. The exhibition room is 40 meters wide. It appears to be endless, as the 80-meter-long projection surfaces on the side walls are visually elongated by mirrors. Visible on the ceiling above the visitors' heads are images of the universe, pictures of galaxies and planets. They illustrate a kind of slow, virtually "timeless" movement in contrast to the turbulent sequences of images projected onto the side walls.

The main theme of the exhibition is the interconnection and integration of traffic systems, for it is the hubs linking air, rail, road and water traffic that make the daily movements of an endless number of people and goods from one place to another possible. Monumental film collages pose penetrating questions about the motives, goals and conditions of mobility. The films themselves show a considerable degree of variation. Collages give way to sequences of recurring images; there are freeze frames and phases in which the visual images disappear, leaving behind only the sounds of movement. Guided by the dynamics of the visual imagery, visitors follow the slight incline of the floor and ultimately leave the exhibition.

**Szenograf: Jean Nouvel, Paris**
**Scenographer: Jean Nouvel, Paris**

**Auf dem Weg in die Ausstellung**
**Approaching the exhibition**

**Einblicke in das »Panorama der Mobilität«**
Views of the "Panorama of Mobility"

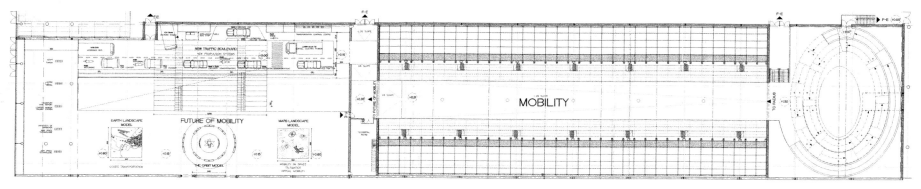

**Grundriss des Ausstellungsbereichs**
Floor plan of the exhibition area

# Zukunft Gesundheit
## Health Futures

Die Rahmenbedingungen für Gesundheit haben sich noch nie so schnell verändert wie heute. Während es im letzten Jahrhundert überwiegend ums Überleben ging, richtet sich das Augenmerk zukünftig vor allem auf die Verbesserung der Lebensqualität.

Eine aufwändige Multimedia-Show mit insgesamt 250 Projektoren führt die Besucher durch eine Reise in die Zukunft. Sie beschäftigt sich mit der Schaffung eines gerechteren Gesundheitssystems für alle. Besondere Schwerpunkte sind die Gesundheitsprobleme in Großstädten, die Erhaltung der Vitalität bis ins hohe Alter und der Kampf gegen Aids oder noch nicht besiegte Infektionskrankheiten wie Malaria oder Kinderlähmung. Doch nicht nur die Bedeutung der körperlichen, sondern auch der seelischen Gesundheit ist Gegenstand der Ausstellung.

Die Ausstellungslandschaft dazu hat der japanische Architekt Toyo Ito entworfen. Sobald Besucher den scheinbar unendlichen, hellen und freundlichen Raum betreten, spüren sie seine entspannende Atmosphäre. Um einen tiefblauen See, in dem sich die auf die umliegenden Leinwände projizierten Bilder mehrfach spiegeln, stehen in frischer Luft 120 Entspannungssessel zur kurzfristigen Erholung bereit. Das Besondere an diesen ebenfalls von Toyo Ito entwickelten Sesseln ist eine Mechanik unter der Polsterung, die für eine Lockerung der Muskulatur sorgt. Man setzt sich in den Sessel und drückt den Startknopf, der Sessel senkt sich in eine waagerechte Position und beginnt mit einem neuartigen Wiegemechanismus eine wohltuende Massage. Nach einigen Minuten richtet er sich selbstständig wieder auf, sodass für den nächsten Besucher Platz frei wird

The conditions affecting health are changing more rapidly today than ever before. While survival was the primary objective for people of the 19th century, our focus will shift in the future toward improving the quality of life.

A multimedia "megashow" featuring some 250 projectors takes visitors on a journey into the future. Theme of the presentation is the quest for a more equitable health-care system for all. Particular emphasis is placed on health problems in major urban centers, on the maintenance of vitality in old age and on the fight against AIDS and other infectious diseases such as malaria and polio. However, the exhibition is concerned not only with the human physical condition but with the health of the mind and spirit as well.

The exhibition landscape was designed by the Japanese architect Toyo Ito. Visitors entering the light, pleasant, seemingly endless room immediately feel a sense of tranquility. Arranged around a deep-blue lake in which the images projected on the surrounding screens are mirrored in multiple reflections are 120 reclining chairs inviting visitors to take a brief rest in the fresh air. A remarkable feature of these recliners, also designed by Toyo Ito, is the apparatus concealed beneath the cushions, which provides a relaxing muscle massage. When a visitor sits down in the chair and presses the start button, the recliner shifts into a horizontal position and begins to apply a comforting massage performed by an innovative rocking mechanism. After a few minutes, the chair returns to its upright position, ready for the next visitor.

**Szenograf: Toyo Ito, Tokio**
Scenographer: Toyo Ito, Tokyo

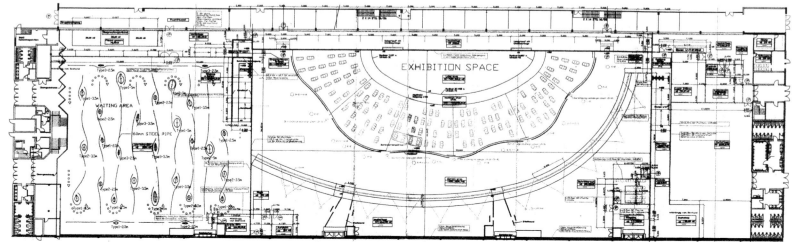

Grundriss des Ausstellungsbereichs
Floor plan of the exhibition area

Entspannungssessel
Relaxing chairs

In der Ausstellungslandschaft
Inside the exhibition

# Energie
## Energy

Wie kann die wachsende Weltbevölkerung auch zukünftig ausreichend mit Energie versorgt werden? Wie können alle verfügbaren Energien sinnvoll genutzt werden, wie lange reichen unsere Rohstoffreserven und welche Ressourcen können wir noch erschließen? Und schließlich: Wie sieht eine nachhaltige globale Energiewirtschaft aus? Auf all diese Fragen versucht die Ausstellung »Energie« Antworten zu geben.

Die Ausstellung des Szenografen Wolfram Wöhr ist so aufgebaut, dass Besucher in die Energiethematik eingeführt werden, als wären sie neugierige Außerirdische. In einem simulierten Raumschiff übermittelt der Bordcomputer Hintergründe, Zahlen, Fakten und Zusammenhänge zum Thema Energie. Eine Rampe führt langsam nach oben, das Raumschiff taucht in die Erdatmosphäre ein. Durch ein Gewitter, in dem Blitze und Entladungen Energie veranschaulichen, gelangen die Besucher in das Zentrum der Ausstellung. Hier fahren sie unter Tage, erleben eine Unterwasserwelt, besuchen ein modernes Kohlekraftwerk, werden auf vielschichtige Weise über Öl, Gas, erneuerbare Energien und Strom informiert und erreichen schließlich den Höhepunkt der Ausstellung, den Lichtzylinder. Hier wird die Energiesituation der Erde in einem beeindruckenden Finale zusammengefasst. Beim Betreten wirkt der große zylindrische Raum zunächst wie ein Rundum-Kino. Dass sie auf einem transparenten Boden stehen, merken Besucher erst, wenn ein ausgeklügeltes Beleuchtungssystem den Blick durch die Glasdecke freigibt. Wie ein Raumfahrer in mehreren Kilometern Höhe blicken sie dann auf die Erde. Für diese perfekte Illusion musste eine 10 x 10 Meter große und 7 Meter tiefe Grube in der Ausstellungshalle ausgehoben werden. Auf eine Halbkugel am Boden der Grube werden Bilder der Erde projiziert. Raffiniert aufgehängte Spiegel an den Grubenwänden vermitteln den Besuchern den Eindruck, als schwebten sie im Raum. Der Lichtzylinder bringt sie zurück in den »Weltraum«, aus dem sie anfangs gekommen sind.

How can we ensure a sufficient supply of energy to a growing global population in the future? How can available energy resources be used with efficiency? How long will our reserves of raw materials last? What new resources will we be able to harness? And finally, what do we expect from a sustainable global energy economy? The "Energy" exhibition seeks to provide answers to all of these questions.

The exhibition, designed by the scenographer Wolfram Wöhr, introduces visitors to the energy issue as if they were curious visitors from another world. In a simulated spacecraft, an on-board computer displays background information, facts, statistics and interrelationships relating to the subject of energy. A ramp rises gradually upward, and the spacecraft enters the earth's atmosphere. Visitors pass through a thunderstorm, witnessing the energy of lightning and electrical discharges, into the center of the exhibition. Here they descend a mine shaft, experience an underwater world, visit a modern coal-fueled power plant and are informed in a variety of ways about oil, gas, renewable energy sources and electricity before finally arriving at the main attraction of the exhibition: the Light Cylinder. Here, the global energy situation is summarized in a compelling finale. At first glance, the large cylindrical room looks like a panoramic movie theater. Visitors do not notice that they are standing on a transparent floor until a complicated lighting system opens the view through the glass plate. Like space travelers hovering several kilometers above the earth, they now look down at the planet. In order to create this perfect illusion it was necessary to dig a pit seven meters deep and ten by ten meters wide in the exhibition hall. Images of the earth are projected onto a hemisphere. An intricate arrangement of mirrors on the walls of the pit gives visitors the impression of floating weightlessly in space. The light cylinder then brings them back into "outer space," from whence they came.

Szenograf: Wolfram Wöhr, München
Scenographer: Wolfram Wöhr, Munich

In der Unterwasserwelt
In the underwater world

Unter Tage
Below ground

**Grundriss des Ausstellungsbereichs**
Floor plan of the exhibition area

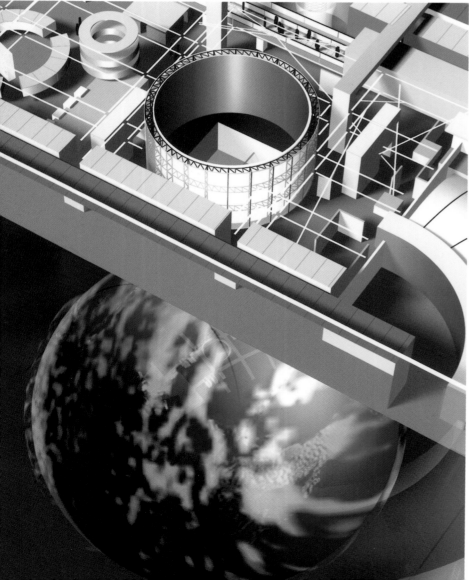

**Modelldarstellung des Lichtzylinders**
Model of the Light Cylinder

**Im Lichtzylinder kommt eine weltweit einmalige Projektionstechnik zum Einsatz.**
The Light Cylinder features projection technology that is unique in the world.

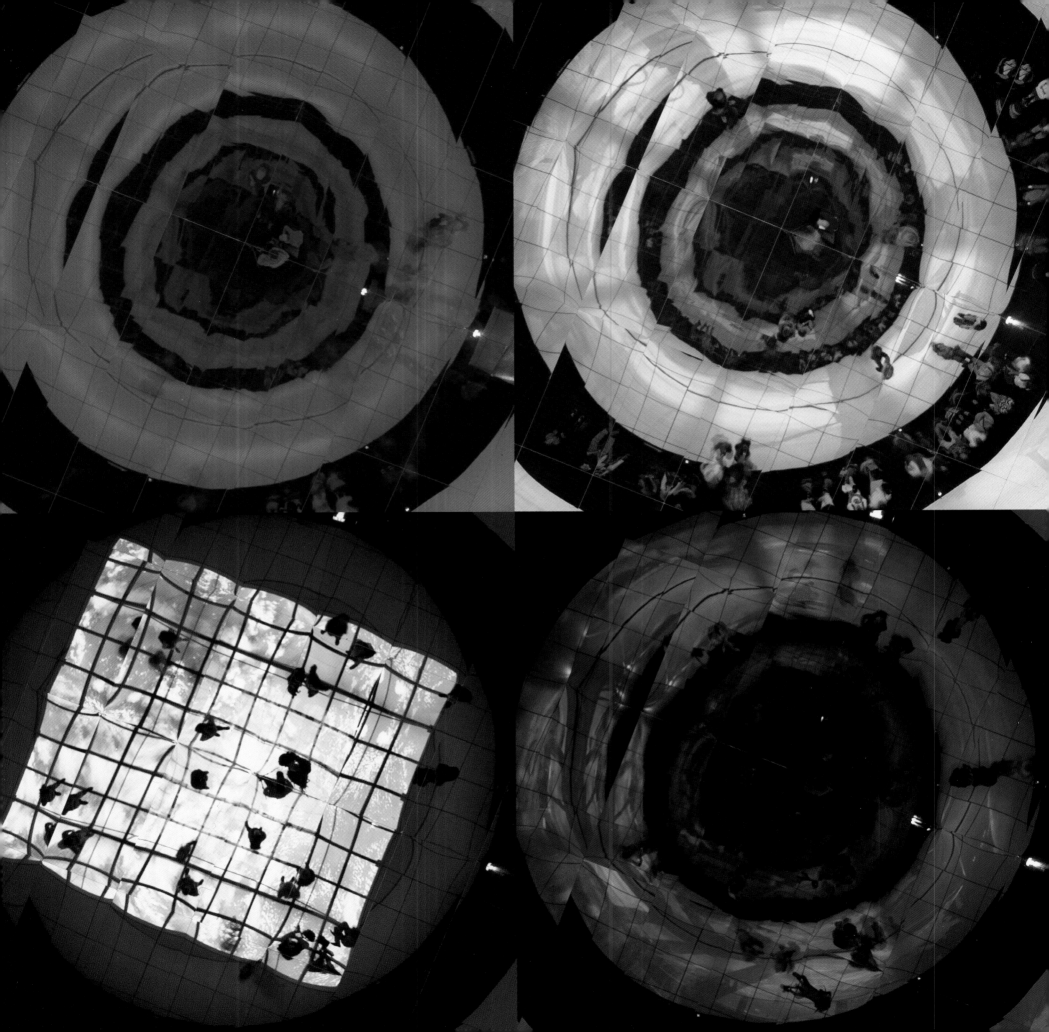

# B. Hallenpräsentationen von Nationen und Organisationen
## B. Hall Presentations of Nations and Organizations

# Afrika
## Africa

Der Kontinent nutzt für seine Präsentation eine komplette Ausstellungshalle mit einer Fläche von 22.000 Quadratmetern. Bereits von außen ist das Gebäude als »Afrikahalle« zu erkennen. Für die Fassade haben afrikanische Künstler farbenfrohe Flächen gestaltet, die an überdimensionale Surf-Segel erinnern. Als weithin sichtbares Wahrzeichen steht ein 30 Meter hoher »Obelisk« in der Mitte der Halle, durchbricht die Decke und ragt weit über das Dach hinaus. Er ist das Ergebnis eines Gestaltungswettbewerbs unter afrikanischen Künstlern und soll als »Symbol des Lebens« die Lebenskraft der Menschen in Afrika sinnbildlich darstellen.

Die gesamte Ausstellung steht unter dem Motto »The Gift of Africa«, wobei die Beiträge einzelner Länder entsprechend ihrer geografischen Lage angeordnet sind. Die äußeren Pole bilden dabei die Gemeinschaftspräsentationen der CILSS-Staaten (neun Länder der Sahel-Zone) und der SADC (14 Staaten der südafrikanischen Entwicklungsgemeinschaft).

Neben den einzelnen Ausstellungsbereichen können die Besucher ein Erlebnisrestaurant besuchen und Kudu, Strauß und Springbock-Steaks kosten oder über einen Basar bummeln.

The continent of Africa uses an entire exhibition hall and 22,000 square meters of floor space for its presentation. The building is recognizable even from outside as "Africa Hall." African artists have decorated the facade with colorful shapes resembling oversized surfboard sails. Visible from a distance is the 30-meter "Obelisk" in the center of the hall, which penetrates the roof and towers high above the building. It is the product of a design competition involving African artists and is meant to represent the vitality and strength of the people of Africa as a "Symbol of Life."

The exhibition as a whole is devoted to the theme of "The Gift of Africa," and the presentations of individual countries are arranged in a configuration corresponding to their geographical locations. The poles at each end are formed by the joint presentations of the CILSS (nine countries of the Sahel Zone) and SADC states (14 countries of the Southern African Development Community).

In addition to visiting the individual exhibition areas, visitors may dine on kudu, ostrich or antelope steaks at the theme restaurant or stroll through an African bazaar.

**Entwurf: MAR Architekten, Düsseldorf**
Design: MAR Architekten, Dusseldorf

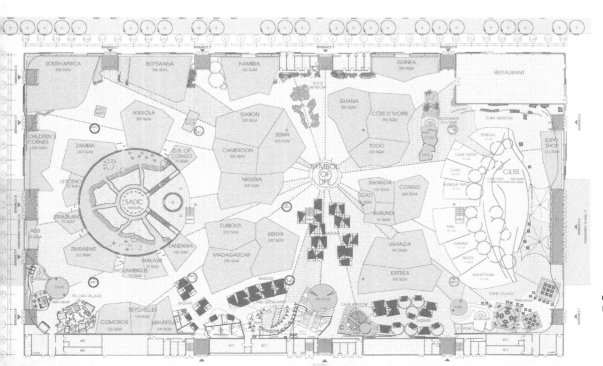

Grundriss der Afrikahalle
Floor plan of Africa Hall

Das »Symbol des Lebens« wächst durch die Hallendecke.
The "Symbol of Life" grows through the roof of the hall.

# Südafrikanische Staaten (SADC)
## Southern African Development Community (SADC)

Die 14 Staaten Angola, Botsuana, Demokratische Republik Kongo, Lesotho, Malawi, Mauritius, Mosambik, Namibia, Sambia, Seychellen, Simbabwe, Südafrika, Swasiland und Tansania haben sich zur Entwicklungsgemeinschaft des südlichen Afrika SADC (Southern African Development Community) zusammengeschlossen, um wirtschaftlich und politisch zu kooperieren. Verbunden sind sie aber auch durch die gemeinsame Sorge um das Wasser, das als zentrales Thema ihre Gemeinschaftspräsentation durchzieht. So können Besucher durch einen Wasserfall einen Wasserraum betreten, dessen Wände zu sprechen anfangen, wenn man sich anlehnt. In einem Labyrinth lädt ein durch Lichteffekte inszeniertes Flussbett dazu ein, ihm zu folgen und sich über die Wasserprojekte der SADC-Staaten zu informieren. Im »Raum der Geschichten« repräsentieren 14 Figuren die Mitgliedsländer. An die Wände projiziert, erzählen sie landestypische Geschichten rund um das Thema Wasser.
Die Ausstellung der SADC-Staaten ist ringförmig angelegt. An den zentralen Raum, den »Raum der Geschichten«, schließt der Ausstellungsbereich an, zu dem fünf Themenräume gehören. Er wird durch eine kreisrunde Wand eingefasst, hinter der als äußerer Ring die Beiträge der einzelnen Mitgliedsstaaten beginnen.

The fourteen nations of Angola, Botswana, the Democratic Republic of the Congo, Lesotho, Malawi, Mauritius, Mozambique, Namibia, the Seychelles, South Africa, Swaziland, Tanzania, Zambia and Zimbabwe have joined together to form the Southern African Development Community (SADC), an organization devoted to economic and political cooperation. They are also united in their common concern with the problem of water, the central theme of their joint presentation. Visitors pass through a waterfall into a water room in which the walls begin to speak whenever someone leans against them. A riverbed simulated with the aid of light effects invites visitors to follow its course and learn about the water projects of the SADC nations along the way. Fourteen figures represent each of the member countries in the "Room of Stories." Projected on the wall, they tell stories from their respective national traditions relating to the theme of water.
The exhibition of the SADC countries is arranged in the form of a ring. Next to the central space, the "Room of Stories," is the main exhibition area comprising five rooms devoted to specific themes. The exhibition area is enclosed by a circular wall. Beyond it, the presentations of the individual member countries form an outer circle.

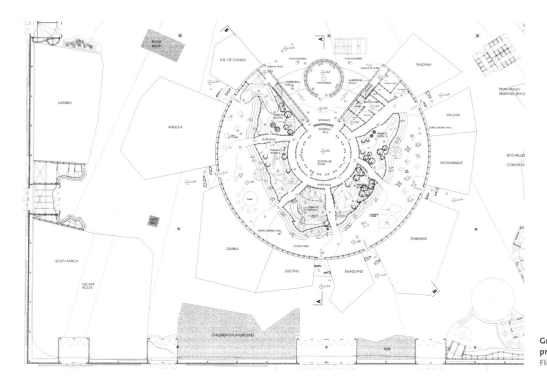

Erster Entwurf: Archevent, Berlin
Weiterentwicklung und Realisierung: HMI Hannover-Messe International GmbH, Hannover
in Zusammenarbeit mit MAR Architekten, Düsseldorf
Original design: Archevent, Berlin
Development and realization: HMI Hannover-Messe International GmbH, Hanover
in cooperation with MAR Architekten, Dusseldorf

Grundriss der SADC-Gemeinschafts-
präsentation
Floor plan of the joint SADC presentation

**Im »Raum der Geschichten«**
In the "Room of Stories"

**Blick in einen Themenraum**
View of a theme exhibition room

# Angola
## Angola

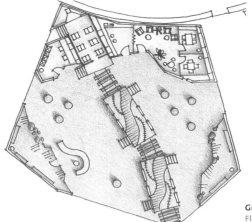

**Grundriss der Präsentation Angolas**
Floor plan of the Angolan presentation

Die Beispiele von Angola und Tansania stehen exemplarisch für die Präsentationen einzelner SADC-Mitgliedsstaaten. Zentral für den angolanischen Beitrag ist die Benguela-Eisenbahn, die längste Bahnlinie des Landes. Sie verbindet die Häfen Lobito und Benguela an der Küste Angolas mit den Kobalt- und Kupferminen der Demokratischen Republik Kongo und Sambias. Vorgestellt werden zum Beispiel die wichtigsten Städte entlang der Bahnlinie und das Projekt des »Lobito-Korridors«, das die wirtschaftliche Neubelebung der Landstriche entlang der Bahnstrecke voranbringen möchte. Entsprechend der thematischen Ausrichtung orientiert sich auch die formale Gestaltung des Beitrags an der Benguela-Eisenbahn: Als Ausstellungsräume dienen drei fast originalgroße Eisenbahnwaggons.

The exhibitions of Angola and Tanzania are interesting examples of the presentations of the individual SADC member states. A central aspect of the Angolan exhibition is the Benguela Railroad, the longest rail line in the country. It connects the ports of Lobito and Benguela on the coast with the cobalt and copper mines of the Democratic Republic of the Congo and Zambia. Focal points include the most important cities along the railroad line and the "Lobito Corridor" project, a program devoted to the economic revitalization of the areas located along the railroad line. In keeping with its thematic focus, the formal design of the presentation also relates to the Benguela Railroad. Three nearly original-sized railroad cars serve as exhibition rooms.

**Entwurf: MAR Architekten, Düsseldorf**
Design: MAR Architekten, Dusseldorf

**Der Ausstellungsbeitrag Angolas**
The Angolan exhibition

# Tansania
## Tanzania

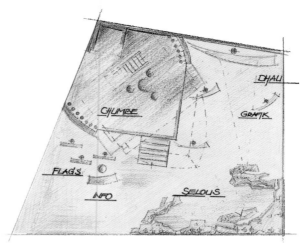

Als eines der reichsten Länder Afrikas zeigt Tansania anhand konkreter Beispiele, wie Tourismus und die Bewahrung der Umwelt miteinander in Einklang gebracht werden können. Die Präsentation des größten Naturschutzgebiets Afrikas und die originalgetreue Rekonstruktion eines Bungalows der Insel Chumbe Island standen bei der Gestaltung des Stands im Vordergrund: So wurde die Fassade des über 6 Meter hohen Bungalows in Originalgröße und mit Originalmaterialien errichtet.

Fotografien von wilden Tieren, von der natürlichen Schönheit des Landes und nicht zuletzt vom Kilimandscharo verweisen auf die Touristenattraktionen Tansanias. Im Boden originalgetreu nachgebildete Fußstapfen von Elefanten, Rhinozerossen, Büffeln und Löwen lassen Besucher zu Fährtenlesern werden.

One of the richest countries of Africa, Tanzania offers concrete examples of a harmonious coexistence between tourism and environmental conservation. The exhibit devoted to Africa's largest nature preserve and the true-to-life reconstruction of a bungalow on Chumbe Island have a direct influence on the design of this stand. The facade of the six-meter-high bungalow was erected in its original size using authentic materials.

Photographs of wild animals, of the natural beauties of the country and of Mount Kilimanjaro call attention to Tanzania's tourist attractions. Life-sized images of the footprints of elephants, rhinoceroses, buffaloes and lions on the floor put visitors in the shoes of game trackers.

**Entwurf: ARGE GFE / Formvielfalt, Aachen**
Design: ARGE GFE / Formvielfalt, Aachen

**Der Ausstellungsbeitrag Tansanias**
The Tanzanian exhibition

# Sahel-Länder (CILSS)
## Sahel Countries (CILSS)

Die neun Mitgliedsländer des CILSS-Zusammenschlusses (Comité permanent inter États de la lutte contre la sécheresse) Burkina Faso, Gambia, Guinea-Bissau, Kap Verde, Mali, Mauretanien, Niger, Senegal und Tschad vergegenwärtigen in ihrem gemeinsamen Beitrag unterschiedliche Aspekte des Lebens in der Sahel-Region. Bereiche wie »Umwelt«, »Ernährung«, »Kultur und Gesellschaft« und »Sahel 21« zeigen Probleme der CILSS-Staaten auf, bieten aber auch Lösungsansätze und vermitteln Kultur und Lebensfreude. Inmitten einer Dünenlandschaft und bunten Markttreibens können sich Besucher über die Geschichte und die aktuellen Probleme der Sahelzone informieren. Zentrale Elemente sind dabei die »Erzählung des Beobab-Baumes« und das »Große Kugelspiel«.

Der Baum, eine 6,5 Meter hohe Nachbildung eines alten Affenbrotbaumes, führt Besucher im Stil westafrikanischer Geschichtenerzähler in die Welt des Sahel ein. Die traditionelle Erzählung wird dabei von modernen Medien und Lichtinszenierungen unterstützt. Im »Großen Kugelspiel«, einem interaktiven Gruppenspiel für vier bis zwölf Personen, können sich Besucher unter anderem mit Themen wie Analphabetentum, Heuschreckenplagen oder unzureichende Stromversorgung auseinander setzen.

Parallel zum gemeinsamen Ausstellungsbereich der Dünenlandschaft werden die Einzelbeiträge der CILSS-Mitgliedsstaaten in einer »Lehmbausiedlung« präsentiert: Zur Hallenmitte orientiert, liegen nebeneinander neun Ausstellungsbereiche in Form von Lehmhäusern, in denen sich die Sahel-Länder individuell darstellen.

In their joint presentation, the nine member states of the CILSS confederation (Comité permanent inter États de la lutte contre la sécheresse) Burkina Faso, Cape Verde, Chad, Gambia, Guinea-Bissau, Mali, Mauritania, Niger and Senegal focus on a number of different aspects of life in the Sahel Zone. Exhibits such as "Environment," "Food," "Culture and Society" and "Sahel 21" show the problems facing the CILSS countries but also offer problem-solving approaches and communicate impressions of the region's culture and the *joie de vivre* of its people. In the midst of lively market activity in a landscape of sand dunes, visitors learn about the history and the current problems of the Sahel Zone. The most prominent elements of the presentation are the "Tale of the Beobob Tree" and the "Big Marble Game."

The tree, a model of an old beobob tree measuring 6.5 meters in height, introduces visitors to world of the Sahel Zone in the manner of West African storytellers. The traditional narrative is complemented by modern media and light shows. In the "Big Marble Game," an interactive game for groups of four to twelve people, visitors deal in play with such topics as illiteracy, locust plagues or insufficient power supply.

Parallel to the joint exhibition, the individual presentations of the CILSS member states are shown in an "Earthen Hut Village." Nine exhibition areas in the shape of earthen huts are arranged near the middle of the hall, each housing the exhibit of one of the Sahel countries.

Entwurf: GFA, Hamburg
Weiterentwicklung: Lippsmeier + Partner, Düsseldorf
Konzept Medien: Thomas Briele
Konzept Grafik: gruppeDrei, Essen
Design: GFA, Hamburg
Further development: Lippsmeier + Partner, Dusseldorf
Media concept: Thomas Briele
Graphics concept: gruppeDrei, Essen

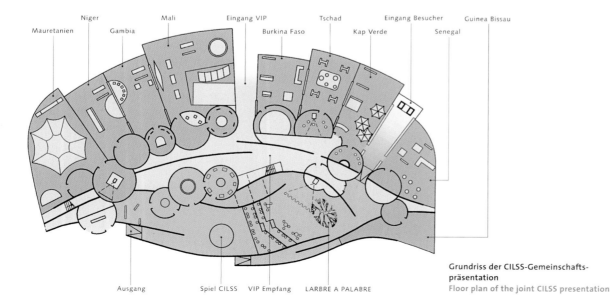

Niger   Mali   Eingang VIP   Tschad   Eingang Besucher   Guinea Bissau
Mauretanien   Gambia   Burkina Faso   Kap Verde   Senegal

Ausgang   Spiel CILSS   VIP Empfang   LARBRE A PALABRE

Grundriss der CILSS-Gemeinschaftspräsentation
Floor plan of the joint CILSS presentation

**Blick in die Dünenlandschaft**
View of the dune landscape

**Der Beobab-Baum auf dem Marktplatz**
The beobob tree in the marketplace

# Kenia
## Kenya

Die Präsentation Kenias liegt im Zentrum der Afrikahalle. In ihrer offenen Gestaltung verbindet sie die Anmutung eines modernen Business-Centers mit Elementen traditioneller Lamu-Architektur. Gemäß dem Leitmotiv »Tradition und Moderne« spielen in der Ausstellung die Naturschönheiten des Landes eine zentrale Rolle. Zugleich wird die Aufmerksamkeit der Besucher auf erfolgreiche Projekte aus den Bereichen Ökotourismus, Heilpflanzen und Schmetterlingszucht gelenkt.

**Entwurf: ARGE GFE/Formvielfalt, Aachen**
Design: ARGE GFE/Formvielfalt, Aachen

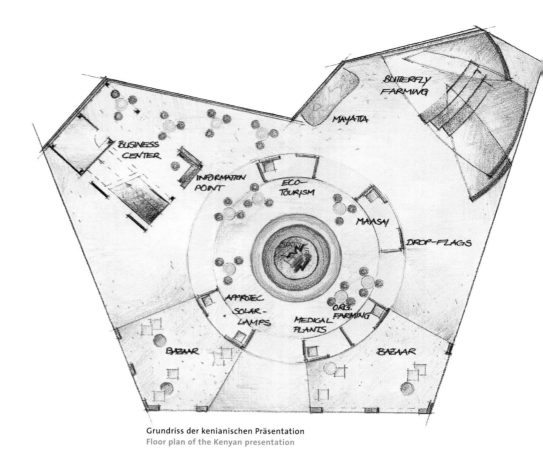

**Grundriss der kenianischen Präsentation**
Floor plan of the Kenyan presentation

Kenya's exhibition is located in the center of Africa Hall. With its open design, it combines the look of a modern business center with elements of traditional Lamu architecture. In keeping with the leitmotif of "Tradition and Modernism," the natural beauties of the country play a prominent role in the exhibition. The visitor's attention is also called to a number of successful projects in the areas of ecotourism, the use of medicinal plants and the breeding of butterflies.

**Gesamtansicht**
Total view

**In der Ausstellung**
Inside the exhibition

# Madagaskar
## Madagascar

**Grundriss der Präsentation Madagaskars**
Floor plan of the Madagascan presentation

Madagaskar lädt seine Besucher zu einer Reise über die Insel ein. Auf einem Rundweg um das Amphitheater, das zentrale Element der Ausstellungsarchitektur, werden die unterschiedlichen Landschaften Madagaskars inszeniert. Felsen, Wüstenlandschaften, die Ostküste mit ihren Resten von Naturwald und den in den dortigen Gewässern lebenden Buckelwalen sowie das Hochland bilden den Lebensraum für eine weltweit einmalige Flora und Fauna. Die Erhaltung dieser einzigartigen Tier- und Pflanzenwelt ist das zentrale Anliegen der Präsentation Madagaskars.

Der Rundgang über die Insel führt Besucher schließlich in das großzügig gestaltete Amphitheater, in dem Computeranimationen und Filmprojektionen modernes Nationalparkmanagement veranschaulichen. In der Nachbildung einer Grotte sind Laute von Tieren zu hören, die nur noch auf Madagaskar leben. Eine Öko-Lodge, ein Basar für den Verkauf von lokalen Produkten und ein Business-Center in Form eines typisch madagassischen Landhauses ergänzen den Auftritt der Insel.

Madagascar invites visitors on a journey across the island. The country's different landscapes are presented along a circular route around the amphitheater, the centerpiece of the exhibition. Rock formations and desert landscapes, the east coast, with its vestiges of natural forest and the humpback whales that frequent its waters, and the highlands are home to a range of flora and fauna that is unique to Madagascar. The preservation of this unparalleled world of animals and plants is the central focus of the country's presentation.

The tour around the island ultimately leads visitors to the lavishly designed amphitheater, where computer animations and films provide illustrations of modern national park management. Visitors to a model grotto hear sounds made by animals found only in Madagascar. An environmental lodge, a bazaar featuring local products and a business center in the form of a typical country house in Madagascar complement the island-country's presentation.

**Entwurf: ARGE GFE / Formvielfalt, Aachen**
Design: ARGE GFE / Formvielfalt, Aachen

**Gesamtansicht**
Total view

**In der Ausstellung**
Inside the exhibition

# Uganda
## Uganda

Schon von weitem erkennbar, kündigt sich Uganda auf einer großen Tafel als »Perle Afrikas« an. Die Ausstellung gliedert sich in zwei unterschiedliche Themenbereiche. In einer Umgebung, die seinen natürlichen Lebensbedingungen nachempfunden ist, begegnen Besucher dem Berggorilla, der als eine der Hauptattraktionen des Landes gilt. Ausführlich werden die Bedrohung seines Lebensraumes und seine Schutzmöglichkeiten erläutert. In einem zweiten großen Ausstellungsabschnitt führt Uganda in den ökologischen Kaffeeanbau und die Kaffeeherstellung ein: Von der grünen Bohne bis zum fertigen Produkt können hier alle Prozesse nachvollzogen und die Ergebnisse probiert werden.

**In der Ausstellung**
Inside the exhibition

**Entwurf: ARGE GFE/Formvielfalt, Aachen**
**Design: ARGE GFE/Formvielfalt, Aachen**

Visible from a great distance, a large sign announces Uganda's presence as the "Pearl of Africa." The exhibition comprises two different theme areas. In an environment modeled on its natural surroundings, visitors encounter the mountain gorilla, regarded as one of the most popular attractions of the country. Observers are informed in great detail about the threat posed to the gorilla's natural habitat and about approaches to effective protection. A second large segment of the exhibition is devoted to ecological methods of coffee-growing and production. Every step in the process from the green bean to the finished product can be observed, and visitors are invited to taste the results.

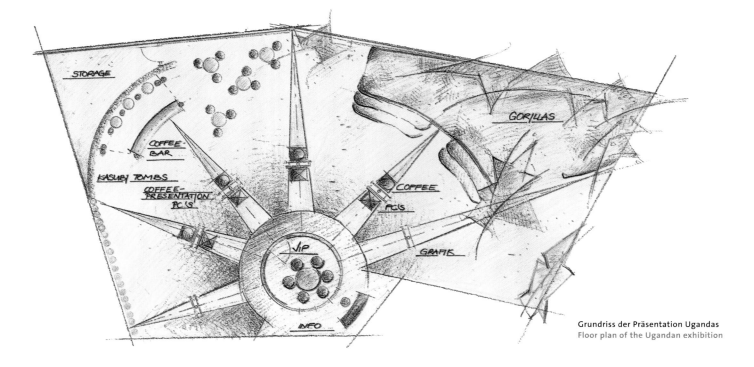

**Grundriss der Präsentation Ugandas**
Floor plan of the Ugandan exhibition

**Gesamtansicht**
Total view

# Österreich
## Austria

Österreich präsentiert sich den Expo-Besuchern als »Land der LebensKunst«. Das Wiener Büro Eichinger oder Knechtl hat die Ausstellung auf zwei unterschiedliche Ebenen verteilt, die rund 5.000 Quadratmeter große Eingangsebene und die darüber liegende 3.200 Quadratmeter große Landschaftsebene. Beide Bereiche ermöglichen mithilfe modernster Medientechnik und inszenierter Bilderwelten einen neuen, »anderen« Blick auf Österreich und thematisieren oft wenig beachtete Seiten der österreichischen Kultur, seiner Menschen und Landschaften. Eine neuartige Präsentationstechnik ermöglicht es den Besuchern, von sieben ausgewählten Aussichtspunkten den Blick über ein 360-Grad-Panorama schweifen zu lassen und auf Salzburg, Wien, das Donautal oder Seen und Wasserfälle zu blicken.

In der unteren Ebene, die über vier Eingänge betreten werden kann, werden Besucher von einem leuchtenden Raumkörper empfangen, dessen äußere Hülle von einem raumhohen Informationsscreen gebildet wird. Wie ein Band führt es in die über der Eingangsebene »schwebende« Landschaft, deren Aufbau aus einer bis zu 20 Meter auskragenden Stahlkonstruktion besteht. Die abstrahierte Landschaft mit ihren weichen und körperbetonten Oberflächen, Lederhügeln oder textilen Strukturen bietet zahlreiche Möglichkeiten auszuruhen, sich zu setzen, hinzulegen oder anzulehnen. Ein umlaufender Horizont mit einer Kombination aus Bewegt- und Standbildern ermöglicht dabei Ausblicke auf die Kulturlandschaft Österreichs. Ergänzt wird die Präsentation durch wechselnde Ausstellungen der einzelnen Bundesländer und eine großzügig angelegte Gastronomielandschaft, in der Expo-Besucher auch den kulinarischen Bereich der österreichischen »LebensKunst« kennen lernen können.

Austria presents itself to Expo visitors as the "Land of the Art of Life." The Vienna architects Eichinger oder Knechtl have distributed the exhibition over two different levels, a large entrance area comprising some 5,000 square meters of space and the landscape level above, covering 3,200 square meters. Each of these sections offers visitors a "different" view of Austria with the aid of state-of-the-art media technology and staged visual worlds, while focusing attention on often neglected aspects of Austrian culture, its people and its landscapes. Innovative presentation technology allows visitors to gaze from any of seven different outlook points and take in a 360-degree panoramic view of the country with images of Salzburg, Vienna, the Danube Valley, lakes and waterfalls.

On the lower level, which has four different entrances, visitors are greeted by a luminous three-dimensional object whose outer shell is formed by an information screen that stretches from floor to ceiling. Like a conveyor belt, it leads up into the "floating" landscape above the entrance area, which is built on a steel structure with an overhang of up to 20 meters. The abstract landscape, with its soft, modeled surfaces, leather hills and textile sculptures, offers many places to stop and rest, to sit or lie down or to lean against something for support. A circular horizon showing a combination of still images and moving pictures offers views of Austria's cultural landscape. The presentation is complemented by alternating exhibitions by the individual Austrian states and an expansive landscape of restaurants and cafés, in which Expo visitors can become acquainted with the culinary side of Austria's "Art of Life" as well.

Grundriss der Eingangsebene
Floor plan of the entrance level

**Architektonischer Entwurf: Eichinger oder Knechtl, Wien**
**Architektonische Ausführungsplanung: Neumann + Partner, Wien**
Architectural design: Eichinger oder Knechtl, Vienna
Architectural planning and realization: Neumann + Partner, Vienna

**In der Eingangsebene**
On the entrance floor

**Blick in die Landschaftsebene**
View of the landscape level

# Liechtenstein
## Liechtenstein

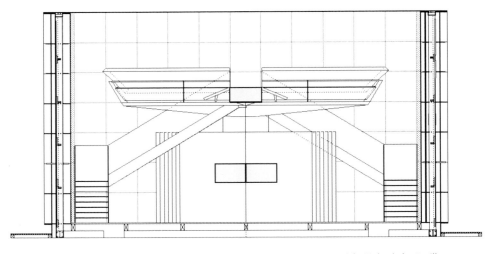

Das Fürstentum Liechtenstein errichtete einen nach allen Seiten geschlossenen Pavillon. Der »lichte Stein« umfasst eine Grundfläche von 13 x 13 Metern und ist 7 Meter hoch. Die hinterleuchtete, transparente Glashülle des quaderförmigen Pavillons symbolisiert Offenheit und Aufgeschlossenheit für alles, was von außen kommt. Diese Fassade, die das äußere Erscheinungsbild des Pavillons prägt, besteht aus geätzten, quadratischen Glasplatten in der Größe von 1 x 1 Meter; das Tragwerk des Pavillons ist in konventioneller Stahlbauweise ausgeführt.

Von den ruhigen Vorplatzbereichen mit Informationsständen, Erholungszonen und einem Café können Besucher den »Liechtenstein« von allen vier Seiten über kleine Rampen aus Holz und durch Steintore betreten: durch den »Wirtschaftsstein«, den »Kulturstein«, den »Finanzstein« und den »Monarchiestein«. Den Namen entsprechend, befinden sich im Innern des Pavillons hinter den Toren jeweils Ausstellungen zu diesen Themen. Durch Zählwerke an den Eingängen ist leicht festzustellen, für welchen Bereich sich die Besucher vorwiegend interessieren.

Der Innenbereich ist klar gegliedert. Die Innenwände sind mit 260 Porträts von Bewohnern Liechtensteins gestaltet. Das Erdgeschoss mit seinem zentralen, kreuzförmig angelegten Ausstellungskern ist durch zwei Treppen mit dem 85 Quadratmeter großen Galeriegeschoss, einer freischwebenden Plattform, verbunden. Hier stehen Informationen zu Umwelt und Entwicklung bereit. Auf vier großen Bodenmonitoren wird ein Landschaftsfilm gezeigt.

Eine Besonderheit stellt die Energieversorgung des Pavillons dar. Dem Grundsatz der Nachhaltigkeit folgend, wird der benötigte Strom für Klima, Licht, Geräte und den Cafébetrieb von einem kleinen Solar- und Windkraftwerk in Liechtenstein in das europäische Stromnetz eingespeist. Der jeweils aktuelle und gesamte Energieverbrauch auf der EXPO 2000 sowie die Energieproduktion in Liechtenstein sind auf Monitoren im Obergeschoss des Pavillons zu sehen.

**Entwurf: Gassner & Seger AG-Atelier für Gestaltung, Vaduz**
Design: Gassner & Seger AG-Atelier für Gestaltung, Vaduz

The principality of Liechtenstein has erected a pavilion that is enclosed on all sides. The "Stone of Light" covers 13 x 13 meters of ground and is seven meters high. Illuminated from within, the transparent glass shell of the cube-shaped building symbolizes openness and receptiveness to the outside world. This facade, the most prominent visual feature of the pavilion, consists of etched square glass plates each measuring one square meter. The pavilion's framework structure is a conventional steel construction.

Visitors can enter the "Liechtenstein" from the quiet outside areas comprising information booths, zones of rest and relaxation and a café over small wooden ramps and through stone gates positioned on all sides of the building, passing through the "Business Stone," the "Culture Stone," the "Finance Stone" and the "Monarchy Stone." Thematic exhibits corresponding to these four named stones are presented behind the gates inside the pavilion. Counters at the entrances indicate which exhibition area has attracted the most visitors.

The inside of the pavilion is clearly structured. The interior walls are decorated with 260 portraits of people from Liechtenstein. The ground floor, with its central, cross-shaped main exhibition area is connected by two stairways to the gallery level (85 square meters), a suspended platform. Visitors to this section receive information about environmental and development issues. A landscape film is shown on four large console monitors.

A unique feature of the pavilion is its energy supply system. In keeping with the principles of conservation and sustainability, the electrical power needed to operate the air-conditioning system, the lights, building equipment and the café is produced by a small solar-wind power plant in Liechtenstein and fed into the European power network. A display of current and cumulative energy consumption at EXPO 2000 and energy production in Liechtenstein is shown on monitors on the upper level of the pavilion.

**Der quaderförmige Pavillon Liechtensteins**
Liechtenstein's cube-shaped pavilion

**Ausstellungsbereich im Erdgeschoss**
Ground floor exhibition area

# Euregio Tirol, Südtirol-Alto Adige, Trentino
## Euregio Tyrol, South Tyrol-Alto Adige, Trentino

Die drei Regionen Tirol, Südtirol-Alto Adige und Trentino haben sich über natio-
nale Grenzen hinweg für ihren gemeinsamen Expo-Auftritt zur Europäischen
Wirtschaftlichen Interessenvereinigung euregio zusammengeschlossen. Unter
dem Motto »Wasser und Berg« versucht euregio Besuchern den bewussten
und intensiven Umgang der Menschen mit der Natur der Region zu vermitteln.
Der Beitrag legt den Schwerpunkt auf lokale Lösungsansätze und die prakti-
sche Auseinandersetzung mit zentralen Zukunftsfragen.
Für die gestalterische Umsetzung des Ausstellungsbeitrags wurde ein internationaler Ideenwettbewerb ausgeschrieben, den ein Team mit dem Künstler
Fabrizio Plessi, dem Trientiner Filmstudio SIRIO und den Architekten Sergio und
Franco Giovanazzi gewonnen hat. Die Präsentation ist in ihrem Erscheinungsbild geprägt von der Form des Dreiecks. Dazu gehört in der Standmitte eine
begehbare Skulptur von Fabrizio Plessi. In dreieckigen Ausstellungsbereichen
werden die Regionen dargestellt. In diesen Dreiecken »fließen« Wasser-Videos
und zeigen die verschiedenen Zustände von Wasser: gefroren in den Glet-
schern Tirols, rauschend in den Wildbächen Südtirols und ruhig in den Seen
des Trentino. Besucher, die sich eingehender über die Regionen informieren
möchten, können in einem »Laubengang« mehr über ihre Vergangenheit
und Gegenwart und in einem anschließenden Parcours auch über die Zukunft
erfahren. Ein Marktplatz mit der Atmosphäre einer typischen Piazza lädt
schließlich zum Ausruhen ein.

The three regions of Tyrol, South Tyrol-Alto Adige und Trentino have opted for
a joint Expo presentation as a cooperative interregional group known as
euregio, the European Union of Economic Interests. Focusing on the theme of
"Water and Mountains," euregio seeks to communicate an appreciation for
the thoughtful and intensive approach to nature and its resources in the
region on the part of the people who live there. The presentation highlights
local solutions and practical attempts to come to grips with key questions
of future importance.
An international competition was conducted for the design of the exhibition.
The winner was a team comprising the artist Fabrizio Plessi, the SIRIO Film
Studio of Trentino and the architects Sergio and Franco Giovanazzi. The dominant form of the presentation is a triangle. In the middle of its base is a walk-in
sculpture by Fabrizio Plessi. Each of the regions is introduced in a triangular
exhibition area. Video clips with images of water "flow" within these trian-
gles, illustrating different states in which water appears: frozen in the Tyrolean
glaciers, rushing in the wild streams of South Tyrol and still in the lakes of
Trentino. Visitors interested in more detailed information about the regions
can learn more about their past and present on a walk through a "pergola" and
about their future in the next exhibit. A marketplace with the atmosphere of
a typical *piazza* invites visitors to stop, rest and relax.

**Entwurf: Architekturbüro Dr. Sergio Giovanazzi, Trento**
**Design: Architects' office of Dr. Sergio Giovanazzi,
Trento**

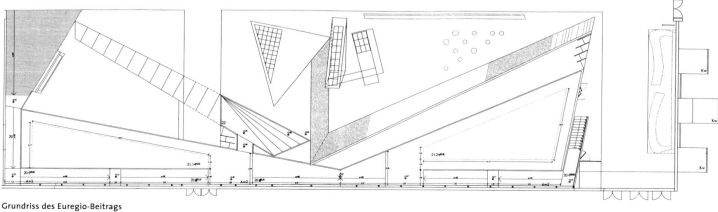

Grundriss des Euregio-Beitrags
Floor plan of the euregio presentation

Die begehbare Skulptur von Fabrizio Plessi
Fabrizio Plessi's walk-in sculpture

Blick in den Laubengang
View of the pergola

Auf dem Marktplatz
At the marketplace

# Moldau
## Moldova

Die Republik Moldau lädt Besucher in ein Haus auf einem Weinberg ein und präsentiert sich damit als wichtiger Erzeuger von landwirtschaftlichen Produkten innerhalb der Gemeinschaft Unabhängiger Staaten (GUS). Sie zeigt aber auch ihre wirtschaftlichen und kulturellen Errungenschaften. Das Haus neben einem alten Brunnen symbolisiert die Aufforderung, das Land zu »besuchen« und besser kennen zu lernen. Besucher werden zunächst auf den Weinberg geführt, wo Kunsthandwerker ihre Arbeiten darbieten und damit Einblicke in alte moldauische Traditionen vermitteln. Aus der landestypisch ausgestatteten »Casa Mare«, der guten Stube des Hauses, gelangen Besucher in einen großen Keller, in dessen Gewölben sich vier Ausstellungsräume befinden. Hier stellt sich die Republik Moldau mit Themen aus den Bereichen Umwelt, Forschung, Geschichte und Wirtschaft vor. Die modernen Präsentationen stehen dabei in einem reizvollen Kontrast zur traditionellen Gestaltung der Räume, die zum Beispiel als Apfel- oder Weinkeller ausgestattet sind.

**In der Ausstellung im Gewölbekeller**
In the exhibition in the vaulted cellar

The Republic of Moldova invites visitors into a house situated in a vineyard, thus underscoring its role as an important agricultural producer within the Commonwealth of Independent States (CIS). But Moldova also proudly presents its economic and cultural achievements. The house next to an old well is a symbolic appeal to tourists to "visit" Moldova and become better acquainted with the country. Visitors are led first to the vineyard, where artisans offer their wares and provide interesting insights into old Moldovan traditions. From the typically furnished "Casa Mare," the living room of the house, visitors descend into a large cellar containing four exhibition areas beneath its vaulted ceilings. Moldova makes its presentation here in thematic exhibits on the environment, scientific research, history and the economy. These modern presentations stand in marked contrast to the traditional design of the rooms, which are set up as fruit or wine cellars, for example.

**Entwurf: Lippsmeier + Partner, Düsseldorf**
Design: Lippsmeier + Partner, Dusseldorf

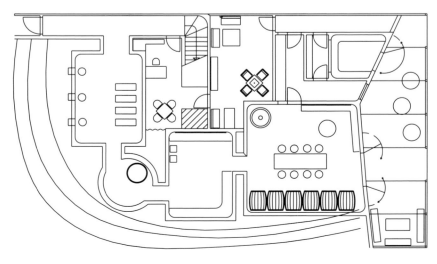

**Grundriss der Präsentation Moldaus**
Floor plan of the Moldavan presentation

**Blick auf den Weinberg**
View of the vineyard

# Paraguay
## Paraguay

Wasser dient als prägendes Gestaltungs-
element.
Water is a significant element of design.

Die Präsentation Paraguays steht unter dem Motto »Wasser – Quelle des Lebens in Paraguay«. Wasser bestimmte die Entwicklung des Landes schon in der Kolonialzeit, denn die Flüsse Paraguay und Paraná waren die zentralen Verkehrswege für die portugiesischen und spanischen Eroberer. Heute bilden sie die Lebensgrundlage für die ländliche Bevölkerung. Auch bei der Energie-gewinnung ist Wasser von zentraler Bedeutung, denn Paraguay bezieht seine gesamte Energie aus der Wasserkraft und besitzt mit den Wasserkraftwerken Itaipú und Yacyretá die größten und modernsten Anlagen der Welt. Anhand eindrucksvoller Bilder können Besucher unmittelbar erfahren, welche Kraft Wasser entwickeln kann.
Entsprechend besteht auch ein Drittel der Fläche des Standes aus Wasser. Den Mittelpunkt bildet ein multimediales Zentrum, in dem die Flora und Fauna des Landes sowie touristische Projekte vorgestellt werden. Um dieses Zentrum herum liegen mehrere Erlebnis- und Informationsbereiche, in denen Besucher Wissenswertes über Geschichte und Kultur erfahren und landestypische Spei-sen und Getränke kosten können.

Paraguay's presentation focuses on the theme of "Water – the Source of Life in Paraguay." Water has always been a shaping force in the country's history, even during colonial times, for the Paraguay and Paraná rivers were the main traffic routes for Spanish and Portuguese explorers. Today, they are the lifelines of the rural population. Water is also a major source of energy, as Paraguay draws all of its electricity from hydroelectric power plants. The Itaipú und Yacyretá plants are the most modern hydroelectric facilities in the world. Photographs offer visitors an impressive demonstration of the potential power of water. Accordingly, one-third of the area covered by the exhibit is covered with water. The heart of the presentation is a multimedia center showing the sights and sounds of the country's flora and fauna and introducing several ongoing proj-ects in the field of tourism. A number of theme-based and informative exhibits are grouped around this center, offering visitors interesting historical and cultural insights and an opportunity to sample typical Paraguayan foods and beverages.

**Entwurf: steindesign Werbeagentur GmbH, Hannover**
Design: steindesign Werbeagentur GmbH, Hanover

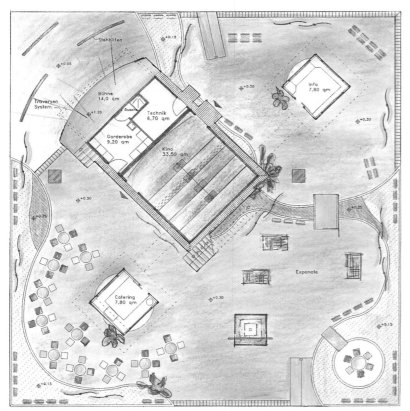

Grundriss der Präsentation Paraguays
Floor plan of the Paraguayan presentation

Blick in die Ausstellung
View of the exhibition

# CARICOM
## CARICOM

Auf einer 1.000 Quadratmeter großen Fläche stellen sich die Inselstaaten der Karibischen Gemeinschaft (CARICOM) wie Barbados, Dominica, Guyana, Jamaika, St. Vincent und die Grenadinen, Trinidad und Tobago vor. Auf vielen kleinen Inseln, umgeben von Wasser, vermitteln die vier Hauptthemen »Paradise« (die Schönheit der Karibik), »Roots« (die reiche kulturelle Vergangenheit), »Transition« (aktuelle Entwicklungen) und »Perspective« (die wirtschaftlichen Perspektiven) die Vielfalt der Karibik-Staaten. Untermalt von Reggae- und Steeldrumrhythmen, werden den Besuchern Eindrücke vom Meer, den Stränden, Vulkanen und dem Regenwald vermittelt. In Form von Mobiles, die über den Köpfen schweben, wird auf die ständige Bedrohung durch Hurrikane und die Lavamassen von Vulkanausbrüchen aufmerksam gemacht. Diese gefährden die Inselstaaten immer wieder aufs Neue und zerstören Ernten und Häuser. Auf einem rund angelegten Marktplatz stellt die Gemeinschaft verschiedene Projekte, etwa aus der Landwirtschaft, vor. Zudem werden Kunsthandwerk und landestypische Gerichte verkauft, während in einer aus Lianen gefertigten Rum-Bar Erfrischungen angeboten werden.

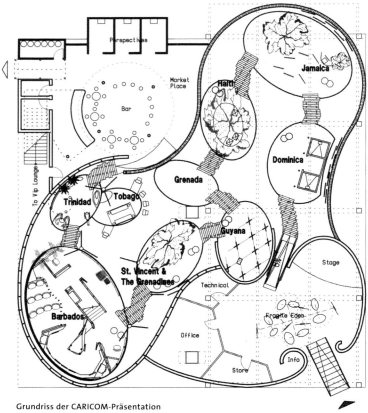

**Grundriss der CARICOM-Präsentation**
Floor plan of the CARICOM presentation

The island countries of the Caribbean Community (CARICOM), such as Barbados, Dominica, Guyana, Jamaica, St. Vincent and the Grenadines, Trinidad and Tobago, make their presentation in an area of some 1,000 square meters. On a number of small islands surrounded by water, the four main themes of "Paradise" (the beauty of the Caribbean region), "Roots" (its rich cultural heritage), "Transitions" (current developments) and "Perspectives" (the economic outlook) communicate an idea of the great diversity of the Caribbean island countries. Visitors are treated to impressions of the sea, the beaches, volcanoes and the rain forest, to the accompaniment of reggae rhythms and steel band music. Mobiles suspended from the ceiling serve as reminders of the constant threat of hurricanes and volcanic eruptions, catastrophes repeatedly visited upon the island countries, causing the destruction of homes and harvests. The Community displays a variety of regional products, including many agricultural specialties, at a circular marketplace, along with handicrafts and typical Caribbean dishes. Refreshments are available in a rum bar built of vines.

**Entwurf: Lippsmeier + Partner, Düsseldorf**
Design: Lippsmeier + Partner, Dusseldorf

**Blick vom Marktplatz auf die Rum-Bar**
View of the Rum Bar from the marketplace

**Die Ausstellungsinseln**
The exhibition islands

# Ausstellungshallen
## Exhibition Halls

Besondere bauliche Veränderungen waren notwendig, um das bestehende Messegelände in ein attraktives Weltausstellungsgelände zu verwandeln. Ein Schwerpunkt der Arbeiten lag darin, die alten mehrgeschossigen Messehallen durch großzügige, lichtdurchflutete Neubauten mit hoher Gestaltqualität zu ersetzen. Diese Aufgabe leitete einen Entwicklungsprozess ein, der großartige, zukunftsweisende Lösungen hervorgebracht hat. Führende Architekten erarbeiteten mit Mut zum Neuen innovative Energiekonzepte, entwickelten neue Tragwerkskonstruktionen und entwarfen im Einklang von Gestaltung und Technik architektonisch anspruchsvolle Gebäude mit hoher Aufenthaltsqualität. Exemplarisch werden hier die Hallen 8/9 und 13 vorgestellt.

Substantial architectural changes were required to transform the existing trade fair grounds into an attractive site for the World Exposition. A major focus of this work was the replacement of the old, multistory trade fair halls with expansive, well-lighted, new buildings of superior design quality. The development process based upon this objective has brought forth magnificent, pioneering solutions. Leading architects with the courage to pursue new approaches created innovative energy concepts, developed new framework constructions and designed outstanding buildings in a harmonious balance of aesthetics and engineering as high-quality settings for visitors and participants. The following sections present Halls 8/9 and 13 as examples of the results achieved.

# Halle 8/9
## Hall 8/9

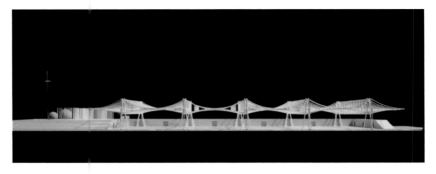

**Modelldarstellung der Hallenkonstruktion**
Model of the hall construction

Mit ihrer Fertigstellung im Frühjahr 1999 wurde die neue Doppelhalle 8/9 zur größten freitragenden Ausstellungshalle Europas. Sie verfügt über eine Ausstellungsfläche von rund 30.000 Quadratmetern, davon 22.050 stützenfrei. Der markante architektonische Eckpunkt für den Süden des Messegeländes entstand nach den Plänen des Hamburger Büros gmp von Gerkan, Marg & Partner. Ein besonderer Blickfang ist das freitragende Holzdach mit seinen fünf sanften Schwüngen. Die Konstruktion ist Hängebrücken entlehnt. Das Dach scheint auf dem Gebäude zu schweben – ein Eindruck, der durch die allseitig transparente Fassade unterstrichen wird. Der hohe Tageslichtanteil, die ressourcenschonende Verwendung von Materialien und der Einsatz von Holz als nachwachsendem Rohstoff belegen den ökologischen Anspruch. Die Konstruktion der 250 Meter langen und 143,5 Meter breiten Doppelhalle besteht aus fünf Hauptträgern im Abstand von 50 Metern und senkrecht dazu verlaufenden Blech-Seilbindern im Abstand von 10 Metern. Die Zweiteilung in Halle 8 und Halle 9 erfolgt durch hängende Schiebewände unter dem mittleren Hauptträger.
Besucher können die Halle ebenerdig vom südlichen Teil des Messeparks aus betreten oder das obere Eingangsplateau an der Hallennordseite nutzen. Diese Eingangsplattform dient gleichzeitig als Gelenk oder Bindeglied zwischen den beiden Teilen des Weltausstellungsgeländes. Von diesem attraktiv gestalteten Platz führt die »Exponale«, die zentrale Brücke, zur Plaza hinüber; eine riesige Freitreppe bildet eine Freilichttribüne zum Messepark und zur Allee der Vereinigten Bäume.

With its completion in the spring of 1999, the new duplex Hall 8/9 became the largest free-standing exhibition hall in Europe. It has a total exhibition floor space of 30,000 square meters, of which 22,050 is free of vertical supports. This prominent architectural cornerstone of the southern sector of the trade fair grounds was built according to plans drafted by the Hamburg architects gmp von Gerkan, Marg and Partners. A particularly striking feature is the cantilevered wooden roof with its five gentle curves. The design is an adaptation of suspension bridge construction. The roof appears to float on top of the building – an impression that is enhanced by the facade, which is transparent on all sides. The large proportion of natural light, the careful use of materials and the selection of wood as a renewable natural resource bear witness to the emphasis placed upon environmental considerations. The structural framework for the duplex hall, which is 250 meters long and 143.5 meters wide, consists of five main girders placed at intervals of 50 meters and perpendicular metal cable trusses ten meters apart. The subdivision of the building into Halls 8 and 9 was accomplished by installing suspended sliding wall beneath the central main girder.
Visitors can enter the hall at ground level from the southern part of the trade fair grounds or from the upper entrance platform on the north side of the hall. This entrance platform also serves as a link joining the two sectors of the World Exposition grounds. The central bridge, known as the "Exponale," leads from this attractive site to the Plaza. A huge outdoor stairway forms an open-air grandstand facing the fair park and United Trees Avenue.

Architekten: gmp von Gerkan, Marg & Partner, Hamburg
Prof. Volkwin Marg
Entwurf: Prof. Volkwin Marg mit Prof. Jörg Schlaich
Wettbewerb: Stephanie Jöbsch, Marc Ziemons
Projektleitung: Torsten Hinz, Marc Ziemons
Mitarbeiter: Ahmet Alkuru, Matthias Holtschmidt, Knut Maass, Stefan Nixdorf, Thomas Schuster, Andrea Vollstedt
Tragwerksplanung: Schlaich, Bergermann & Partner, Stuttgart
Prof. Jörg Schlaich

Architects: gmp von Gerkan, Marg & Partner, Hamburg
Prof. Volkwin Marg
Design: Prof. Volkwin Marg in cooperation with Prof. Jörg Schlaich
Competition: Stephanie Jöbsch, Marc Ziemons
Project management: Torsten Hinz, Marc Ziemons
Staff: Ahmet Alkuru, Matthias Holtschmidt, Knut Maass, Stefan Nixdorf, Thomas Schuster, Andrea Vollstedt
Structural framework design: Schlaich, Bergermann & Partner, Stuttgart
Prof. Jörg Schlaich

**Blick von Nordosten**
View from the northeast

**Von der Eingangszone über der Halle 8
führen Treppen hinab in die Halle 9.**
Stairs lead from the entrance area over
Hall 8 down to Hall 9.

**Direkt an die Halle schließt die Freitreppe an.**
The open stairway is located right next to the hall.

# Halle 13
## Hall 13

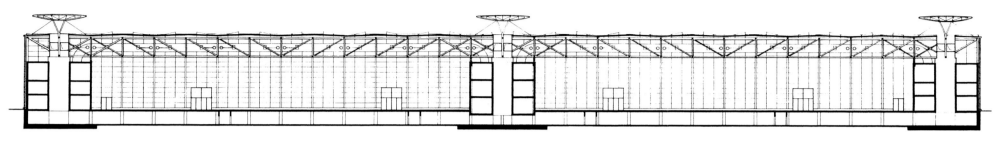

Längsschnitt durch die Halle
Longitudinal section view of the hall

Die Halle 13 aus dem Jahre 1997 liegt im Westen des Ausstellungsgeländes an der Allee der Vereinigten Bäume. Sie zeichnet sich durch ihr zurückhaltendes Erscheinungsbild, eine klare Form, innovative Haustechnik und Umweltfreundlichkeit aus. Das 225 x 120 Meter große Gebäude der Münchner Architekten Ackermann + Partner hat zu allen Seiten hin transparente Fassaden und besteht primär aus einem Stahlträgerrost, der auf sechs Installationskernen aus Beton aufliegt. Bis auf diese Techniksäulen, die gleichzeitig der Aussteifung in vertikaler und horizontaler Richtung dienen, ist die Halle stützenfrei und kann für unterschiedliche Nutzungen flexibel aufgeteilt werden. Das quadratische Raster von 7,5 auf 7,5 Meter resultiert aus der konstruktiven und wirtschaftlichen Optimierung des eingesetzten Materials. Die Sekundärstruktur bilden vorgefertigte Holzkassetten im Abstand von 3,75 Metern. Die Rasterfelder werden je nach Bedarf als technische Elemente für die Gebäudeausrüstung eingesetzt. Mut zum Experiment hat laut Kurt Ackermann das innovative Lüftungssystem der Halle 13 hervorgebracht. Verbrauchte Hallenluft wird durch ein System aus so genannten Venturi-Flügeln auf dem Dach durch Unterdruck abgesaugt. Dieses natürliche Lüftungskonzept führt zusammen mit der optimalen Ausnutzung des Tageslichts durch ein blendfreies Oberlichtsystem zu einer maximalen Energieeinsparung. Recycelbare Baustoffe wurden entsprechend ihrer konstruktiven Aufgaben zum Beispiel in der Decken- und Fassadenkonstruktion und in dem Ausbauraster sinnvoll eingesetzt, wodurch auch der Materialaufwand minimiert wurde. Die Halle 13 ist ein zeitgemäßes Symbol konstruktiver Intelligenz.

Built in 1997, Hall 13 stands in the western sector of the World Exposition grounds on United Trees Avenue. It is characterized by its unpretentious appearance, its clear lines, its innovative building engineering systems and its environmentally sound design. Measuring 225 x 120 meters, this building designed by the Munich architects Ackermann and Partners has transparent facades on all sides and consists primarily of a steel-girder grate resting on six concrete foundation pads. Except for the building engineering columns, which also provided vertical and horizontal stability, the hall is free of vertical supports and can be configured flexibly for different types of use. The square 7.5 x 7.5 grid pattern is the product of the optimum constructive and economical use of materials. The secondary structure consists of prefabricated wooden modules set at intervals of 3.75 meters. The fields in the grid are used as technical elements for building equipment as specific needs dictate. According to Kurt Ackermann, the innovative ventilation system in Hall 13 is the product of willingness to experiment. Stale hall air is drawn off by a system of so-called Venturi flaps on the roof, which operate on the basis of the natural pressure gradient. This natural ventilation concept, coupled with the optimum exploitation of available daylight through a non-glare skylight system, promotes maximum energy savings. Recyclable building materials were incorporated wherever feasible, in the ceilings, facades and in superstructure modules, for example, thus minimizing the total investment in materials. Hall 13 is a modern-day symbol of architectural intelligence.

**Architekten: Ackermann + Partner, München**
**Prof. Kurt Ackermann, Peter Ackermann**
**Mitarbeiter: Ying Chang, Hannelore Huber, Barbara Karl,**
**Beate Kuntz, Herbert Markert, Reiner Nagel, Susanne**
**Nobis, Dagmar Plankermann, Horst Raab, Heinz Riegel**
**Tragwerksplanung: Schlaich, Bergermann & Partner,**
**Stuttgart**
**Architects: Ackermann + Partner, Munich**
**Prof. Kurt Ackermann, Peter Ackermann**
**Staff: Ying Chang, Hannelore Huber, Barbara Karl, Beate**
**Kuntz, Herbert Markert, Reiner Nagel, Susanne Nobis,**
**Dagmar Plankermann, Horst Raab, Heinz Riegel**
**Structural framework design: Schlaich, Bergermann &**
**Partner, Stuttgart**

Die Südfassade der Halle wird durch feststehende, vorgesetzte Sonnenschutzlamellen zusätzlich gegliedert.
The hall's south facade is given added structure by fixed sunshade slats mounted on its exterior.

Während der Weltausstellung wird ein Teil
der Halle als Eingangsbereich genutzt.
A part of the hall is to be used as an
entrance area during the World Exposition.

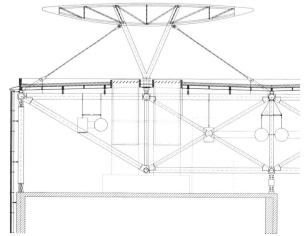

Schnitt durch einen Venturi-Flügel
Sectional view through a Venturi flap

Nordfassade entlang der Allee der
Vereinigten Bäume
The north facade facing United Trees
Avenue

# Servicegebäude und Public Design
## Service Buildings and Public Design

# Eingang Süd
## South Entrance

Das Weltausstellungsgelände ist über insgesamt sechs Eingänge zu erreichen. Die Eingänge West, Nordost und Ost sind in Gebäude integriert, der Eingang Nord wurde als bestehender Eingang zum Messegelände übernommen, und die Eingänge Nordwest und Süd wurden als temporäre Einrichtungen geplant. Der sechste, der neu errichtete Eingang Süd, wird hier exemplarisch vorgestellt. Er bildet zusammen mit dem Seerestaurant den baulichen Abschluss der Westschiene des Pavillongeländes Ost. Die Zugangsfunktion wird durch eine markante Torsituation mit flankierenden Gebäudeteilen gebildet. Die homogen wirkenden Gebäudekörper bestehen aus Raummodulen in Stahlrahmenbauweise, ihre Fassaden sind geprägt durch vorgestellte Sonnenschutzelemente. Diese geschosshohen, regalartigen Holzkassetten haben einen umlaufenden, 15 Zentimeter starken Holzrahmen mit eingesetzten, flach geneigten, 15 Zentimeter breiten Holzlamellen aus transparent lasiertem Nadelholz. Der von den Gebäuden eingefasste Eingang erinnert in seiner Ausführung an ein altes Stadttor in einer Stadtmauer, die filigrane Stahl-Vordach-Konstruktion unterstützt diesen Tor-Charakter zusätzlich. Der Eingang wurde so dimensioniert, dass er in der Hauptanreisezeit von rund 35.000 Besuchern genutzt werden kann.

Im südlichen Teil des Eingangsgebäudes liegt ein Café-Restaurant, das mit seiner stegähnlichen Terrasse in den angrenzenden See beziehungsweise in die Wassergärten ragt. Die anderen Gebäudebereiche werden von der Zugangskontrolle, von Sicherheitseinrichtungen, Information und Merchandising oder von Serviceeinrichtungen wie beispielsweise der Gepäckaufbewahrung genutzt.

The grounds of the World Exposition are accessible through six entrances. The West, Northeast and East Entrances are incorporated into standing buildings, the existing entrance to the trade fair grounds was retained as the North Entrance, and the Northwest and South Entrances were designed as temporary gates. The sixth gate, the newly erected South Entrance, is described here as an example. Together with the Lakeside Restaurant, it forms the architectural boundary of the western sector of the East Pavilion Site. Its function as a point of access is marked by a prominent gateway configuration flanked by building segments. The homogeneous buildings consist of three-dimensional steel-framework modules and facades with mounted sunscreens. These one-story high, shelflike wooden units are enclosed in 15-centimeter-thick wooden frames containing inset, 15-centimeter-wide, flat softwood slats with a transparent varnish finish. The design of the entrance framed by the building is reminiscent of an old gate in a city wall, and the filigreed steel canopy construction lends further emphasis to this impression. The entrance was made large enough to accommodate approximately 35,000 visitors during the most popular arrival times.

Located in the southern section of the entrance building is a café-restaurant with a pier-style patio that extends over the adjacent lake and into the Aquatic Gardens. The other parts of the building are occupied by the admissions control section, security facilities, the Information and Merchandising Departments and by service facilities such as the luggage deposit room.

Entwurf: Garriock & Associates, Uetze
Design: Garriock & Associates, Uetze

Blick vom Vorplatz durch das Eingangstor
View of the square through the entrance

Der Gastronomiebereich des Eingangsgebäudes ragt in den See.
The lakefront restaurant area of the entrance building

# Vorplatz Eingang Süd
# Square at the South Entrance

**Entwurf: Landschaftsarchitekt Kamel Louafi, Berlin**
**Design: Landscape architect Kamel Louafi, Berlin**

**Der Kanal begrenzt den Platz im Süden.**
The canal forms the southern boundary
of the square.

Entsprechend seiner Lage und Umgebung ist dem Eingang Süd ein großzügiger Platz vorgelagert. Die räumliche Komposition des Vorplatzes ist geprägt durch die künstliche Anhöhe des Expo-Parks, die Ausrichtung der Fußgängerbrücke, den Himmelsturm, den Wasserkanal, durch eine Sitztreppe zwischen dem Kanal und der Brücke sowie durch eine nördlich davon angeordnete Pappelreihe. Von der Brücke und der Sitztreppe aus können Besucher sowohl den Eingang als auch die Öffnung des Parks zur Landschaft überblicken. Die Schnittstelle zwischen Sitztreppe und Brücke bildet eine »Spanische Wand« mit blauer Mosaikkeramik. Die Pappeln nördlich des Eingangs sind im regelmäßigen Abstand von 10 Metern angeordnet und bieten damit in den Zwischenräumen Platz für Fahrradständer und Servicekioske. Ein Regen- und Sonnendach gewährt Wartenden Schutz vor Witterungseinflüssen.

Der Platz ist zwischen der Pappelreihe, der Fußgängerbrücke, dem Kanal und dem Eingangsgebäude durch ein 5 x 5-Meter-Raster von Metallplatten und Beleuchtungskörpern strukturiert, die in die bitumenhaltige Deckschicht eingelassen sind. Als Orientierungshilfe für Behinderte wurde entlang des Wasserkanals im Abstand von 1 Meter ein Steinband mit deutlich gerillter Oberfläche verlegt, das gleichzeitig als Entwässerungslinie ausgebildet ist. Die einzelnen Gestaltungselemente fügen sich zu einem Gesamtbild zusammen und definieren den Vorplatz als einen Bereich mit hoher Aufenthaltsqualität.

In keeping with its location and surroundings, a large square has been laid out in front of the South Entrance. The spatial boundaries of the square defined by the man-made hill of Expo Park, the pedestrian bridge, the Sky Tower, the canal, the amphitheater-style stairs between the canal and the bridge and a row of poplars to the north. Visitors standing on the bridge or sitting on the stairs have a view of both the entrance and the point at which the park opens into the landscape. The interface linking the amphitheater stairs and the bridge is a "Spanish Wall" covered with blue mosaic tiles. The poplars to the north of the entrance are spaced at regular intervals of ten meters and thus provide space for bicycle stands and service kiosks. A combination rain-and-sun canopy offers waiting visitors shelter in inclement weather.

The area of the square bordered by the poplars, the pedestrian bridge, the canal and the entrance building is structured by a gridwork pattern of metal plates measuring five by five meters and flush lamps set into the bituminous paving surface. A paved pathway with a grooved surface was laid along the canal (at a distance of one meter from the water) as an aid to orientation for the disabled. It also serves as a water drainage line. The individual elements of design meld together into a harmonious whole that contributes to the high quality of the square as a setting for visitors.

**Säulenförmige Pappeln und die Überdachung prägen den Vorplatz im Norden.**
Columnar poplars and the roof are the most striking features of the northern end of the square.

# Modulares Kiosksystem
# Modular Kiosk System

Ein dichtes Netz von kleinen Serviceeinrichtungen überzieht das Weltausstellungsgelände. Das modulare Baukastensystem dieser Kioske ermöglicht ein hohes Maß an Vorfertigung und flexiblen Nutzungen, etwa als Gastronomie-Stände, Book-Stores, Sanitäreinrichtungen, Tageskassen oder Servicemodule für Getränke- oder Snackautomaten. Unterschiedliche Funktionspaneele wie Türöffnungen, Fenstereinheiten, Klappläden oder Kassenfronten in einem Grundraster von 1 x 1 Meter bieten eine große Variationsbreite. Durch die Tafelbauweise aus 6 Zentimeter starken Massivholzplatten war eine einfache Vormontage der Paneele möglich; nach der Demontage sind die Einzelelemente in neuer Kombination wieder verwendbar. Die Signalisation der jeweiligen Nutzung erfolgt über bedruckte textile Fahnen im Rastermaß, die mit Querstäben und Gewindespannern an die Verbindungsknoten angeschraubt und jederzeit austauschbar sind. Werden die normalen L-Stahlprofile an den Außenecken der Baukörper durch U-Profile ersetzt, ist eine Addition der Kioske zu größeren Einheiten möglich. Neben der 16 Quadratmeter großen Grundversion sind auch kleinere Servicemodule mit 6 und 8 Quadratmetern Grundfläche im Einsatz. Aus dem gleichen Baukastenprinzip bestehen auch die 100 und 150 Quadratmeter großen Merchandising-Stores aus Glas- und Holzelementen sowie die 144 Quadratmeter großen Info-Pavillons mit umlaufender Holzsitzbank und Tafeloberfläche.

The grounds of the World Exposition are covered by a dense network of small service facilities. The modular kiosk system permits a substantial degree of prefabrication and provides for flexibility of use – as refreshment stands, book shops, sanitary facilities, ticket booths or service units for beverage and snack machines. Different types of functional panels, including door frames, window units, shutters or cashier's windows in basic one-by-one-meter units provide for considerable variability. The use of uniform elements made of six-centimeter-thick whole-wood sheets made it possible to preassemble the panels easily. Once dismantled, the individual elements can be reused in new combinations. Printed textile flags in modular dimensions hung on crosspieces and attached to connection points with threaded bolts indicate the specific function of each kiosk. The flags can be changed at any time. Replacement of the standard L-shaped steel profiles on the outside corners of the structures with U-shaped profiles makes it possible to connect the kiosks together to form larger units. Aside from the large basic version with 16 square meters of floor space, smaller service modules with six or eight square meters of floor space are also in use. The wood-and-glass merchandising stores (with floor spaces of 100 or 150 square meters) and the information pavilions (144 square meters) with wrap-around benches and tables are constructed on the basis of the same modular principle.

Entwurf: Wiege Entwicklungs GmbH, Bad Münder
Fritz Frenkler, Anette Ponholzer
mit Pergola GmbH & Co. KG, Hannover
Design: Wiege Entwicklungs GmbH, Bad Münder
Fritz Frenkler, Anette Ponholzer
in cooperation with Pergola GmbH & Co. KG, Hanover

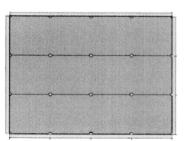

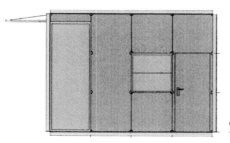

Grundraster des Kiosksystems
The basic configuration of the kiosk system

Einer der rund 30 Gastronomie-Stände auf
dem Weltausstellungsgelände
One of some 30 food and beverage stands
on the grounds of the World Exposition

Die Info-Pavillons sind zentrale Elemente
der Besucherinformation.
The info pavilions are key components of
the visitor information system.

# Schirmüberdachungen
# Umbrella Canopies

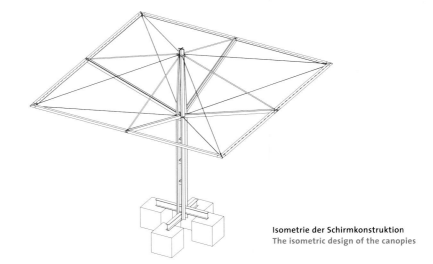

Isometrie der Schirmkonstruktion
The isometric design of the canopies

In Ergänzung zu den Kioskelementen wurden Schirmüberdachungen entwickelt, die Besuchern Schutz vor Sonne oder Regen bieten. Ihr Konstruktionsprinzip ermöglicht die Montage von nach innen oder außen geneigten Membranen und bietet damit ein breites Spektrum unterschiedlicher Erscheinungsformen. Die Tragstruktur der Schirme besteht aus entrostetem, grundiertem und zweifach beschichtetem Stahl. Die einzelnen Konstruktionselemente wurden im Werk vorgefertigt und vor Ort über Schraubverbindungen miteinander verbunden. Jeder Schirm lagert auf Fertigteilfundamenten mit den Abmessungen 80 x 80 x 80 Zentimeter und ist über Gewindeanker mit diesen verbunden. Die Baumwollmembranen sind linienförmig an den Konstruktionselementen befestigt. Die nach innen geneigte Membran ist am Randträger und am Hauptträger angebracht. Bei dieser Form fließt Regenwasser zur Hauptstütze und wird über einen Einlauftopf in das innen liegende Regenfallrohr geleitet. Die nach außen geneigte Membran ist am Randträger und Druckrohr befestigt. Hier wird das Regenwasser im Bereich des Randträgers in einem aufgedoppelten L-förmigen Aluminiumblech gesammelt und über den Hauptträger in das Fallrohr der räumlichen Hauptstütze geführt. Die einzelnen Elemente der Schirme einschließlich der Fundamente können zerstörungsfrei abgebaut und wieder verwendet werden.

Umbrella canopies were developed as an addition to the kiosk elements to provide shelter for visitors against sun and rain. They are designed to accommodate convex or concave shell membranes and thus provide for a wide range of different visual configurations. The supporting structure for the umbrella canopies is made of rust-proof, primed steel with two protective coatings. The individual elements were prefabricated by the manufacturer and assembled with bolt connections on site. Each umbrella canopy stands on a prefabricated footing stone measuring 80 x 80 x 80 centimeters, to which it is firmly attached by threaded anchors. The cotton coverings are fastened to and aligned with the structural elements. The concave membrane coverings are attached to an edge support and the main support. In this type of umbrella, rainwater flows toward the main support and runs into the inside drainpipe through a collection pan. The convex membranes are attached to edge supports and pressure tubes. In these units, rainwater is collected near the edge of the membrane in a gutter formed by a pair of L-shaped aluminum profiles and diverted via the main support into the drainpipe of the three-dimensional main support. All parts of the umbrella canopies, including the footing stones, can be dismantled and removed without damage and used at other locations.

Architekten: Schulitz + Partner, Braunschweig
Tragwerksplanung: Martin Sifflingen – Consulting
Engineers, Braunschweig
Architects: Schulitz + Partner, Braunschweig
Supporting structure design: Martin Sifflingen –
Consulting Engineers, Braunschweig

Die Schirme kommen auf dem Expo-Gelände in unterschiedlichen Variationen zum Einsatz.
The canopies appear in a number of different variations on the Expo grounds.

# Gastronomiegebäude und Möblierung
# Restaurant Buildings and Furnishings

Die insgesamt zwölf Gastronomiegebäude liegen verteilt über die Pavillon-gelände West und Ost. Zwar sind sie unterschiedlich groß, wurden aber alle nach demselben modularen Holzbausystem errichtet. Dieses System besteht aus dem Gastbereich, einem eingeschossigen Hallenteil als Holzständer-konstruktion mit Gebäudehülle, und einem zweigeschossigen rückwärtigen Nebenbereich mit eingestellten Raumzellen innerhalb der Ausfachungen der Gebäudekonstruktion. Eine zweigeschossige Massivholzwand ist in die Holzständerkonstruktion eingespannt und trennt den Gastraum von den Serviceräumen. Die Glasfassade ist eine Holz-Glas-Konstruktion mit einer Feld-aufteilung von 1,7 x 1,7 Meter. Türen und Fenster ermöglichen eine natürliche Belüftung, die Beschattung des Gastraumes erfolgt von innen. Ein filigran ge-stalteter Dachreiter verläuft über die gesamte Länge des vorderen Gebäude-teils, nimmt die nötigen Zuluftkanäle auf und beinhaltet auch zwei seitliche Fensterbänder. Die Dachfläche besteht aus einer Sperrholzplatte, einer 4 Zenti-meter starken Isolierschicht und Dachfolie. Die Randbereiche zu den Ein-gängen sind mit Doppelstegplatten teilweise transluzent gedeckt. Die Raum-module im zweigeschossigen Nebenbereich sind auf die Holzständerkonstruk-tion aufgelegt und werden über Holzstege mit den entsprechenden Treppen und Geländern erschlossen.

Die temporär genutzten Gastronomiegebäude sind so aufgebaut, dass sie nach der Weltausstellung demontiert und an andere Stelle wieder verwendet wer-den können.

Twelve restaurant buildings are distributed over the East and West Pavilion Sites. Although they differ in size, all are based upon the same modular wood-en construction system. This system comprises a guest area, a one-story hall segment as a wooden support structure with building shell and a two-story rear auxiliary section with cells built into the spaces provided by the build-ing structure. A two-story wooden wall is inserted into the wooden support structure and separates the guest area from the service areas. The glass facade is a wood-and-glass construction with openings measuring 1.7 x 1.7 meters. Doors and windows provide for natural ventilation, the guest area is shaded from inside. A filigreed roof turret runs along the entire length of the front part of the building, enclosing the necessary fresh-air vents and incorporating two bands of side windows. The roof surface consists of plywood sheeting, a four-centimeter layer of insulation and roofing foil. The edges around the en-trances are covered with double-webbed plates, some of which are translucent. The modules in the two-story auxiliary area are set on top of the wooden support structure and accessed via wooden walkways with steps and railings. The temporary restaurant buildings are designed to be dismantled after the World Exposition and reused at new locations.

**Entwurf der Gastronomiegebäude:**
**Pergola GmbH & Co. KG, Hannover**
**Design of the restaurant buildings:**
**Pergola GmbH & Co. KG, Hanover**

**Blick auf die Eingangsfront eines Gastro-nomiegebäudes**
View of the front entrance of a restaurant building

**Stuhl »Tom Vac«**
A "Tom Vac" chair

**»Eames Plastic Chair«**
An "Eames Plastic Chair"

**»Expo-Table«**
An "Expo Table"

Die Ausstattungselemente der Gastronomie wurden nach funktionalen und ökologischen Kriterien ausgewählt. Die Tische und Stühle sind stapelbar und damit leicht und flexibel zu handhaben. Ihre Konstruktion folgt dem Prinzip der Reduktion, ihr Erscheinungsbild unterstützt kommunikatives Verhalten. Der Stuhl »Tom Vac«, ein Entwurf von Ron Arad, hat eine Sitzschale mit Wellenstruktur aus durchgefärbtem Polypropylen. Sein Vierbein-Stahlrohruntergestell ist verchromt und pulverbeschichtet und ermöglicht das Stapeln von bis zu fünf Stühlen. Durch die verwendeten Materialien kann der Stuhl auch im Freien genutzt werden.

The furnishing elements in the restaurant buildings were selected on the basis of functional and environmental criteria. The tables and chairs can be stacked for easy, flexible handling. They are designed in accordance with the principle of reduction, and their configuration fosters communication.
The "Tom Vac" chair, designed by Ron Arad, has an undulating surface made of tinted polypropylene. Its four-legged steel-tube stand construction has a chrome, powder-coated surface and permits the chairs to be stacked in groups of up to five. The chair materials are weather-resistant and can be used outdoors.

**Entwurf: Ron Arad**
**Design: Ron Arad**

Alternativ zu dem Modell »Tom Vac« wird in der Gastronomie stellenweise auch der in den Veranstaltungsstätten eingesetzte Stuhl »Eames Plastic Chair« genutzt. Der von dem Designerpaar Charles und Ray Eames vor rund 50 Jahren entwickelte Stuhl besitzt ebenfalls eine durchgefärbte Sitzschale aus Polypropylen. Er wird in verschiedenen Ausführungen angeboten: mit einem stapelbaren Vierbein-Stahlrohruntergestell mit und ohne Reihenkupplung sowie mit einem nicht-stapelbaren, verstrebten Stahldrahtuntergestell.

As an alternative to the "Tom Vac" model, some of the restaurants and event venues use the "Eames Plastic Chair." Developed by the designers Charles and Ray Eames some 50 years ago, these chairs also have a tinted seat made of polypropylene. They are available in different versions: with a stackable four-legged steel-tube stand construction, with or without row connectors, and with a non-stackable, strutted, steel-wire stand construction.

**Entwurf: Charles und Ray Eames**
**Design: Charles and Ray Eames**

Als ideale Ergänzung zu den formschönen und bequemen Stühlen dient der von Vitra entwickelte »Expo-Table«. Den stapelbaren Bistrotisch gibt es mit runder und quadratischer Tischfläche, jeweils mit einem Durchmesser oder einer Kantenlänge von 70, 80 und 90 Zentimetern. Mit seinen pulverbeschichteten Stahlrohreinzelfüßen und der gegen Hitze und Feuchtigkeit beständigen Tischplatte wird der »Expo-Table« auch im Freien eingesetzt.

The ideal complement to the attractive and comfortable chairs is the "Expo Table" designed by Vitra. This stackable bistro table is available with a round or square top in diameters or edge lengths of 70, 80 and 90 centimeters. With its powder-coated individual steel tube legs and the heat- and moisture-resistant tabletop, the "Expo Table" can also be used outdoors.

**Entwurf: Vitra, Weil am Rhein /**
**Büro-Concept Klingenberg, Hannover**
**Design: Vitra, Weil am Rhein /**
**Büro-Concept Klingenberg, Hanover**

# Möblierung des öffentlichen Raumes
## Furnishings in Public Spaces

Das hochwertige Sitzmöbelsystem »Level 2000« bietet mit seinen unterschiedlichen Elementen sehr flexible Nutzungsmöglichkeiten. Das Spektrum reicht von Einzelsitzen ohne Lehnen bis zu einer Bank für vier Personen mit Rücken- und Armlehnen, die in zahlreichen Formen kombiniert werden können. In immer neuen Zusammenstellungen stehen die Bänke den Besuchern auf dem Weltausstellungsgelände zur Verfügung. Die Sitz- und Rückenflächen können mit unterschiedlichen Materialien ausgestattet werden; ein besonderes Merkmal des Systems ist der nachträglich vor Ort mögliche Austausch einzelner Flächen. Die Tragkonstruktion der Bänke besteht zu fast 100 Prozent aus recyceltem Aluminium. Die Sitz- und Rückenflächen der Grundversion bestehen aus Stahlblech, dessen spezielle Langlochung das Erscheinungsbild der Bänke prägt und einen schnellen Ablauf von Regenwasser und eine gute Belüftung gewährleistet. Das Basismaterial ist oberflächenvorbehandelt und im Farbton »Graualuminium« spezialfarbbeschichtet.

Die Fahrradbügel »Level 2000« haben mit dem Sitzmöbelsystem nicht nur den Namen, sondern auch das Material gemeinsam: Das zentrale Stangenpressprofil besteht aus nahezu 100 Prozent recyceltem Aluminium, die Ständer sind oberflächenvorbehandelt und spezialfarbbeschichtet. In den zwei Längsnuten des Stangenprofils sind jeweils zwei Bügel als Anlehn- beziehungsweise Anschlusshilfe befestigt, sodass von beiden Seiten Fahrräder an dem Rahmen angeschlossen und optimal gesichert werden können. Sind mehrere Fahrradständer in einer Reihe aufgestellt, werden sie mit durchlaufenden Rohren verbunden, die gleichzeitig die Position der Vorderräder bestimmen. Eine Verlängerung des Stangenprofils ermöglicht auch die Befestigung von Elementen des Leit- und Orientierungssystems.

The high-quality "Level 2000" seating-furniture system offers a variety of different elements for multipurpose use. The spectrum ranges from single chairs without backs to benches with backs and arm rests. The latter type accommodates four persons, and all can be combined in numerous different ways. These benches are made available to visitors in many different configurations on the grounds of the World Exposition. The seats and backs can be covered with different materials. A unique feature of the system is the interchangeability of the seat and back elements, which can be replaced as desired on site. Nearly 100 percent of the material used in the bench support constructions is recycled aluminum. The seats and backs of the basic version are made of sheet steel with a special longitudinal perforation that gives them an unmistakable look and also ensures rapid rainwater runoff and good ventilation. The basic material is surface-treated and coated with a special "aluminum-gray" paint.

The "Level 2000" bicycle racks share more than a name with the seating-furniture system. They are also made of the same material. The central extruded bar segment consists almost entirely of recycled aluminum. The stands are surface-treated and given a special coating of paint. Pairs of brackets are attached as leaning or locking braces to the two longitudinal grooves of the bar segment on each side, so that bicycles can be fit and locked into the rack and reliably secured. Where several bicycle stands are arranged in a row, they are connected by a single pipe that also fixes the position of the front wheels. An extension of the bar segment also makes it possible to attach elements of the Guidance and Orientation System to the bicycle racks

Entwurf »Level 2000«: Wiege Entwicklungs GmbH,
Bad Münder
Fritz Frenkler, Anette Ponholzer
mit Mabeg Kreuschner GmbH & Co. KG, Soest
Ausrüster: Mabeg Kreuschner GmbH & Co. KG, Soest
Design for "Level 2000": Wiege Entwicklungs GmbH,
Bad Münder
Fritz Frenkler, Anette Ponholzer
in cooperation with Mabeg Kreuschner GmbH & Co. KG,
Soest
Supplier: Mabeg Kreuschner GmbH & Co. KG, Soest

**Sitzbank »Level 2000«**
A "Level 2000" bench

**Fahrradbügel »Level 2000«**
A "Level 2000" bicycle rack

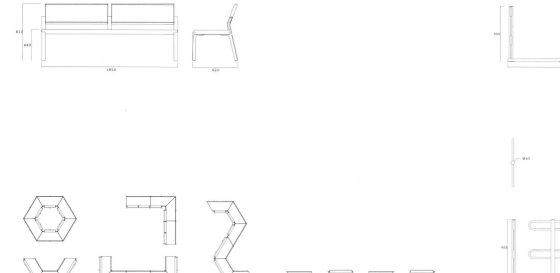

**Grundrisse**
Floor plans

**Grundrisse**
Floor plans

# Masterplan Licht
# Lighting Master Plan

Der Masterplan Licht wurde so entworfen, dass er die unterschiedlichen Licht-verhältnisse – vom bewölkten Himmel über die Dämmerung bis zur völligen Dunkelheit – sinnvoll mit Kunstlicht ergänzt und gleichzeitig gestalterisch nutzt. Er schafft ein dichtes Netz, welches das gesamte Weltausstellungs-gelände mit Lichtquellen überspannt. Die speziell entwickelte Expo-Leuchten-familie sorgt dabei für das Grundlicht auf dem Gelände und bildet das ge-stalterische Rückgrat. Diese Außenleuchten ermöglichen Orientierung, heben Achsen oder Kreuzungsbereiche hervor und gliedern Verkehrsflächen. Sie haben ein sachlich orientiertes Erscheinungsbild und drängen sich nicht in den Vordergrund. Sie lassen verschiedene Lichtcharakteristika und verschiedene Lichtpunkthöhen zu. Ihre Höhe reicht in vier Stufen von Licht in 1 Meter Höhe bis zu 16 Meter hohen Masten, die beispielsweise zur Beleuchtung der Park-plätze eingesetzt werden. Die Lichtpunkthöhe beeinflusst die Lichtatmosphäre. Ein hoher Lichtpunkt verbreitet ein gleichmäßiges, aber eher anonym wirken-des Licht, ein niedriger Lichtpunkt schafft ansprechendes Licht und eine ver-traute Atmosphäre. Jeder der zahlreichen Geländebereiche wird entsprechend seiner Funktion und Gestaltung individuell beleuchtet. Das Funktionslicht der Expo-Leuchten wird gezielt durch Stimmungs- und Gestaltungsbeleuchtung wie beispielsweise durch die im Boden eingelassenen Expo-Marks oder Solar-gräser ergänzt. So sorgt der Masterplan Licht für ein variantenreiches und gleichzeitig immer stimmiges Gesamtbild.

The Lighting Master Plan was drafted in such a way that it provides for the effective use of artificial light under different outside light conditions – from cloudy skies to dusk to complete darkness – to ensure sufficient illumina-tion and to enhance the visual effects of the Expo grounds and facilities. The result is a dense network of lighting elements that covers the entire complex. The Expo lamp series designed especially for the World Exposition supplies the basic lighting for the grounds and represents the aesthetic backbone of the overall design. These outdoor lights serve as aids to orientation, emphasize axes and intersections and structure traffic areas. They have an unobtrusive appearance and do not attract attention. They allow for different light charac-teristics and different light-focus points. They range in height from one meter to the 16-meter-high masts used, for example, to illuminate the parking lots. The light-focus level influences the light atmosphere. A high light-focus point distributes a uniform but impersonal light, while a low light-focus point cre-ates an appealing lighting effect and an atmosphere of familiarity. Each of the many different areas on the grounds is furnished with the amount and quality of light that suits its function and design. The functional lighting provided by the Expo lamps is systematically complemented by mood and design lighting, such as the Expo Marks set in the ground or the solar grasses. Thus the Master Lighting Plan provides for a highly varied yet consistently appropriate overall lighting scheme.

**Entwurf: Ulrike Brandi Licht, Hamburg**
**Mitarbeiter: Ulrike Brandi, Mariana Müller-Wiefel, Oliver Ost**
**Expo-Leuchten: Sill, Berlin**
Design: Ulrike Brandi Licht, Hamburg
Staff: Ulrike Brandi, Mariana Müller-Wiefel, Oliver Ost
Expo lamps: Sill, Berlin

**Expo-Leuchten am Europa Boulevard auf dem Pavillongelände Ost**
Expo lamps along Europa Boulevard on the East Pavilion Site

Der Masterplan Licht bietet einen Über-blick über die Beleuchtung der unter-schiedlichen Ausstellungsbereiche des Weltausstellungsgeländes.
The Master Lighting Plan provides an over-view of the lighting scheme for the various exhibition areas on the World Exposition Site.

EXPO2000
HANNOVER

0    100m    200m    300m    400m

# Leuchten
# Lights and Lamps

Die Expo-Marks sind dekorative Lichtelemente, die zur Betonung einzelner Bereiche beispielsweise an Eingängen oder auf Plätzen eingesetzt werden. Die Bodeneinbauleuchten versorgen sich selbst mit Energie und sind damit unabhängig von einer Elektroinstallation: Die Spannungsversorgung erfolgt über ein Fotovoltaikmodul unterhalb der Glasabdeckplatte, einen Spannungswandler, eine Ladeschaltung und ein Akku-Modul. An den Seitenflächen zwischen dem Fotovoltaikmodul und der Glasplatte angeordnete Linsendioden in unterschiedlichen Farben geben ihr Licht horizontal ab. Die Glasplatte ist mit einem Motiv, hier dem Expo-Logo, in einem Punktraster weiß bedruckt. Dadurch wird eine Totalreflexion des Lichts unterbrochen, sodass das Licht nach oben austreten kann. Eine Ablaufsteuerung macht unterschiedliche Farb- und Lichtspiele möglich; ein integrierter Dämmerungsschalter aktiviert das Lichtelement am Abend.

The Expo Marks are decorative lighting elements used to highlight specific areas such as entrances or squares. These built-in flush lamps generate their own energy and thus require no electrical installation. Current for these lamps is produced by a photovoltaic module beneath the glass cover plate, a voltage converter, a charging circuit and a rechargeable battery unit. Lens diodes of different colors positioned on the sides between the photovoltaic module and the glass plate emit light in a horizontal direction. The glass cover plate bears a motif printed in a dot-matrix pattern – in this case the Expo logo. This defracts the total reflection of the light, directing light upward. A program control system makes it possible to create different effects of light and color. The lighting unit is activated at night by an integrated dusk sensor-switch.

**Entwurf: Dinnebier Licht, Wuppertal**
**Design: Dinnebier-Licht, Wuppertal**

Expo-Marks
Expo Marks

**Solargräser im Expo-See**
Solar grasses at Expo Lake

Solargräser aus federndem Edelstahl betonen abends den Expo-See am Hermesturm. Ihre 9 Meter langen, filigranen Stängel treten optisch zurück. Sichtbar sind vor allem die Blüten mit der fotovoltaischen Lichteinheit und ihre Schatten. Die Solarmodule laden sich tagsüber auf und beginnen in der Dämmerung ihre Energie als Licht abzugeben. Zum einen sind die Spitzen der Gräser beleuchtet, zum anderen erzeugen präzise fokussierte Spotlights Projektionen von 1 Meter Durchmesser, die durch die Bewegung des Windes ellipsenförmig über den Boden wandern. Die Gräser sind mit Wurzeln aus Edelstahl, die auch den Energiespeicher enthalten, fest im Boden verankert. Die Solargräser sind so im See verteilt, dass die Wasserfläche die nötige Distanz schafft, damit die Besucher die Installation ganz überblicken können.

Solar grasses made of flexible stainless steel highlight Expo Lake near the Hermes Tower during the hours of darkness. Their nine-meter-long filigreed stalks are unobtrusive in appearance. The readily visible elements are the blossoms, equipped with a photovoltaic lighting unit, and their shadows. The solar modules charge themselves during the day and begin emitting their energy as light at dusk. The tips of the grasses are illuminated, and precisely focused spotlights generate projections measuring one meter in diameter, which wander over the ground as ellipses of light in response to movements caused by the wind. The grasses are firmly anchored in the ground by stainless-steel roots, which also contain the rechargeable batteries. These solar grasses are distributed in the lake in such a way that the water's surface establishes distance sufficient to allow visitors a full view of the installation.

**Entwurf: Christoph Behling, London**
**Design: Christoph Behling, London**

# Entsorgungskonzept
## Waste Disposal System

**Wastecontainer**
A waste container

Für das komplette Entsorgungsmanagement der Weltausstellung ist die Duales System Deutschland AG, Weltpartner der EXPO 2000, verantwortlich. Erstmals werden auf einer Veranstaltung dieser Größenordnung Abfalltrennung und der Aufbau von Wertstoffkreisläufen konsequent umgesetzt. Das Duale System erstellt für die Arbeitsphasen Aufbau, Betrieb und Rückbau der EXPO individuelle Entsorgungskonzepte, die alle anfallenden Materialfraktionen einbeziehen. Für den Expo-Besucher werden auf dem gesamten Gelände Leichtverpackungen (LVP), Papier, Pappe, Karton (PPK) sowie, nach Farben getrennt, Glas gesammelt und anschließend einer Verwertung zugeführt; zusätzlich werden die Restabfälle erfasst. Für die Expo-Teilnehmer und Konzessionäre wie Restaurants und Imbissverkäufer besteht zudem die Möglichkeit der getrennten Erfassung von Bio- und Sonderabfall. Um Besuchern, die mit dem System der Abfalltrennung weniger vertraut sind, zu verdeutlichen, in welche Behälter die verschiedenen Abfälle eingeworfen werden, wurden leicht verständliche Piktogramme entwickelt.

Das Entsorgungssystem besteht aus drei »Sammelelementen« unterschiedlicher Größe. In 1.500 Abfallbehältern auf dem Gelände, die mit einem Aschenbecher kombiniert sind, werden Leichtverpackungen und Restabfall gesammelt, zudem an 95 Standorten in Depotcontainern Glas und Papier. Die größten Einheiten sind die modular aufgebauten Waste-Guard-Stationen, in denen die anfallenden Abfälle aus den Behältern und Containern zusammengeführt werden. Alle Einrichtungen wurden eigens für die EXPO entwickelt; ihre Materialien Edelstahl und Recycling-Kunststoff prägen das »saubere« Erscheinungsbild des Gesamtauftritts des Unternehmens mit dem Grünen Punkt. Alle Flächen und Behälter werden mehrmals täglich gereinigt, der Abtransport der Materialien erfolgt ausschließlich nachts.

Sole responsibility for waste management at the World Exposition is in the hands of Duales System Deutschland AG, global partner of EXPO 2000. For the very first time at an event of this magnitude, consistent waste separation and material recycling systems have been put into operation. Duales System has developed individualized waste-management concepts for all three phases of EXPO 2000: preparation, exposition operations and reconversion. These concepts take into account all types of waste materials. Lightweight packaging, paper and cardboard will be separated and recycled. Glass will be collected, separated by color and recycled. Residual waste will be collected and processed as well. Expo participants and concessionaires, such as restaurant and snack-bar operators, will also be able to collect biodegradable and hazardous waste materials separately. Easily understandable pictograms have been developed for the purposes of showing visitors who may not be completely familiar with the waste-separation system which containers to use for the disposal of specific waste materials.

The waste disposal system consists of a large number of "collection elements" in three different sizes. Lightweight packaging materials and residual waste are collected in 1,500 trash bins distributed throughout the grounds. Collection containers for glass and paper are also positioned at 95 different locations. The largest units are the modular Waste-Guard Stations in which waste from the bins and containers is collected. All of these items were developed especially for EXPO 2000. Made of stainless steel and recycled plastic, their appearance underscores the "clean" overall image of the company identified by the green dot. All areas are cleaned several times a day, along with all bins and containers. Waste material transports take place only at night.

**Entwurf der Container und Waste-Guard-Stationen:**
**yellowcircle, Köln**
**Design of containers and Waste-Guard stations:**
**yellowcircle, Cologne**

**Depotcontainer**
A depot container

**Waste-Guard-Station**
A Waste-Guard station

# Leit- und Orientierungssystem
## Guidance and Orientation System

Als Bestandteil des Gestaltungskonzeptes der EXPO 2000 hilft das Leit- und Orientierungssystem den Besuchern, sich zu informieren und räumlich zu orientieren. Bei der Beschilderung wurde größter Wert auf das Erscheinungsbild gelegt. Die Formate der Schilder, die Konstruktion der Träger, die Farben, die Schriftwahl und das Layout sind genauestens aufeinander abgestimmt.
Zu den Grundelementen gehören die durchgängig verwendete Schrift »Thesis« und die Farbkombination Blau und Weiß, die aufgrund des Kontrastes beispielsweise für Piktogramme oder die Führungsbeschilderung benutzt wird. Für Informationseinrichtungen und Lagepläne wurde die signalhaft wirkende Farbe Gelb in Verbindung mit Grau gewählt.
Grundsätzlich wird zwischen Führungs-, Bereichs- und Sonderbeschilderung unterschieden. Hauptelemente sind dabei die ortsmarkierenden Masten und die quadratischen Informationstafeln mit Richtungsangaben, die hochformatigen Informationsfahnen der Gebäude- und Pavillonbeschriftungen, die Piktogramme der Dienstleistungen und der Lageplan. Bei der Hallenbeschriftung weisen hochformatige Transparente durch unterschiedliche Farben auf die jeweiligen Inhalte hin.

An integral part of the overall design concept for EXPO 2000, the Guidance and Orientation System assists visitors in obtaining information and finding their way about the grounds. Significant emphasis was placed upon the appearance of signs. The shape and size, the construction of signposts, colors, print types and layout of all signs are precisely coordinated.
The basic elements include the "Thesis" print font used on all signs and the combination of blue and white – which is well suited for pictograms and directional signs by virtue of its marked contrast. The signal color yellow is combined with gray for information facilities and maps.
A categorical distinction is made between directional signs, identification signs and special-purpose signs. The main elements are masts identifying sites, square information panels with directional indicators, vertical-format information banners on buildings and pavilions, pictograms identifying service facilities and map items. Different colored banners in vertical formats provide information about the contents of exhibition halls.

**Entwurf: Büro für Gestaltung Prof. Eberhard Stauß**
**Ursula Wangler, München**
Design: Büro für Gestaltung Prof. Eberhard Stauss
Ursula Wangler, Munich

Hallen- und Gebäudebeschriftung
Hall and building identification

**Führungsbeschilderung**
Guide signs

**Führungsbeschilderung der Serviceeinrichtungen**
Guide signs for service facilities

**Piktorgrammtransparent an einem Infostand**
Pictogram banner at an info stand

**Pavillonbeschilderung**
Pavilion identification

# Verkehrsprojekte
## Traffic and Transportation Projects

Damit Besucher aus aller Welt schnell und bequem zum Expo-Gelände anreisen können, wurde vor allem der öffentliche Nahverkehr benutzerfreundlich und gleichzeitig ökologisch verträglich gestaltet. Die Verkehrsinfrastruktur der Region Hannover wurde zu diesem Zweck weiter verbessert, wobei 90 Prozent der Mittel in den Ausbau des Schienennetzes im Nah- und Fernbereich investiert wurden. Architektonisch wurden dabei neue Maßstäbe gesetzt und die notwendigen neuen Verkehrsgebäude adäquat gestaltet. Der kombinierte Fern- und S-Bahnhof Laatzen, der daran anschließende Skywalk als Zubringer zum Weltausstellungsgelände, die Endhaltestelle der neuen Stadtbahn-Linie D und der Heliport bieten Reisenden großen Komfort und hohe architektonische Qualität.

In order to ensure visitors from around the world quick and comfortable access to the EXPO grounds, considerable investments were made in the design of the public transportation system with an eye to user-convenience and principles of environmental protection. The traffic and transportation infrastructure in the Hanover region was improved with that end in mind, and 90 percent of investments were funneled into the expansion of the local and long-distance railway network. In the process, new architectural standards were set, and necessary new transportation buildings with suitable design features were erected. The combined long-distance railway and light rail transit station Laatzen, the connecting Skywalk which conveys visitors to the World Exposition grounds, the terminal for the new light rail transit line D and the heliport offer travelers a maximum of comfort and architectural quality.

# Bahnhof Hannover-Messe / Laatzen
# Hannover-Messe / Laatzen Railway Station

Das Erscheinungsbild des neuen Bahnhofs wird hauptsächlich durch sein gebogenes Dach geprägt. Mit zwei räumlichen Fachwerkbindern überspannt es die Hallenebene auf einer Länge von rund 90 Metern und weist mit seinem höchsten Punkt in Richtung Weltausstellungsgelände. Der Bahnhof ist auf eine Nutzung durch 180.000 Reisende täglich ausgerichtet. Zur sicheren und leistungsfähigen Abwicklung der Verkehrsströme wurden die Bahnsteige auf einer Länge von 125 Metern zweigeschossig ausgebildet. Die Bahnhofshalle liegt über den Ferngleisen und beinhaltet die Serviceeinrichtungen der Deutschen Bahn AG wie Reisezentrum, Reisefrische, Service Point und Schließfachanlage sowie Bereiche für private Dienstleister. Die massive Sockelstruktur der Bahnhofshalle findet als »Stadtloggia« ihre Fortsetzung über den Bahnhofsvorplatz und entlang der angrenzenden Straße. Wie bei vielen historischen Vorbildern sind die Sockelbereiche des Bahnhofs in Naturstein ausgebildet, das Hallendach besteht aus Stahl und Holz, und die Fassaden sind aus Stahl und Glas.

The most prominent visual feature of the new railway station is its arched roof. Supported by two three-dimensional latticework beams, it spans the station area along a stretch of some 90 meters and points at its highest level toward the World Exposition grounds. The railway station is designed to accommodate as many as 180,000 travelers per day. In the interest of the safe and efficient management of moving traffic, platforms were built on two levels, each 125 meters long. The station lobby lies above the long-distance tracks and houses the service facilities of the Deutsche Bahn AG, including a travel center, sanitary facilities, a service point and luggage lockers as well as spaces for private service providers. The massive base structure of the station lobby extends as a "city loggia" across the station square and along the adjacent street. As in many of its historical predecessors, the base of the railway station is built of natural stone. The roof is made of steel and wood and the facades of steel and glass.

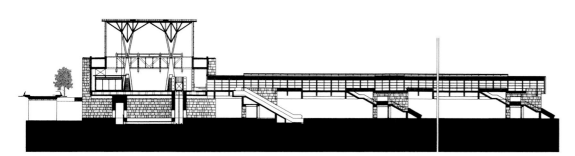

**Querschnitt**
Cross section

**Architekten: Architekten Gössler, Hamburg**
**Freischaffende Architekten und Stadtplaner**
**Dipl.-Ing. Bernhard Gössler, mag. arch. Daniel Gössler,**
**Dipl.-Ing. Kerstin Döring, Dipl.-Ing. Martin Kreienbaum**
**Bauherr: DB Station & Service AG, Hannover**
**Architects: Architekten Gössler, Hamburg**
**Freelance architects and urban planners**
**Dipl.-Ing. Bernhard Gössler, mag. arch. Daniel Gössler,**
**Dipl.-Ing. Kerstin Döring, Dipl.-Ing. Martin Kreienbaum**
**Client: DB Station & Service AG, Hanover**

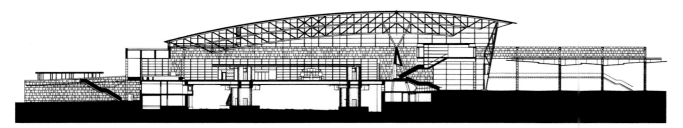

**Längsschnitt**
Longitudinal section

**Südfassade**
The south facade

**Hinter den zweigeschossigen Bahnsteigen
erhebt sich das gebogene Dach.**
The sweeping curve of the roof rises above
the dual-level railway platforms.

Der Bahnhofsvorplatz ist als »Stadtloggia«
ausgebildet.
The station plaza is designed as a "city
loggia."

# Skywalk
# Skywalk

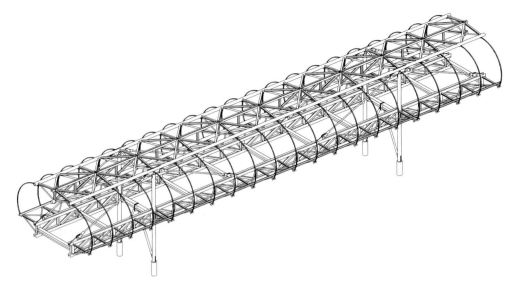

Isometrie – Fachwerkträger und
Stahlrippen bilden die Konstruktion des
Skywalk.
Isometric structure: The Skywalk is con-
structed of lattice girders and steel ribs.

Zwischen dem Bahnhof und dem Eingang West des Weltausstellungsgeländes bietet der 340 Meter lange Skywalk Expo-Besuchern eine schnelle und wetter-geschützte Fußgängerverbindung. Der Entwurf für diese gläserne, aufge-ständerte Transportröhre stammt von dem Braunschweiger Architekturbüro Schulitz + Partner. In der 500 Tonnen schweren Stahlkonstruktion können auf zwei Laufbändern stündlich rund 9.000 Besucher befördert werden. Die Zahl der Stützen des Skywalk wurde so gering wie möglich gehalten, da er über eine Straße führt und der Verkehr nicht behindert werden sollte. Die Konstruk-tion besteht aus der abgespannten Transportebene in 6 Metern Höhe mit Spannweiten von 20, 24 und 28 Metern. Um eine Verformung der Stützen durch die Abspannung zu verhindern, ist ein Druckglied als Viergurtträger in die Dachebene eingefügt, das die horizontalen Kräfte kurzschließt, die Spannweite der Glasfassade auf 4,5 Meter verringert und deren filigrane Ausführung ermöglicht.

The 340-meter-long Skywalk linking the railway station and the West Entrance to the World Exposition Site offers Expo visitors a quick pedestrian connection and protection against inclement weather. This elevated glass tunnel was designed by the architects Schulitz + Partner of Braunschweig. Two rolling sidewalks in the steel structure, which weighs 500 tons, are capable of moving some 9,000 visitors per hour through the Skywalk. The designers limited the number of vertical supports to the extent possible in order to avoid hindering the flow of traffic, as the Skywalk passes over a major street. The structure consists of the guyed transport level six meters above the ground with widths of 20, 24 and 28 meters. In order to prevent deformation of the supports result-ing from the guyed construction, a four-belt beam was built into the roof level as a pusher element to short-circuit the horizontal forces and reduce the width of the glass facade by 4.5 meters, making possible its filigreed design.

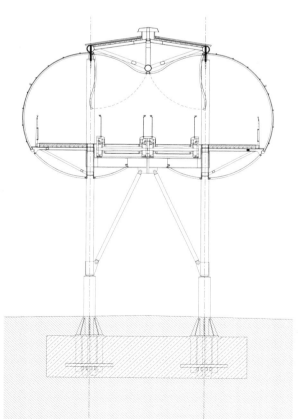

Schnitt durch den Skywalk – in der Mitte
zwischen den Hauptträgern der Fachwerk-
konstruktion liegen die Laufbänder, seitlich
kragen zwei Laufstege aus.
Cross-sectional view of the Skywalk: The
rolling walkways are positioned in the
middle between the steel girders. Two
walkways extend from the sides.

Architekten: Schulitz + Partner, Braunschweig
Bauherr: DB Station & Service AG, Hannover
Prof. Helmut C. Schulitz, Stefan Worbes,
Johannes König, Matthias Rätzel
Tragwerksplanung: RFR, Paris
Architects: Schulitz + Partner, Braunschweig
Client: DB Station & Service AG, Hanover
Prof. Helmut C. Schulitz, Stefan Worbes, Johannes
König, Matthias Rätzel
Framework structure design: RFR, Paris

Der Skywalk beginnt unmittelbar vor dem Bahnhof.
The Skywalk entrance just outside the railway station

Die filigrane Konstruktion trägt entschei-
dend zur ansprechenden Gestaltung des
Skywalk bei.
The filigreed construction contributes to
the overall appeal of the Skywalk's design.

Der Skywalk ermöglicht durch seine großzügige Verglasung einen uneingeschränk-
ten Blick nach draußen.
The glass walls of the Skywalk offer an
unrestricted view of the surrounding area.

In 6 Metern Höhe werden
Expo-Besucher zum
Weltausstellungsgelände
gebracht.
Expo visitors approach the
grounds of the World Exposition six meters above
ground level.

# Stadtbahn-Haltestelle D-Linie
## Light Rail Transit Terminal, Line D

Die neue Stadtbahn-Haltestelle im Osten des Weltausstellungsgeländes hat eine besondere Gestalt bekommen. Die hannoverschen Architekten Bertram und Bünemann haben eine elegante Konstruktion aus Stahl und Glas entworfen, die sich mit ihrer geschwungenen Dachform perfekt der Umgebung anpasst. Die Haltestelle liegt am Hang und überbrückt einen Höhenunterschied von 5 Metern. Mit ihrer Länge von rund 100 Metern ist sie auf ein großes Fahrgastaufkommen ausgerichtet. In Spitzenzeiten verkehren die Bahnen hier im Minutentakt.

The new light rail transit terminal in the eastern section of the World Exposition Site was given a very unique look. The Hanover architects Bertram and Bünemann designed an elegant structure of steel and glass that fits perfectly into its surroundings with its curving roof form. The terminal is situated on a hillside and bridges a drop in elevation of five meters. Nearly 100 meters long, it is designed to accommodate large numbers of travelers. At peak times, trains arrive and depart every minute from this station.

**Architekten: Bertram-Bünemann-Partner-GmbH, Hannover**
**Architects: Bertram-Bünemann-Partner-GmbH, Hanover**

**Mit ihrer offenen und einladenden Gestaltung bereitet die Stadtbahn-Station Besuchern der Weltausstellung einen freundlichen Empfang.**
**The open and inviting design of the light rail transit station presents a friendly welcoming face to Expo visitors.**

**Silberpfeile bringen täglich Tausende von Fahrgästen zur neuen Expo-Haltestelle.**
**"Silver Arrows" bring thousands of visitors to the new Expo station daily.**

# Vorplatz Stadtbahn-Haltestelle D-Linie
## Square at the Light Rail Transit Terminal, Line D

Als Übergang von der Stadtbahn-Haltestelle zur Brücke Ost und zur Plaza wurde die dazwischen liegende Fläche als geschlossener Platz mit leichtem Gefälle gestaltet. Da eine begrenzende Randbebauung fehlt, wurde der Platz in Form eines Erdkörpers nach Süden überhöht und nach Norden geneigt. Die Bewegungsachse liegt zwischen Bahnhof und Brücke. Der dreieckige Platz ist so angelegt, dass im Norden 40 Taxis und 18 Busse halten können, im Westen gibt es 600 Fahrradständer. Durch diese Aufteilung können Fußgänger, ungehindert vom Verkehr, den Platz überqueren. Begrünt ist der Platz im Bereich des Bus-Terminals mit Linden, in der Mitte stehen Palmenkübel im selben Raster wie 190 Fahnenmasten. Dieses Raster nimmt Bezug auf die Gestaltung der Brücke. Die Platzmitte ist mit den gleichen Betonvorsatzsteinen gepflastert wie die Plaza, an der Westseite liegt strapazierfähiger Schotterrasen.

The area between the light rail transit terminal, the East Bridge and the Plaza was designed as a gently sloping enclosed square to facilitate visitor movement between these points. Because there are no buildings marking the boundaries of the area, the square was given the form of an earth mound rising toward the south and sloping toward the north. This places the axis of movement between the railway station and the bridge. The triangular square is designed with space for 40 taxis and 18 buses. Six hundred bicycle stands have been set up on the western side. This configuration enables pedestrians to cross the square without being impeded by vehicle traffic. Linden trees have been planted on the square near the bus terminal, and planted palms are distributed in the same pattern as the 190 flagpoles in its center. This pattern echoes the design of the bridge. The middle portion of the square is paved with the same concrete facing stones as the Plaza. A rugged graveled lawn has been laid out on the western side.

**Entwurf: WES Wehberg, Eppinger, Schmidtke & Partner, Hamburg**
**Design: WES Wehberg, Eppinger, Schmidtke & Partner, Hamburg**

**Fußgänger gehen über den Platz durch ein Fahnenmeer.**
Pedestrians cross the plaza through a sea of flags.

**Blick von der Haltestelle über den Platz**
View of the station across the plaza

# Heliport
## Heliport

Der Heliport liegt östlich des Weltausstellungsgeländes; er wurde mit seiner einfachen quadratischen Grundform jedoch so konzipiert, dass er an unterschiedlichen Standorten zum Einsatz kommen und versetzt werden kann. Seine turmartige Ausbildung verleiht dem Gebäude Prägnanz, die unterschiedlichen Nutzungsbereiche sind übereinander gestapelt. Durch die offene Gestaltung ergeben sich vielfältige vertikale Blickbeziehungen, und die Materialkombination aus Metall und Buchenholz bietet reizvolle Kontraste. Um den Innenraum freizuhalten, wurde die Vertikalerschließung um den Turm geführt – und bildet damit ein gestaltprägendes Element. Der Turm ist aus Schale und Kern gebildet, wobei der Kern als verglastes Stahlgerüst die Nutzungsebenen umfasst. Darum liegt eine Schale, die mit TZ-Rosten verkleidet ist. Die Primärkonstruktion besteht aus mehrteiligen Tragelementen, die aus Profilstahl zusammengesetzt sind. Die Aussteifung erfolgt über Windverbände und Deckenscheiben.

The heliport is located to the east of the World Exposition Site. Due to its simple, square base configuration, however, it can be moved and deployed at different locations. The building's tower extension lends it a particularly striking quality. The various functional areas are stacked on several floors. The open design offers a variety of different views, and the combination of metal and beechwood in the construction creates appealing contrasts. The vertical access route was placed in the tower section in order to keep the interior open and thus becomes a significant design feature. The tower consists of a core and a shell. The glassed-in steel-framework structure of the core encloses the functional levels. Around it is a shell lined on the outside with TZ-alloy grates. The primary structure consists of supporting elements assembled from multiple profile-steel parts. The structure is stabilized by transverse bracing and ceiling plates.

**Architekten: Glaser + Krautwald Architekten, Braunschweig**
**Dipl.-Ing. Peter Glaser, Dipl.-Ing. Thomas Krautwald**
**Architects: Glaser + Krautwald Architekten, Braunschweig**
**Dipl.-Ing. Peter Glaser, Dipl.-Ing. Thomas Krautwald**

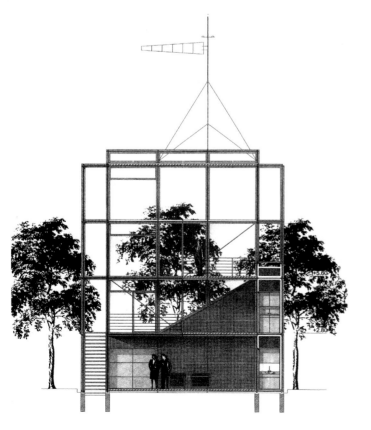

**Schnitt durch das Gebäude**
Cross section of the building

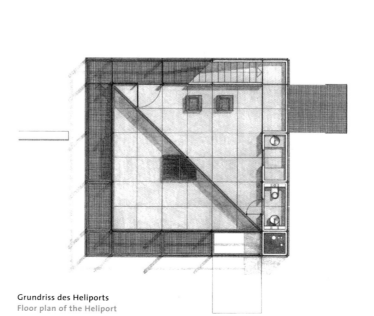

**Grundriss des Heliports**
Floor plan of the Heliport

Der Heliport ist geprägt durch seine offene Gestaltung.
The heliport presents a strikingly open appearance.

Die Verkleidung aus Buchenholz verleiht den Innenräumen einen ansprechenden Charakter.
The beechwood walls inside the building heighten the appeal of the interior.

Die dreieckige Form der oberen Ebenen ermöglicht interessante Blickbeziehungen.
The triangular shape of the upper levels offers a number of fascinating views.

# Register
Index

# Architekten, Designer und Kontaktarchitekten
## Architects, Designers and Contact Architects

# Bildnachweis
# Photo Credits

Ackermann + Partner  242, 244 unten bottom

ARGE KVHH  17 unten bottom, 20 unten bottom, 22 unten bottom, 24

artemedia ag  152

AS & P Albert Speer & Partner  13

Ulrike Brandi Licht  259

Buchhalla + Partner  184

Büro für Gestaltung  9

Atelier Brückner/DSD  108

Luis Guillermo Camargo  112 links oben und unten top left and bottom

Deutsche Telekom/EXPO 2000, Produktion ART+COM AG
 Umschlagseiten front pages

euregio EXPO 2000  228

EXPO GmbH  16, 192, 198 unten bottom, 200, 206

FOJAB arkitekter  166

Fotoform Plus GmbH  255 oben Mitte top middle

Glaser + Krautwald  278

gmp von Gerkan, Marg & Partner  44, 45 unten bottom

Architekten Gössler/Deutsche Bahn AG  267

Herzog + Partner  26, 27

H + Z Bildagentur Hannover, Fotografen photographers: Heinrich Hecht, Karsten Koch, Maurice Korbel, Thomas Nowak, Manoel Nunes, Marc Theis 15, 17 oben top, 18, 19, 20 oben top, 21, 22 oben top, 23, 25, 28, 29, 32, 33, 34, 35, 37, 40, 41, 43, 45 oben top, 46 unten bottom, 47, 48, 49, 50/51, 52, 53, 54, 55, 56, 57, 58, 59, 60, 61, 62, 63, 64, 65, 69, 71, 72 oben top, 73, 75, 76 oben top, 77, 78, 79, 80, 81, 83, 84 oben top, 85, 86, 87, 88 unten bottom, 89, 91, 92 oben top, 93, 95, 96 oben top, 97, 98, 99, 100, 101, 102, 103, 105, 106, 107, 109, 111, 112 rechts right, 113, 116, 117, 118 unten bottom, 119, 120, 121, 123, 125, 127, 129, 130, 131, 132 unten bottom, 133, 134, 135, 137, 138, 139, 140, 141, 142 unten bottom, 143, 145, 146 unten bottom, 147, 149, 151, 153, 155, 156 unten bottom, 157, 158 unten bottom, 159, 160, 161, 163, 164, 165, 167, 168, 169, 171, 172, 173, 174, 175, 177, 179, 181, 182 oben top, 183, 185, 187, 188 oben top, 189, 193, 194, 195, 197, 198 oben top, 199, 201, 202, 203, 205, 207, 211, 213, 214 unten bottom, 215 unten bottom, 217, 219, 220 unten bottom, 221, 223, 225, 227, 229, 230, 231, 233, 235, 237, 238, 241, 243, 244 oben top, 245, 246, 247, 248, 249, 251, 252 unten bottom, 253, 254, 255 links und rechts left and right, 257 oben links und rechts top left and right, 258, 260, 261, 262, 263, 264, 265, 268, 269, 273, 274, 275, 276, 277, 279, 280, 281

H. Leiska  38, 239, 240

Michael Lindner  39

Kamel Louafi  30/31, 36

Pergola GmbH + Co. KG/Wiege Entwicklungs GmbH/EXPO GmbH  250

SARC Architects Ltd.  126, 128

Schulitz + Partner  42, 252 oben top, 270, 271, 272

SIAT Architektur + Technik  74, 76 unten bottom

Tschorz & Tschorz/Deutsche Post  186, 188 unten bottom

Wiege Entwicklungs GmbH/Mabeg Kreuschner GmbH + Co. KG/EXPO GmbH 257 unten bottom

Zeichnungen der Architekten und Modelldarstellungen freigegeben durch den Abteilungs-Generalkommissar des Landes Australien (Seite 68), Belgien (Seite 118 oben), Dänemark (Seite 122), Estland (Seite 124), Griechenland (Seite 132 oben), Irland (Seite 136), Japan (Seite 82, 84 unten), Korea (Seite 88 oben), Kroatien (Seite 146 oben), Lettland (Seite 148), Liechtenstein (Seite 226), Litauen (Seite 150), Mexiko (Seite 90, 92 unten), Niederlande (Seite 156 oben), Norwegen (Seite 158 oben), Monaco (Seite 152), Österreich (Seite 224), Paraguay (Seite 234), Portugal (Seite 162), Spanien (Seite 170), Ungarn (Seite 176, 178), Venezuela (Seite 104), Vereinigte Arabische Emirate (Seite 180, 182 unten) und ZERI (Seite 110, 112)

Zeichnungen der Architekten und Modelldarstellungen freigegeben durch die Gesellschaft für Technische Zusammenarbeit (GTZ) GmbH: Bhutan (Seite 70, 72 unten), Jemen (Seite 142 oben), Jordanien (Seite 144), Nepal (Seite 96 unten), Afrika (Seite 210), CILSS (Seite 216), SADC (Seite 212), CARICOM (Seite 236), Angola (Seite 214 oben), Kenia (Seite 218), Madagaskar (Seite 220 oben), Tansania (Seite 215 oben), Uganda (Seite 222) und Moldau (Seite 232)

Architects' drawings and model renderings courtesy of the Commissioner General of Section of the individual countries: Australia (page 68), Belgium (page 118 top), Denmark (page 122), Estonia (page 124), Greece (page 132 top), Ireland (page 136), Japan (pages 82, 84 bottom), Korea (page 88 top), Croatia (page 146 top), Latvia (page 148), Liechtenstein (page 226), Lithuania (page 150), Mexico (page 90, 92 bottom), The Netherlands (page 156 top), Norway (page 158 top), Monaco (page 152), Austria (page 224), Paraguay (page 234), Portugal (page 162), Spain (page 170), Hungary (pages 176, 178), Venezuela (page 104), United Arab Emirates (pages 180, 182 bottom), and ZERI (page 110, 112)

Architects' drawings and model renderings courtesy of the German Technical Cooperation Corporation (GTZ) GmbH: Bhutan (pages 70, 72 bottom), Yemen (page 142 top), Jordan (page 144), Nepal (page 96 bottom), Africa (page 210), CILSS (page 216), SADC (page 212), CARICOM (page 236), Angola (page 214 top), Kenya (page 218), Madagascar (page 220 top), Tanzania (page 215 top), Uganda (page 222), and Moldova (page 232)

Die deutsche Gesellschaft für technische Zusammenarbeit (GTZ) GmbH ist in rund 2.700 Entwicklungshilfe-Projekten in 130 Ländern aktiv. Auch bei der EXPO 2000 unterstützt sie zahlreiche Nationen und ermöglichte ihnen durch die Übernahme der Planungsleistungen und durch finanzielle Unterstützung den Bau von Ausstellungsständen oder eigenen Pavillons. Die GTZ handelt dabei im Auftrag des Bundesministeriums für wirtschaftliche Zusammenarbeit und Entwicklung (BMZ). Bauherren sind in allen Fällen die jeweiligen Länder oder Staatengemeinschaften.

In dem vorliegenden Buch sind dies im Rahmen der Hallenpräsentationen die Afrikahalle, die Gemeinschaftspräsentationen von SADC, CILSS und CARICOM sowie die Länderstände von Angola, Tansania, Kenia, Madagaskar, Uganda und Moldau. Bei den Nationenpavillons handelt es sich um die Länder Äthiopien, Bhutan, Jemen, Jordanien, Nepal, Rumänien und Sri Lanka.

The German Technical Cooperation Corporation (GTZ) GmbH is active in around 2,700 developmental aid projects in 130 countries. At EXPO 2000 it also supports numerous countries, and by taking charge of planning and offering financial support made it possible for them to build exhibition stands or their own pavilions. The GTZ operates in this capacity on the behalf of the Federal Ministry of Economic Cooperation and Development (BMZ). In all cases the clients are the respective countries or groups of states.

In the present book, hall presentations supported by the GTZ are the Africa Hall, the group presentations of SADC, CILSS, and CARICOM, as well as the country stands of Angola, Tanzania, Kenya, Madagascar, Uganda, and Moldova. The countries which received support for their national pavilions are Ethiopia, Bhutan, Yemen, Jordan, Nepal, Rumania and Sri Lanka.

ONE WORLD

EINE INITIATIVE DER DEUTSCHEN ENTWICKLUNGSPOLITIK

Herausgeber  Editor
EXPO 2000 Hannover GmbH
Gesellschaft zur Vorbereitung und Durchführung der Weltausstellung
EXPO 2000 in Hannover mbH
D-30510 Hannover
EXPO 2000 Hannover GmbH
Corporation for the Organization and Realization of the World Exposition
EXPO 2000 in Hanover mbH
30510 Hanover, Germany

Bereich Planen und Bauen  Planning and Construction
Hubertus von Bothmer
Regina Lücker

Redaktion und Text  Editing and Text
Martina Flamme-Jasper, Hannover

Redaktionsschluss Text  Deadline Text
14. April 2000  April 14, 2000

Lektorat  Copy-edited by
A. C. W., Köln (deutsch); Tas Skorupa, Berlin (englisch)

Übersetzung  Translation
John Southard, Groß-Umstadt

Grafische Gestaltung  Graphic design
Johannes Sternstein, Stuttgart

Satz  Typesetting
Graphisches Atelier Sternstein, Stuttgart

Reproduktion  Reproduction
C + S Repro, Filderstadt

Gesamtherstellung  Printed by
Dr. Cantz'sche Druckerei, Ostfildern-Ruit

Erschienen im  Published by
Hatje Cantz Verlag
Senefelderstraße 12
D-73760 Ostfildern
T. ++49/(0)711/44 05-0
F. ++49/(0)711/44 05-220
Internet: www.hatjecantz.de

Distribution in the US
DAP, Distributed Art Publishers
155 Avenue of the Americas, Second Floor
New York, NY 10013
T. 001-212-627 1999
F. 001-212-627 9484

ISBN 3-7757-0924-X